Professional
Travel
Agency
Management

Professional Travel Agency Management

CHUCK Y. GEE
School of Travel Industry Management
University of Hawaii

KEVIN B. BOBERG
College of Business Administration and Economics
New Mexico State University

DEXTER J. L. CHOY
School of Travel Industry Management
University of Hawaii

JAMES C. MAKENS
Babcock Graduate School of Management
Wake Forest University

PRENTICE HALL, Englewood Cliffs, New Jersey 07632

Library of Congress Cataloging-in-Publication Data

Professional travel agency management / Chuck Y. Gee.
    p.   cm.
  Includes bibliographical references.
  ISBN 0-13-725557-8
  1. Travel agents--Vocational guidance.   I. Gee, Chuck Y.
G154.P75 1990
338.4'791'02373--dc20   89-38970
                                                             CIP

Editorial/production supervision: Merrill Peterson
Interior design: Joan Stone
Cover design: Lundgren Graphics
Cover photo: Tony Stone, Worldwide
Manufacturing buyer: Dave Dickey

© 1990 by Prentice-Hall, Inc.
A Division of Simon & Schuster
Englewood Cliffs, New Jersey 07632

Printed in the United States of America

10 9 8 7 6 5 4 3 2 1

ISBN 0-13-725557-8

Prentice-Hall International (UK) Limited, *London*
Prentice-Hall of Australia Pty. Limited, *Sydney*
Prentice-Hall Canada Inc., *Toronto*
Prentice-Hall Hispanoamericana, S.A., *Mexico*
Prentice-Hall of India Private Limited, *New Delhi*
Prentice-Hall of Japan, Inc., *Tokyo*
Simon & Schuster Asia Pte. Ltd., *Singapore*
Editora Prentice-Hall do Brasil, Ltda., *Rio de Janeiro*

DEDICATED TO THE MEMORY OF

D. STUART FUJIYOSHI

President, American Society of Travel Agents
Hawaii Chapter, 1982 to 1984

whose legacy was the advancement of the
travel agency profession in the Hawaiian community
and his support of higher education in
Travel Industry Management

Contents

chapter 3
Types of Travel Operations   46

chapter 4
Retail Travel Agency Operations   60

chapter 5
Travel Agency Marketing   76

chapter 6
Agency Organization and Office Management   110

chapter 7
Personnel Administration   154

chapter 8
Travel Agency Accounting   190

chapter 9
Financial Analysis and Controls   208

chapter 10
Travel Agency Automation   226

chapter 11
Legal Aspects and the Management of Risk   255

chapter 12
Future Aspects in the Industry   282

Foreword

The travel agency industry of today is vastly different from the one that I entered 23 years ago. We have grown from a small group of "Mom and Pop" shops, numbering 6,000, to over 31,000 locations, generating in excess of $42 billion each year in airline sales alone.

Recent changes brought about by airline deregulation, experimentation with other forms of distribution, a technological explosion, and the emergence of a small but highly powerful group of mega agents have made the management of a travel agency increasingly complex and difficult. Travel agents and suppliers alike continually attempt to redefine their role in this changing environment.

Successful agency managers not only require general business skills such as marketing, accounting, and personnel management, together with a keen understanding of how the travel industry operates, but also need an awareness of the various environmental factors which affect them, including government and regulatory actions, the market place, and the role of the overall economy on travel behavior.

Professional Travel Agency Management is a college level text which approaches travel agency operations from a management perspective and deals with the complex issues facing managers. The fact that many community colleges, and more recently four year colleges, are now offering courses in travel agency management certainly attests to the need for increased professionalism throughout the industry.

As a primary trade association representing travel agents exclusively, the Association of Retail Travel Agents (ARTA) strongly supports all efforts to provide better educated managers who will lead the industry in the future.

The late Dr. Herman Kahn predicted that the travel industry would be the world's foremost revenue producer by the year 2000. Today, it represents 6.4% of America's Gross National Product, and it continues to grow at a rapid pace. While many opportunities exist for a very rewarding career in the industry, the future is nonetheless cloaked in uncertainty. It will take educated and astute management to rise to the challenge, define the travel industry of tomorrow, and ensure validation of Dr. Kahn's prediction.

Ronald A. Santana
President and Chief Executive Officer
Association of Retail Travel Agents

Preface

Under a climate of fierce competition and shifting industry dynamics, the management of travel agencies is a constant challenge. Today, managers must not only know the technical aspects of travel agency operations but also have an understanding of the agency as it exists within a larger business, governmental, and social environment. In response to new industry requirements, programs and courses on travel agency management have emerged all over the country in colleges, universities, and, in particular, community colleges.

Professional Travel Agency Management addresses the need for a college level text emphasizing the management of travel agencies. Various books on the market describe how to open an agency or focus on some particular aspect such as accounting or personnel; many excellent "how-to" training manuals have also been written. None of these, however, are written from a broad, management perspective. With *Professional Travel Agency Management*, it is our intent to fill this gap. The text is a product and culmination of several years of research and analysis of the travel agency business and its changing dynamics. While the book is partly descriptive, at least in terms of agency operations and current conditions, it was the intention of the authors to bridge academic observations with general information and specific examples from the industry itself.

A number of topics in the text, organized under major subject areas and by chapters, cover such functions as marketing, accounting, automation, personnel administration, and legal aspects. Chapter 3, entitled "Types of Travel Operations," discusses the complex and varied relationships that link travel agents with travel suppliers, tour operators, tour wholesalers, and others involved in the travel distribution system. The final chapter identifies and discusses issues that are likely to have a major impact on future agency operations.

Many individuals and organizations contributed to the writing of this text. Carolyn Cain, Research Specialist at the School of Travel Industry Management, assisted with preliminary research and drafted significant portions of the book. The Airlines Reporting Corporation (ARC) was extremely helpful in providing statistics and information on the current status of the regulatory relationship between ARC and travel agents. The legal chapter was reviewed by Alexander Anolik, Esq., of Alexander Anolik Law Corporation, who is president of the International Forum of Travel and Tourism Advocates. Keri Tanaka handled the word processing for the final draft of the manuscript. To these people, the authors owe a large debt of gratitude. Other persons or organizations the authors wish to acknowledge for their efforts and/or contribution of materials for the text are Bonnie Kogos and Zenith Travel, Bonnie Barry of the Association of Retail Travel Agents (ARTA), the Institute of Certified Travel Agents (ICTA), the American Society of Travel Agents (ASTA), Garber Travel, American Airlines, *Travel Weekly*, and *The Travel Agent*.

Professional Travel Agency Management is meant to provide a basic understanding of the various components that must be considered in the management of a travel agency. We hope the text will serve to encourage more individuals to enter this exciting and challenging field.

Chuck Y. Gee
Kevin B. Boberg
Dexter J. L. Choy
James C. Makens

chapter 1

Introduction to Travel Agencies

LEARNING OBJECTIVES

- To understand the travel agent's role as a primary intermediary within the travel industry
- To appreciate the expanding scope and nature of the travel industry and the areas that are and will be the most profitable for travel agents
- To understand how various travel agencies differ in structure
- To explain how deregulation, the loss of exclusivity, and advances in technology have affected the travel industry

KEY TERMS

- Airlines Reporting Corporation (ARC)
- American Automobile Association (AAA)
- American Society of Travel Agents (ASTA)
- Association of Retail Travel Agents (ARTA)
- Business Travel Department (BTD)
- Business Traveler
- Bypass Activities
- Commercial Accounts
- Commission
- Competitive Marketing Decision
- Consortiums
- Cooperatives
- Corporate Travel

- Cruises
- Deregulation
- Direct Selling
- Domestic versus International Bookings
- Exclusivity
- Fly–Drive Package
- Franchise
- National Passenger Traffic Association (NPTA)

- Outbound Traffic
- Rebating
- Sliding Commission Scale
- Teleshopping
- Tour Package
- The Travel Distribution System
- Videotex

INTRODUCTION

The travel industry represents one of the most significant sectors of the worldwide economy. Spending for domestic and international tourism is over $2 trillion annually, or $5.5 billion per day. The travel industry is considered by many to be the largest business in the world.[1] Despite bouts with recession and inflation, terrorism, dollar fluctuations, and many other factors that stand as obstacles to the growth of tourism, people in both developed and developing nations place a high priority on travel.

The travel agent, who provides a sales outlet for air carriers, hotels, car rental firms, major attractions, event organizers, and other travel suppliers, represents an important intermediary within the travel industry. Annual travel agent sales in the United States presently total more than $50 billion, which clearly demonstrates the travel agent's vital function.

The U.S. travel agency industry grew from fewer than 8000 agency locations in 1970 to over 31,000 in 1988 (including satellite ticket printers), representing a healthy annual average growth rate of over 9 percent. (See Figure 1.1.) The advent of jet aircraft in the late 1950s, airline deregulation in the late 1970s, and the introduction of computerized reservation systems (CRS) have been major factors contributing to the growth in travel and tourism, which in turn spurred the rapid growth of travel agency services. Most analysts predict, however, that the number of travel agencies will soon begin to level off, with the number of new entrants closely matched by agency defaults and voluntary withdrawals.

Recent changes within the travel industry have resulted in the travel agency business becoming increasingly more sophisticated and competitive. The original agencies were primarily "mom and pop" businesses established as independent ticket outlets for a particular airline. Travel agencies now sell a variety of travel services and serve as counselors for both pleasure and business travelers. Some agencies, however, have chosen to specialize in a specific area of travel, for example, to serve the needs of a specific

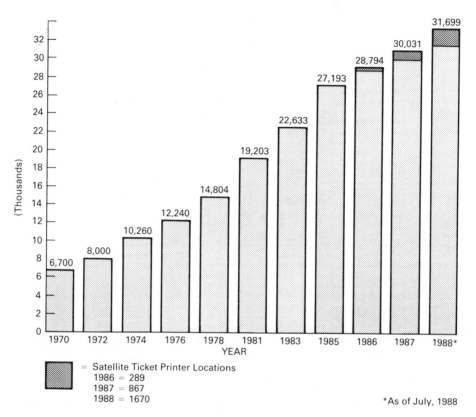

FIGURE 1.1 Number of travel agencies in the United States

Source: Somerset Waters, *Travel Industry World Yearbook—The Big Picture 1987*, New York: Child & Waters, Inc. p. 114, and *Travel Weekly's Louis Harris Survey*, June 1986, p. 34.

ethnic group, specialize in cruise-only travel, offer professional assistance in planning meetings, or help develop corporate motivational programs, using travel as the incentive.

THE TRAVEL DISTRIBUTION SYSTEM

With respect to the entire travel industry, the distribution system may be defined as the process of producing, marketing, selling, and delivering travel-related services from travel suppliers to consumers. In this process, travel agents serve as intermediaries between travel suppliers and ultimate consumers. They sell the products offered by travel suppliers such as airlines, cruise ships, railroads, bus companies, car rental firms, hotels, and sightseeing operators to the general public, often adding special services and customizing arrangements according to client needs.

There are two general types of travel agents—wholesale and retail. A wholesaler specializes in organizing the various components of a tour that are sold to the public through a network of retail agents. While this textbook is principally concerned with travel agencies at the retail level, it is important to note that wholesalers often operate as retailers; that is, they organize tour packages and sell them directly to the consumer as well. A retail agency may also arrange some of its own packages and in this way act as a wholesaler. In fact, approximately 25 percent of travel agent retailers, primarily the larger agencies, function also as wholesalers. (The various types of travel operations and their interrelationships are discussed further in Chapter 3.)

A great deal of speculation exists regarding the effects of deregulation and increased information technology on the travel distribution system. Some changes have already taken place, but the long-term outcome is uncertain.

A recent survey indicates that purchasers of travel products employ the services of travel agents for three basic reasons: (1) convenience, (2) counseling, and (3) the assumption that an agent's services are free.[2] Travel agents can be particularly helpful to vacationers seeking new travel destinations and experiences. Surveys indicate that almost half of those visiting travel agencies do not have precise plans concerning a vacation destination. Vacationers usually know the *kind* of holiday or recreation they like, for instance, ocean, beach, and sunshine versus visiting museums and opera houses, but they are not always sure about alternative vacation destinations that will fit their budget and special vacation needs.

Since travel agents are influential in the selection of vacation destinations, they are important marketing intermediaries for nations, states, and such visitor attractions as theme parks, historic preserves, or major events. Consequently, cities, states, and counties actively compete to host the meetings of the American Society of Travel Agents (ASTA), the Association of Retail Travel Agents (ARTA), and the National Tour Association (NTA), as well as other travel trade associations. Hosting such meetings provides destinations with an opportunity to show travel agents and tour operators what they offer as potential vacation sites.

A travel agent's influence on the traveler becomes more pronounced in selecting the specific components of a trip: airline, hotel, car rental, package tours, and so on. Even 40 percent of the business travelers who utilize the services of a travel agency ask their agents for specific hotel recommendations.[3] Understandably, then, travel suppliers continually barrage travel agents with various types of attractive promotional information. For the suppliers of air transport, international hotel accommodations, cruise ship holidays, and packaged tours, travel agents are the primary source of sales generation. Packaged-tour operators and cruise lines, for instance, rely on travel agencies for 90 percent or more of their sales (see Table 1.1).

TABLE 1.1 SUPPLIER DEPENDENCE ON U.S. TRAVEL AGENTS

	Estimated percent of volume booked by agents
Airlines	67% (domestic)
	80% (international)
Hotels	18% (domestic)
	79% (international)
Cruise lines	92%
Rail	28%
Bus	Less than 10%
Rental cars/vehicles	40%
Packaged tours	90%

Source: Somerset Waters, *Travel Industry World Yearbook—The Big Picture 1987,* New York: Child & Waters, Inc., and *Travel Weekly's Louis Harris Survey,* June 1986, p. 116.

PRODUCT LINE

Air Transportation

Although travel agents sell many travel products, they remain heavily dependent upon air travel sales. Indeed, it was the advent of commercial jet air travel that spawned the tremendous growth in the consumer travel industry and, subsequently, in the travel agency industry. Currently, nearly two-thirds of the travel agency industry's gross income is derived from the sale of airline tickets. (See Figure 1.2.)

With deregulation and travel agents' loss of exclusivity in the sale of airline tickets, many analysts feel the long-term relationship that travel agents have had with airlines may be changing. Airlines, in looking at alternative distribution systems, appear to be advertising more directly to the public and less to the travel trade. Meanwhile, travel agents complain about the constant fluctuation in airfares (estimated at 25,000 changes daily), the lack of sufficient information from the airlines, and the fact that they must pay more attention to carrier consumer advertising to keep abreast of new rates.

Water Transportation

During the era of the Grand Tour (seventeenth, eighteenth, and nineteenth centuries) and up to the time of World War II, water transportation was a key component in the travel plans of almost every long-haul traveler. The

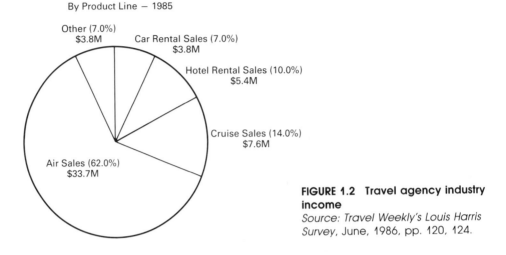

FIGURE 1.2 **Travel agency industry income**
Source: Travel Weekly's Louis Harris Survey, June, 1986, pp. 120, 124.

introduction of transoceanic commercial jet travel, however, seemed to herald the extinction of the passenger ship industry. Although the use of ships for the sole purpose of transporting passengers from one destination to another remains minimal, the 1970s witnessed the resurgence of the use of cruise ships by both passengers and travel agencies, and ocean travel has since experienced a rebirth.

Cruise ship ticket sales represents the second largest source of income for travel agents and is the segment with the highest growth rate. The cruise ship industry is heavily dependent upon travel agents, with all but 8 or 10 percent of the sales for cruise ship vacations made through travel agents; some cruise lines, in fact, have a firm policy of requiring passengers to buy their tickets through a travel agency. Individual cruise lines sponsor a substantial number of industry promotions, which facilitates the job of selling ocean vacations. Cruises are also easily booked and receive high marks of satisfaction from customers. For these reasons, many agencies have increased their involvement with cruise line ticket sales.

Accommodations

Travel agents also make hotel and resort reservations for clients, which represent a stable component in travel agents' annual revenues stream and rank third in importance for the production of agency revenue. Although relations between travel agents and hotels have been satisfactory, the payment, or rather nonpayment, of hotel commissions continues to present problems, as many agents are never paid their due commission, even with the increase in centralized hotel commission systems.

Vehicle Rentals

Car and other vehicle rentals represent the fourth major component of travel agency sales. Many agents find that selling car rentals can make a substantial contribution to their commissions with minimal additional effort. However, retail agents still have difficulty understanding car rental payment policies. Insufficient computerized information, changing rates, unpaid commissions, and low commissions on discounted corporate rentals are common irritants to the agent–car rental firm relationship.

Other Services

Other income-producing services offered by travel agencies include motor-coach and rail travel sales, sightseeing tours, sale of travelers cheques, passport photos, attractions, and entertainment services. The sale of travel insurance is also a means of diversifying and increasing agency revenue.

Domestic versus International Bookings

Travel agencies within the United States depend upon domestic travel for the majority of their sales. Domestic travel sales, as a percentage of total travel sales, have increased steadily since 1970 and currently represent approximately 70 percent of U.S. travel agency business. (See Figure 1.3.) The reverse is often true for travel agencies in many other countries in Western Europe, East Asia, and Central America, where international travel may represent close to 80 percent of the bookings.

The large number of domestic bookings is due to the size and economic structure of the United States. A nation that spans four time zones cannot be easily traveled without airlines. Moreover, many business trips in the United States require overnight or longer travel, creating a need for the services of travel agencies. In small countries such as the Netherlands, Singapore, and Costa Rica, on the other hand, travelers can drive across the nation and return the same day. With a variety of U.S. vacation destinations ranging from desert to mountains to seashore, many American pleasure travelers see little reason to vacation in other countries. Americans enjoy traveling in their own country and take over one and a quarter billion person-trips per year to domestic destinations 100 miles or more away from home. Sixty-five percent of all U.S. residents took one or more such trips during 1987.[4]

The Business Traveler

The business traveler is a valuable customer for travel agencies, as close to 90 percent of the agencies handle commercial accounts. Business travel today (including combined business and pleasure) currently represents over

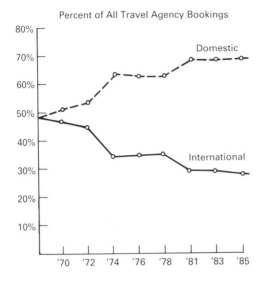

Percent of All Travel Agency Bookings

FIGURE 1.3 Trends in international versus domestic bookings
Source: Travel Weekly's Louis Harris Survey, June, 1986, p. 70.

50 percent of travel agency bookings.[5] Agencies frequently find that business clients are the most loyal customers, since over 75 percent of the business bookings come from repeat customers.

Travel agencies, particularly the smaller ones, are finding it increasingly difficult to break into the business travel scene. There is a positive correlation between agency size and the percentage of business travel handled. The current trend is for businesses to consolidate their corporate travel needs and put them out to bid as commercial travel accounts. Bigger agencies are in a better position to bid because their increased volume results in more overrides or bonuses from the airlines, and they are able to pass these savings on to the commercial account. Competition is so stiff for commercial accounts that many agencies offer such special services as delivering tickets and providing limousine service to the airport for their business clients. A major benefit from pursuing commercial accounts is that business clients will often use the same agency for their pleasure travel.

Income tax changes with respect to business travel can seriously affect travel agents. Legislative decisions regarding limitations on the deductibility of business meals and entertainment, on the deductibility of familiarization trips, and on convention spending have a significant impact on commercial travel and consequently commercial account income.

TRAVEL AGENCY OWNERSHIP AND STRUCTURE

Nearly two-thirds of all travel agencies are incorporated. Twenty percent are sole proprietorships, and the remainder are branch offices and partnerships. In recent years, there have been two pronounced trends with respect to travel agency structure: (1) the decline of the mid-size agency and (2) the proliferation of cooperatives and consortiums.

Agency Size

Large agencies with annual sales over $5 million, comprising 15 percent of total agencies in 1986,[6] have done well under deregulation due to over-rides—the ability to negotiate benefits from suppliers—and economies of scale. Smaller agencies, those with a volume under $2 million, comprising 66 percent of the total, have survived on the basis of offering more personalized service or by carving out new specialized niches and keeping their overhead low. By contrast, the mid-size agencies, with sales volume between $2 million and $5 million, have been declining in recent years, many having lost their bigger accounts to larger agencies. Because of the necessity of absorbing substantial business overhead without the needed volume provided by large accounts, many agencies have left the business altogether, while others have been acquired. Mid-size agencies accounted for 43 percent of all sales in 1983, but this figure dropped to around 19 percent in 1986. (See Table 1.2.) Meanwhile big agencies, often referred to as mega-agencies, continue to get bigger through acquisition and merger.

Cooperatives and Consortiums

Cooperatives and consortiums have been the answer for many small and mid-size agencies trying to survive. During the late 1960s, co-ops began to enter the travel agency picture when operators of international tours offered incentive override plans to individual agents on a sliding scale based on annual sales volume. The purpose of the cooperative was to negotiate a sliding commission scale that would put members in a higher bracket. Tour operators without an override policy were pressured by the co-op to establish such a policy. In this respect, the basic function of the co-op or consortium was and still is to act as a pressure group to gain higher commissions. The difference between these two groups is that a cooperative is owned by its membership, whereas a consortium is a voluntary association. Both charge a membership fee—initial consortium membership fees, for instance, may run from 200 to several thousands of dollars—and require ongoing contributions for advertising programs.

Since deregulation, competition for consumer travel dollars has increased, and the use of co-ops and consortiums has proliferated. In 1985, over one-third of all agencies were affiliated with a consortium, a share that is expected to grow to 50 percent in the near future.[7] In addition to increased purchasing power and supplier discounts, co-ops and consortiums provide other services, such as marketing campaigns, prospecting for large nationwide accounts, seminars, training programs, twenty-four-hour toll-free line service for clients, and other networking advantages.

TABLE 1.2   1986 ASTA SURVEY OF AGENCY SIZE

Sales	Percentage of agencies
Small	
$499,000 and less	14.7%
$500,000 to 999,999	24.1%
$1,000,000 to $1,900,000	27.1%
Medium	
$2,000,000 to 4,900,000	19.1%
Large	
$5,000,000 to 9,900,000	5.2%
$10,000,000 and up	9.8%

Source: John Dalton, "Surveying Meaning of Industry Statistics," *Travel Trade*, July 29, 1987, p. 18.

Co-ops and consortiums follow the basic theory of strength in numbers, and some analysts predict that these organizations may start to join together to achieve additional size. The potential benefits notwithstanding, several problems exist with co-ops and consortiums, including the charge that decisions are often made that benefit some agencies more than others. For example, when two or more member agencies bid for competitive business within the same geographic area, potential conflict of interest may arise as a result of common membership within the consortium. Consortiums, moreover, are undergoing a transition in the marketplace similar to the experience of other members of the travel industry. Suppliers are increasingly holding back on overrides unless market share is gained by that channel. Suppliers are becoming skilled in analyzing consortium production and comparing it to the rest of the market. If market share has not increased by giving a preferred vendor or distributor override, some are simply discontinuing the override. Only consortiums that have the ability to enforce or persuade directive selling are consequently assured of survival. This is sometimes called "focusing the volume of the consortium."[8]

Franchise

Franchise affiliations provide a different option for agencies. In this situation, the agency acquires the franchise brand name and makes regular royalty payments to use the name and other services. One of the disadvantages of the franchise option, in addition to a large purchase fee of between $30,000 and $70,000, is the loss of autonomy for the individual agency. Some franchises have, in fact, complained that franchised offices are almost impossible to manage and to control and are reverting to company-owned stores.

Under a deregulated business environment the travel agency industry is likely to experience a growth of nationwide and even worldwide chains. Many observers opine that these chains will be similar in form to those in the lodging and real estate industries, where well-managed, strong chains of independents have proven workable. Independent agencies have expressed interest in joining chains to enjoy the benefits of strong advertising and a corporate image. Management training, business counsel, buying assistance, group insurance, lead referrals, and shared on-line computers represent some of the benefits available to agencies through a strong chain affiliation.

Trends in Grouping

The trend toward grouping in the travel agency industry is reflective of other types of retailers, such as supermarkets and department stores, which experienced the move toward large, mass marketing over the past three decades. Smaller retailers have generally gone in one of three directions: They have attempted to reach a specialized market, they have regrouped to gain more purchasing power, or they have fallen by the wayside. This pattern has been true for travel agencies as well, with a record 437 defaults in 1986. Most agencies, however, are proving their resiliency, adjusting to the changes facing the industry and altering the way they do business. And they continue to grow: In a survey of the American Society of Travel Agents (ASTA), 43 percent of agencies stated plans to expand their businesses in the near future.[9]

Location

Until recently, the principal location of travel agencies has been within cities, but suburban locations, however, now account for 47 percent. Agency growth appears to be following the migration of corporations and their employees from the cities to the suburbs. Agencies located in cities now account for only 42 percent of all agencies, while 11 percent are located in town and rural areas.[10]

A CHANGING ENVIRONMENT

Deregulation and Competition

In 1978 the U.S. Congress began a process of "deregulation." The philosophy behind deregulation was to provide increased competition among private companies by reducing or eliminating government restrictions. The government's goal was to promote competitive practices for the ultimate benefit of the consumer. Industries that were highly regulated—ground and air transportation, financial services industries such as banking, and telecommunications—were targeted. The deregulation of the air transportation industry meant that routes and fares would no longer be determined by the Civil Aeronautics Board (CAB), resulting in heavy price competition among airlines and a new freedom for carriers to select routes. Deregulation not only opened the door for new carriers to join the competition but resulted in the bankruptcy of many existing carriers unable to adapt to the new open environment. Deregulation's effect on the travel agency industry has been profound enough to actually change the way the industry does business.

Loss of antitrust immunity. In a deregulated environment, airlines are no longer protected from antitrust laws. During the forty years under intense regulation, airlines had been encouraged to ignore certain antitrust laws. This immunity extended to travel agents through the airline trade associations. Airlines now operate in an environment of competition enforced by antitrust laws, instead of regulation from the CAB. The extent of deregulation is evidenced by the fact that the CAB itself was phased out of existence on January 1, 1985. The airline association that regulated travel agencies, the Airline Traffic Conference (ATC), was also dissolved and has been replaced with another association, the Airlines Reporting Corporation (ARC).

Loss of exclusivity. Deregulation has had a profound impact on the issue of agency "exclusivity." Travel agents had historically been granted exclusivity in the sale of airline tickets, which in essence meant that besides the airlines, only travel agents were allowed to sell air tickets. Such exclusivity precluded other entries, for instance, financial institutions or department stores, from selling air travel and meant that business travel departments (BTDs) in large corporations could not receive commissions. The U.S. Department of Justice and the National Passenger Traffic Association (NPTA) (an association of business travel departments) were opposed to exclusivity and urged the elimination of the rule.

The issue came to a head in what was known as the CAB's Competitive Marketing Case Decision of 1982. The final decision on the case centered around the conclusion that the exclusivity provisions substantially reduced competition in the air transportation industry and exclusivity rights were not necessary to secure the benefits of accreditation that were derived from the airline's association with travel agencies. The final ruling was that the benefits of the provisions did not justify their retention and thus travel agents lost exclusivity, effective from 1984 on.

The full effects of the loss of exclusivity have not yet been felt. While financial institutions, business travel departments, and even supermarkets can now sell airline tickets, most airlines are still professing allegiance to travel agencies. It has been argued that the agency retail system works well and that market forces are such that this is still the most efficient system for the carriers to use.

But the ruling has provided the groundwork for changing the entire distribution system of airline ticket sales and for drastically altering the long-accepted partnership between agents and carriers. The fact is that suppliers will support travel agents only as long as they believe it is in their best interest. Now that airlines can form any type of commission, override, or bonus arrangement they wish (many had provided overrides anyway under the table), they will heavily favor volume producers. Airlines are at least considering other outlets for distributing their product, particularly to the commercial market, and have offered "exclusive rates" to preferred accounts, which was not possible prior to the Competitive Marketing Decision.

In addition to changing the relationship travel agencies have with airlines, deregulation may also change the relationship agencies have with other travel suppliers.

New Competitors

Financial institutions and retailers are beginning to take a stronger interest in selling travel services. Sears, Roebuck and Company, one of the nation's

Ask Mr. Foster Travel Service was founded in 1888 in St. Augustine, Fla., at this Cordova Corner location. At the time of this photo, circa 1905, Ask Mr. Foster had 25 offices in the U.S.

largest retailers of goods and services, formed the Sears Discount Travel Club in January, 1987 with an initial membership of 35,000 and an expected enrollment of 100,000 members paying a $45 fee by the end of 1987. The Sears Discount Travel Club, as its name implies, offers club members a wide choice of trips at deeply discounted prices. With a full array of deeply discounted trips, mailing lists that read like telephone books, and state-of-the-art marketing techniques, Sears projects similar growth through the next decade. [11]

Threat of Direct Selling

Bypass activities.   An important issue currently facing travel agencies is direct selling by the suppliers to the consumer. One survey indicates that bypass activities are currently the number one concern of travel agents.[12] Bypass activities include promotion of 800 numbers for direct sales, couponing in consumer advertising by cruise lines and tour operators, and direct mail campaigns, activities that tend to change the agent-supplier relationship from one based on partnership to one that is adversarial and competitive in nature. Some travel agents are becoming more the agent of the buyer (consumer) than of the seller, as the relationship with the latter becomes less secure.

Rising costs of distribution and sales.   Soaring distribution expenses for the various suppliers are at the root of this bypass trend. For instance, the increase in distribution expenses for airlines is attributed to a number of factors, including (1) the increasing provision of overrides by airlines, (2) the cost of participating in automated distribution systems, and (3) increased transactional costs due to constantly changing fares. Airlines incur costs of 14 to 18 percent of their gross revenues from ticket sales by travel agencies. By contrast, airlines try to keep costs at 5 percent for their airport and city ticket offices.[13] Table 1.3, which shows the total commissions paid by major U.S. carriers, illustrates how substantial these commissions are in aggregate amounts. In 1986 total travel agency commissions received from all airlines on air ticket sales through the ARC reached $3.2 billion.[14]

The travel agency industry is now pressed to prove its system is more cost effective than the suppliers'. If airlines decide to issue all or most of their own tickets, they would also have to perform agency functions such as handling refunds and reissues and providing at least minimal counseling. The cost of providing these services is high, and salaries are generally higher in the airlines than the travel agency industry. Consequently, airlines are likely to find it more cost effective to continue to use travel agents. Abandoning a system of sales networking that has worked well for many years might thus give airlines pause for consideration.

**TABLE 1.3   COMMISSIONS PAID BY MAJOR U.S.
CARRIERS—1985**

Carrier/market	Commission paid
American domestic	$ 389,639,000
American Latin America	23,275,000
American Atlantic	15,611,000
Continental domestic	94,315,000
Continental Latin American	4,350,000
Continental Atlantic	3,258,000
Continental Pacific	23,001,000
Delta domestic	339,415,000
Delta Atlantic	12,408,000
Delta Latin America	5,358,000
Eastern domestic/Canada	319,088,364
Eastern Latin America	30,539,415
Eastern Atlantic	368,259
Northwest domestic	110,569,000
Northwest Atlantic	22,366,000
Northwest Pacific	160,616,000
Pan Am domestic	46,532,000
Pam Am Atlantic	121,684,000
Pan Am Latin America	38,142,000
Pan Am Pacific	92,155,000
Piedmont	80,617,992
Republic	130,332,000
TWA domestic	158,493,346
TWA Atlantic	137,177,273
United domestic	384,353,184
United Pacific	26,179,719
USAir	118,949,000
Western domestic	90,286,000
Western Latin America	4,163,000
Total	$2,983,241,552

Source: Roland Leiser, "Commission payments Increasing at Slower Rate." *The Travel Agent,* April 28, 1986, p. 1.

Responses to Change

In response to the changing environment and increased competition, some agencies have begun to charge a fee to customers for the servives they provide. The fee-for-service practice, however, has been slow to catch on. A more common practice is rebating, or sharing commissions with clients, particularly corporate clients. Industry observers predict that travel agents will one day need to either charge a standard service fee or operate on a system of buying and reselling ticket stocks, similar to other retailers who buy at wholesale and sell at retail.

Ward Grenelle Foster, founder of Ask Mr. Foster Travel Service, makes his annual visit to the Flagler Street office in Miami, Fla., in 1925. The travel agents behind the desk were known as "Foster Girls," employees hired by Foster himself prior to 1937.

Traditionally, travel agents have been concerned primarily with outbound traffic, that is, serving the needs of those who travel from home for business or pleasure. In view of possible changes in the travel environment, however, many agencies may find it profitable to emphasize inbound traffic as a way of increasing and diversifying their revenue base. This will require substantially more client involvement and managerial talent than writing a ticket. A concentration on inbound traffic could necessitate expertise in such areas as convention and meeting planning, incentive planning, tour promotion, motivational programs, and networking with outbound producers in other areas or countries.

As the travel industry has grown in complexity, the level of professionalism in travel agencies has also grown. The days of running a travel agency as a sideline activity or as a small family enterprise are coming to an end. Today it is essential for all but the smallest travel agencies to use automated on-line reservation systems to provide the quality of service demanded by clients. While smaller agencies will continue to offer personalized service and can benefit from specialization, only larger, well-managed agencies can support the financial requirements of an automated office with increased staffs of professional employees. The trend is clearly toward large professional agencies with sophisticated equipment and personnel and increased purchasing power.

Effects of Information Technology

Increased productivity. Automation within the travel agency industry has contributed to much progress in decreasing operational costs and increasing agency productivity. From 1978 to 1985, the number of agencies using automated reservation systems grew from 69 percent to 90 percent.[15] Automation is now spreading to other agency functions as well, especially accounting, as agencies are adapting personal computers and microcomputers for word processing, mailing list management, and other functions.

Agencies report that a trained agent using a CRT can produce almost $120,000 more in annual sales than a similar employee without automated equipment.[16] Clearly, automation has enabled travel agencies to grow in size and productivity; however, it has not led to a reduction in personnel. In fact, the majority of agencies with automated systems have either retained or increased their number of employees.

Traveler benefits. Information technology has also benefited the traveler directly. Airlines and other travel suppliers are now making rates and schedules directly available to consumers through linkups with personal computers at home and the office. Videotex, which feeds descriptive information and pictures to video screens, is another innovation. Teleshopping as it currently functions can be beneficial to the travel agency because products are booked by the consumer but processed by the travel agent so that the commission will be credited to the vendor agency.

While some of these electronic information systems are attractive to the customer for their convenience and timesavings, teleshopping and videotex have been slow to develop in the United States. Some consumers feel they are too impersonal and cannot provide professional counseling, and other consumers are hesitant to rely on their computers when travel agents offer the service without passing on charges. A fear within the industry itself, however, is that as people become more proficient with computers, and as the systems become more refined and accessible, the travel retailer could eventually be bypassed altogether. In such case, the role of the travel agent as professional counselor may become more pronounced in the selling of vacation destinations.

TRAVEL IN THE UNITED STATES

Low Public Usage of Travel Agency Services

Although travel agents are important travel industry intermediaries, they currently serve only a minority of the traveling public. The majority of the $50 billion-plus generated by travel agents annually goes to airlines, cruise ships, and hotels. However, in any given year, international and domestic travelers in the United States may spend nine times that amount;[17] thus, only a small percentage of total U.S. travel industry sales is actually generated by travel agents. In contrast to a country like Japan where almost *all* travelers use travel agents to arrange travel plans, in the United States only 20 percent of the traveling public uses travel agents.[18] The percentage of U.S. travelers using agents for international travel, however, is much higher. A primary reason for the less frequent use of travel agents by Americans is that the majority of travel in the United States is done by personal vehicle. (See Table 1.4.) Close to 400 million trips are taken by travelers annually in automobiles, trucks, or recreational vehicles, according to one study, but only a very small percentage of persons taking these trips (approximately 3 percent) currently uses the services of a travel agent.[19]

Untapped potential.   The travel agency industry evidently has not explored possible opportunities to serve the majority of Americans who travel in their own vehicles. During the gas shortage of the early 1970s, for instance, many road travelers became clients of travel agencies when they were unable to use their own automobiles and opted for fly-drive packages that permitted them to fly to a destination and rent an automobile or recreational vehicle. Travel agencies can offer creative and competitively priced travel services to this market. As competition increases for the sale of airline tickets, cruise ship tickets, and hotel rooms, travel agencies may be forced to explore the personal motor vehicle traveler market. The American Automobile Association (AAA), with annual sales of over $1.3 billion, is best known as an auto travel agency and has served the vehicle traveler market

TABLE 1.4 MODE OF TRANSPORTATION FOR TRAVEL IN THE UNITED STATES—1987

	Percent of travel
Auto, truck, recreation vehicle, motorcycle	80.1
Airplane	18.0
Bus	1.2
Train	.7

Source: Transportation Policy Associates. *Transportation in America—1986 Report*, Washington, D.C., March 1988, p. 8.

for several decades. The AAA provides emergency road service, trip routing, maps, car rental discounts, the AAA hotel guide, tours, and cruise default insurance, in addition to the more traditional travel agent products such as airline, cruise, and hotel sales. In 1983 it came to an agreement with American Express for AAA agencies to offer no-fee travelers cheques; in 1984 travelers cheques issued by AAA totaled over $1.6 billion.[20]

The motor vehicle traveler market might very well be receptive to some form of professional counseling from travel agents. Expanding the range of services or products offered to motor vehicle travelers may be necessary for the long-term viability of the travel agency industry.

The Economy and Shifting Travel Behavior

While Americans have a hefty appetite for travel, they view pleasure travel as a discretionary expenditure and tend to change travel consumption behavior in recessionary periods. Pleasure travel is also in competition with durable consumer goods. As Americans began to recover from the recession in 1983, instead of traveling many purchased consumer durables (such as refrigerators, TVs, and automobiles) that had been deferred during bad times. By 1985 and 1986, however, Americans were traveling again in substantial numbers, thanks to a stronger economy, a host of travel bargains, and changing demographics.

Business travel also declines in recessions as organizations attempt to conserve cash. Business travelers who continue to fly during these periods are often prohibited from flying first class or staying in expensive hotels, which reduces the cost of their airline tickets and hotel rooms and, in turn, the commissions received by travel agents. In short, it is evident that the welfare of the travel industry, including travel agencies, is inextricably tied to the national and world economy.

SUMMARY

The travel agency business is no longer an enterprise for amateurs. Over the last twenty-five years, travel agencies have changed and survived by demonstrating resiliency in meeting tough challenges. The mom and pop establishments of yesteryear are rapidly evolving into large professional travel organizations. Those who originally opened agencies "just for the fun of it" are finding the industry increasingly complex. Successful travel agencies will change to meet competitive threats and opportunities and match the needs of a new travel market, with the need to incorporate flexibility, creativity, innovation, determination, and professionalism into their businesses. As this occurs, travel agencies must compete with airlines, hotels, and other members of the travel industry for the best available managerial talent to assure their continuing viability as a business form in the twenty-first century.

DISCUSSION QUESTIONS

1. How has "deregulation" affected the travel agency industry? What changes are still likely to occur within this industry as a result of deregulation?

2. What are the primary sources of income for travel agencies? Discuss any problems associated with these sources.

3. What is the relative importance to travel agencies of international versus domestic bookings?

4. What are the trends in the type of ownership and size of travel agencies?

5. What does "loss of exclusivity" mean to the travel agency industry? Discuss its potential impact upon travel agencies.

6. Why does "direct selling" continue to pose a threat to travel agencies?

7. Discuss the possible future effects of automation, rebating, and information technology to travel agencies.

ENDNOTES

[1]Somerset Waters, *Travel Industry World Yearbook—The Big Picture*, (New York: Child and Waters, 1987), p. 6.

[2]Archie Wilson, "Public: Agents Best in Convenience, Advice, Cost," *The Travel Agent*, April 11, 1985, p. 1.

[3]U.S. Travel Data Center, *Hotel Line, Hotel and Travel Index*, Spring, 1987, p.1.

[4]U.S. Travel Data Center, "Travel Tab 1988," Washington, DC, June 1988, p. 2.

[5]*Travel Weekly's Louis Harris Survey*, p. 9.

[6]John Dalton, "Surveying Meaning of Industry Statistics," *Travel Trade*, July 29, 1987, p. 18.

[7]Barbara Sturken, "Marrying for Money," *Travel Weekly Focus on Business Travel*, August, 1986, p. 8.

[8]Jack Bell, "Consortium Pros and Cons: When Should an Agency Enlist," *Travel Age West*, October 27, 1986, p. 132.

[9]Fran Durbin, "ASTA Finds Nearly 43% of Agencies Will Expand," *Travel Weekly*, April 28, 1986, p. 1.

[10]*Travel Weekly's Louis Harris Survey*, p. 49.

[11]Peder Zane, "Sears Travel Club Selling Strong," *The Travel Agent*, October 12, 1987, p. 65.

[12]"Major Agent Concern Is Direct Dealing, Survey Finds," *The Travel Agent*, June 19, 1986, p. 1.

[13]Bill Bartman, "Will High Cost Destroy Distribution System?" *The Travel Agent*, July 29, 1985, p. 1.

[14]Waters, *Travel Industry World Yearbook*, p. 114.

[15]*Travel Weekly's Louis Harris Survey*, p. 24.

[16]Ibid., p. 24.

[17]Somerset Waters, *Travel Industry World Yearbook—The Big Picture 1986*, (New York: Child and Waters, 1986), p. 13.

[18]*Travel Weekly's Louis Harris Survey*, p. 92.

[19]Karen Rubin, "Why Agents Have Hardly Scratched the Surface," *The Travel Agent*, August 26, 1985, p. 9.

[20]Roland Leiser, "AAA: It's More Than Just Cars," *The Travel Agent*, December 14, 1987, p. 58.

chapter **2**

Establishment of a Travel Agency

LEARNING OBJECTIVES

- To understand the importance of a business plan
- To know the various elements that go into preparing a business plan
- To appreciate the many activities involved in establishing an agency
- To comprehend the regulatory relationship between agents and suppliers

KEY TERMS

- Adhesion Contract
- Agent Reporting Agreement
- Air Transport Association
- ARC Audit
- Area Settlement Plan
- Barriers to Entry
- Business Plan
- Conference Appointments
- Corporate Philosophy
- Corporation
- Financial Projections
- Independent Arbitration Panel
- *Industry Agents' Handbook* (ARC)
- International Airlines Travel Agent Network (IATAN)
- International Air Transport Association (IATA)
- Irrevocable Letter of Credit
- Licenses and Certification
- Limited Partnership
- Mission Statement
- Organizational Chart
- Partnership

- Passenger Network Services Corporation (PNSC)
- Product Expansion
- Pro forma
- Sales Forecast
- S Corporation
- Travel Agent Arbiter
- Travel Agent Handbook (IATAN)
- Vertical Integration

INTRODUCTION

Historically, the travel agency business has been a relatively easy one to establish. It required little investment capital or technical knowledge to own or operate a small travel agency. The result was that many travel agencies were little more than hobbies for their owners who, in many cases, were also the operators.

Travel agencies were and remain relatively easy to establish for the following reasons:

- No product or raw material inventory is required.
- Offices can be leased, often in lower-rent areas.
- Office equipment can be leased.
- Business can be operated at a comparatively lower "break-even" point.
- Licensing requirements are far less stringent than for many professions (for example, medicine, dentistry, law, accounting).

Given these factors and the perceived benefits of working in the industry, it is little wonder that, despite fierce competition, growth in the number of travel agencies has remained close to 10 percent per year over the past two decades.

NEED FOR A BUSINESS PLAN

The relative ease of market entry can lull a travel agency manager into complacency and a belief that success is assured. Nothing could be further from the truth. The passing years since deregulation have been challenging ones for all travel agencies, and the future is clouded in uncertainty. What is certain is that competitive conditions will intensify and greater levels of management expertise will be required for success in the travel agency business.

Planning is a major key to success for any travel agency, particularly a newcomer. A business plan is essential for several reasons.

Bankers and other financial backers require business plans. A financial backer assumes willingness to accept risk based on (a) the reputation of the applicant and his or her experience in the travel agency industry; (b) the applicant's success and reliability in previous business undertakings; (c) the personal financial net worth of the applicant; and (d) assessment of the applicant's business plan.

Anyone planning to open a travel agency is likely to be optimistic about future success, but often the decision is based on emotional reasons rather than objective analysis. A business plan forces the entrepreneur to analyze the opportunity from a business perspective and possibly avert potential disasters. After analyzing the situation, some may decide not to enter the travel agency business. These entrepreneurs can then select another more appropriate business—perhaps something less complex and more profitable—without wasting time, capital, or reputation.

Individuals who elect to open a travel agency after constructing a business plan will be more aware of the problems and risks they face. The business plan will force them to examine the reasons for wanting to start the agency and whether they have the necessary qualifications and/or drive to succeed. In researching for the business plan, they are more likely to understand that a travel agency generally does not generate a huge return on investment and that owners and managers tend to be too busy with day-to-day operations to take extensive advantage of travel benefits. If the decision is made to continue with opening an agency, the business plan will serve as road map to guide new owners in their managerial functions.

The business plan is essentially a plan of operation, providing all the information necessary to run the business. Specific components of the business plan include

- Name of agency
- Ownership
- Location and building
- Philosophy and mission statement
- Organization chart
- Industry and market analysis
- Strategic plan
- Sales forecast
- Licenses and certification
- Conference appointments

These elements will be discussed in the sections that follow.

Name of Agency

It is important to select a name that has the following attributes:

- It is easily remembered by clients.
- It is easily pronounced.

- It is easily spelled and written.
- It looks impressive in print and on signs.
- It reinforces the desired image.
- It has permanence and is not trendy.
- It does not infringe upon the name of others and is not the same name as a previous unsuccessful agency.

On this last point, it is important to ensure that the proposed name can be legally used and is not already the possession of another person or business. This requires checking with the state's incorporation department.

Ownership

Serious consideration must be given to the issue of ownership, which may be in the form of an individual proprietorship, a partnership, a limited partnership, or a corporation. These terms will be explained later in the chapter. It is worth mentioning, however, that many travel agencies comprising multiple owners have experienced serious problems due to conflict among owners, including those who only have minority interests in the business.

During the formation period of a new travel agency, friends and relatives frequently become excited about seeing themselves as co-owners of a glamorous new business. Unfortunately, the hard reality of daily business problems soon unfolds, and many lose interest. It is generally best to keep the number of owners at a minimum, but if multiple owners are desired, a corporate form of business organization should be selected for the agency.

Entrepreneurs have been known to promise partial ownership to accountants, lawyers, and consultants in exchange for their services in helping to form the agency. Such professionals will seldom wish to continue donating services once the agency has been formed. If each, as co-owner must be consulted prior to making decisions, the decision-making process will be a slow one. Examples abound of co-owners who started as friends and departed as enemies; they should therefore be carefully selected. An attorney experienced in establishing new business enterprises should be consulted before potential co-owners enter into an agreement.

Location and Building

A business plan includes a description of the location and the building where the agency will be housed. Location can be a critical factor if walk-in traffic is expected. A ground floor location with a good window area for displays, as well as location in a busy commercial area, is essential to attract walk-ins (it is mandatory in some countries). If walk-in traffic is not an issue, a location that requires lower rent and maintenance may be suitable. Other factors to consider include adequate parking, the number of other travel agencies located in the immediate area, and proximity to businesses and middle- and upper-class neighborhoods. Both location and the building itself must match the objectives of the agency.

Until the business is well established, most new travel agencies are well advised to lease rather than buy the office property. The services of an experienced commercial real estate professional, who helps with lease negotiations and provides guidance to avert potential problems, can be invaluable in directing the entrepreneur to suitable locations. Commercial real estate companies have retail leasing specialists whose task is to assist clients with these needs.

Philosophy and Mission Statement

Successful business ventures operate under a statement of what the business is intended to be and philosophical statements concerning how the business will be operated, and these need to be clearly thought out and written as a guide. Exhibit 2.1 provides an example of a mission statement for a travel agency specifying how the agency will conduct its business.

Organization Chart

Efficiency of operation and minimization of internal conflict depend upon a clear understanding of the authority, responsibilities, and titles of all individuals within the travel agency. An organization chart is the common method of visually depicting this organizational design. A description of the titles and responsibilities of all employees should accompany the chart. (Organization charts will be further discussed in Chapter 6.)

Most travel agencies begin with only a few persons and gradually add employees and management levels as the business grows. Sometimes a spouse, relative, or friend of one of the original key people serves the company on a part-time basis. The role and responsibilities of this individual as well as such professionals as accountants and lawyers should be understood and described. In the absence of clear understanding, these individuals sometimes assume management responsibilities on an ex officio basis, which can lead to conflict if relationships are not clearly understood.

Industry and Market Analysis

The business plan should include a description and analysis of the travel agency industry. A good analysis requires interviews with knowledgeable persons from associations that represent travel agencies, suppliers such as hotels and airlines, government agencies, and competitors. Industry publications can also provide a great deal of information. The analysis of the industry will provide a "macro" perspective and enable an entrepreneur to understand important trends and possible opportunities.

EXHIBIT 2.1 Example of a Mission Statement

PAX TRAVEL AGENCY
MISSION STATEMENT

The PAX Travel Agency has a basic mission to provide its clientele with a full range of travel services—both business and pleasure, primarily at the deluxe level—handled in a competent, professional manner. To fulfill this mission, our management and staff will work together, acting in accordance with the highest standards and ethics of the travel profession, dealing fairly with our travel suppliers as well as our clients. We will also strive for constant self-education in travel product knowledge and be ever alert to rapid changes in the dynamic travel industry in order to provide PAX Travel Agency's clients with correct up-to-the-minute information and appropriate advice suited to each client's particular needs. By providing high-quality service and building a solid and loyal client base, *profit*, which is the life blood of all businesses, will be assured.

Although a travel agency will be affected by national trends, most of its income is derived from the local market, and frequently conditions within the local market are quite different from the national picture. An analysis of the local market should contain the following:

1. *Competition.* All competitors, including nontraditional travel agents such as discount travel agencies and department store travel clubs, should be described. The description should consider perceived strengths and weaknesses, customer base, competitive strategies used, turnover trends such as bankruptcies, and entrance of new travel agencies during the past three years. An assessment as to whether or not the community can realistically support the agency and the competitive advantages of the proposed agency should be made.

2. *Market Trends.* It is critical to have a clear understanding of the local market and how it is changing. In some markets, government accounts are very important; in others, pleasure and commercial travel business may be distributed among a broad base of clients. It may be foolish to enter a market dominated by only a few clients, such as large corporations and government agencies. Increasingly, clients of this type are dictating to travel agencies their own terms of doing business. In some cases, agencies have been asked to return all commissions to the client and to work on a monthly fee instead.

3. *Market Segments.* Travel agencies are increasingly being forced to find market niches rather than attempting to serve the entire general public

as well as the commerical sector. Travel agencies have been successful in selecting specialized market niches such as an ethnic market or the religious market. There are, for example, travel agencies specializing in the overseas Chinese market to the People's Republic of China and a southeastern travel agency that specializes in arranging group travel for church members to religious seminars and conferences. The market analysis portion of the business plan should identify opportunities that exist in terms of serving particular market segments.

4. *Barriers to Entry.* Barriers to entry exist in some markets. The existence of too many large travel agencies or lack of affordable office space in good locations might prove to be significant barriers and should be considered in the local market analysis.

Strategic Plan

Based on the industry and market analysis and the overall goals for the agency, a business strategy must be selected. Strategy entails how best to utilize limited resources to maximize profits and obtain other agency goals given the environment and the competition. Strategic planning then can be defined as the determination of the future status of the business with specific reference to its products, its profitability, its size, its rate of innovation, and its relationship with owners, managers, employees, and so on. The process of planning assists travel agency management in reaching better decisions regarding all aspects of operation.[1]

1. *Product-Market Matrix.* The product-market matrix is a major component or outcome of the agency's strategic planning. The matrix identifies which products the agency will be selling and to whom they will be sold. It is important to segment both products and markets in order to determine differences in resource requirements such as personnel, facilities, and marketing. The matrix in Figure 2.1 provides a simplified way for analyzing product-market decisions.

2. *Environmental Forecast.* Forecasts of the future environment are a major basis of planning and should be made explicit during the planning process. A small agency lacking the resources to conduct its own research and expensive forecasts can utilize available data and forecasting results available through trade publications and local business organizations.

3. *Growth Directions.* For both short-term and long-term planning, agency management should determine future growth directions and the resources this will require. There are basically three options available to agencies seeking growth: market expansion, product expansion, and vertical integration. *Market expansion* involves selling existing products to new markets. *Product expansion* means adding new products com-

| | Outbound | | | | | | | | | | | | | | Inbound | | | |
| | Commercial Independent | | | | Comm. Corp. | | Commercial Nonprofit | | | | | | Pleasure/ Personal | | Group | | | |
	Professional	Sales-Distribution	Manufacturing	Other	Individual	Group	Schools: Indiv.	Schools: Group	Gov't.: Indiv.	Gov't.: Group	Quasi-Public: Indiv.	Quasi-Public: Group	FIT	GIT	Conf. Business	Pleasure	International	Domestic
Air Transportation																		
Train																		
Auto Rental																		
Hotel																		
Package Tours																		
Own Tours																		
Cruise																		
Travel Insurance																		
Financial Services																		
Recreation																		
Incentive																		
Group Planning																		

FIGURE 2.1 Product-market matrix

patible with the agency's existing product line. For a strictly retail agency, *vertical integration* involves expanding beyond retailing activities, for example, wholesaling, designing and operating tours, and incentive travel. Anticipated growth directions should be specified as part of the strategic plan.

Sales Forecast

Bankers and other money lenders are not interested in vague statements and usually require facts and figures regarding the prospective business. A travel agency business plan should include an estimated sales forecast for each month of the year. Sales are likely to fluctuate quite drastically between months and seasons, depending upon the location of the agency and its clientele. Financial projections and the determination of future cash flows are based on these monthly estimates; therefore, the sales forecast must be realistic. Consideration must also be given to the time lag between sales and receipt of commissions and the implication of credit card sales, as these will seriously affect cash flows.

Sales forecasts should include revenues from all possible sources. Revenue from fees and commissions from the various types of insurance options are becoming important to travel agencies and may account for a substantial portion of future revenue. Financial projections will be discussed at a later point in the chapter.

Licenses and Certification

To open a travel agency in the United States, individuals are not required to hold a college degree or a professional certification. Other countries may have different requirements; for instance, in some countries, no one is allowed to work in an agency unless they have passed the examination set by the local authority. These and other requirements should be stated in the business plan, as well as the costs and time associated with obtaining licenses and professional certification. Travel agencies in the United States and elsewhere may also be required to have a sales tax license or a retail merchant's license.

Conference Appointments

Travel agencies are required to obtain *appointments* from associations representing international and domestic airlines. Appointments authorize travel agencies to serve as sales agents for carriers and allow the agencies to write tickets and collect commissions from the carriers. Travel agents are also guided by the regulations established by these international and domestic associations. Later in this chapter, we will examine the relationships that ensue from this regulatory function.

ADDITIONAL PREOPENING ACTIVITIES

A number of other activities must be completed prior to opening the agency. If a manager is to be selected, this should be done as early in the planning process as possible, so that the manager can then be included in preopening decision-making matters and help to select other agency staff members. The design of a company logo needs to be commissioned and appropriate stationary, business cards, and business forms printed. The office layout should be designed and office furniture and required equipment purchased. A safe (burglar proof and bolted to the floor) and minimum telephone lines (at least three) will need installation and a safety deposit box should be arranged.

Commonly used index catalogues will be required as office references; these include the *Travel Planner,* the *Hotel and Travel Index,* the *Official Steamship Guide International,* and the *Official Hotel and Resort Guide.* The *Official Airline Guide,* a key index for travel agents seeking information on airlines, routes, and fares, now offer an electronic edition. Subscriptions to such trade magazines as *The Travel Agent, Travel Weekly,* and *ASTA Agency Management* should be ordered.

Brochures for hotels, tours, attractions, and so on will also be needed, and travel suppliers are generally more than willing to provide such information. For international travel, letters of request to the various National Tourism Organizations (NTOs) can yield a significant amount of material. Additionally, a supply of the various visa application forms for the many countries clients will travel to is needed.

Opening a new agency will require many other activities as well: opening a bank account and setting up an accounting system; selecting a computer reservation system (CRS), negotiating the computer contract, and ordering automated equipment; arranging for insurance; and planning for the grand opening in terms of advertising, publicity, and other promotional activities.

Since the majority of travel agency sales are made in air transportation, some arrangement with the various airlines will be necessary to obtain ticket stock to be used in the interim while waiting for official appointment from the conferences.

PURCHASING AN EXISTING AGENCY

The entrepreneur who has decided to enter the travel agency industry, should give at least some consideration to the possibility of acquiring an established agency as a viable option. There are several advantages to entering the travel agency business in this way, particularly for a newcomer to the industry. The seller of the agency can generally provide the buyer with the benefit of experience, besides an office which is already staffed and equipped, and with a ready clientele. Conference appointments can be easily transferred instead of having to apply and wait for new appointments, avoiding a lag period without cash flow from airline commissions. By acquiring an existing agency, a new owner will most likely inherit the ongoing sales volume and profit, thereby gaining an earlier return on investment. If the agency has not been profitable, the new owner will at least know what shortfalls he or she will have to overcome to turn the agency around.

Choosing the option of purchasing an existing agency is, however, not without its drawbacks. For one thing, more upfront capital is generally required and the new owner runs the risk of having paid more for the agency than it is actually worth. The new owner may need to pay off financial notes over a period of years, which can seriously affect his or her financial statements.

A seller who is anxious to unload his or her business may not voluntarily reveal everything in discussing the agency's business situation: The principle of caveat emptor (let the buyer beware) applies. Assuming that both parties are experienced businesspersons, the seller is under no obligation to disclose more than he or she is asked by the potential buyer about the business operations unless it is material or unless the withholding of such information is tantamount to misrepresentation. Consideration must, therefore, be given to the motives behind the existing owner's decision to sell, and questioning should be thorough. In purchasing an established agency, the new owner must realize that he or she is purchasing the agency's weaknesses as well as its strong points. A poor location, bad reputation, and internal staffing problems, for example, will stay with the agency even though ownership has changed hands. And for that matter, there are no guarantees that key employees and/or clients will remain with the agency.

Besides the foregoing, the new owner should analyze the volume of sales in view of the industry analysis as well as growth rates and profits, as well as check conference appointments to ensure they are in good standing. Attention should also be directed toward the agency's long-term potential, the status of automation, the terms of the lease, and the abilities of the existing staff.

TRAVEL AGENCY OWNERSHIP

As discussed under the business plan section, the legal form of business in which the agency will be operated is an important consideration. The common travel agency structures are discussed below.

Proprietorship

A proprietorship is a business that is owned by one person, who is the sole person and has sole rights to profits but is liable for all the debts of the business. The sole proprietorship is the easiest to establish and dissolve; it has no existence apart from its owner. The advantages to this type of structure are

- Low cost to organize
- Easier record keeping
- Deduction of losses from owner's personal income
- Need to file just one tax return

Disadvantages to the sole proprietorship include

- Liability of owner for all debts
- Personal taxing of profits
- Difficulty in attracting additional investors
- Termination of business upon death of owner
- Lack of the full tax benefits that accrue to corporations[2]

Partnership

A partnership is a simple form of business with an agreement among own-ers as to who has the right to manage the operation and share in the profits. Each partner assumes the unlimited obligation to be personally responsible for all liabilities of the enterprise. The advantages and disadvantages of the partnership form of business are basically the same as for sole proprietor-ships. Additional advantages, however, include more availability of capital, better use of labor, and possibly improved management. The potential for personality and philosophical clashes between partners leading to divided management decisions is one of the major drawbacks to a partnership. Po-tential partners should be compatible and reputable, particularly because of the unlimited liability arising from the business-related acts of partners.

Every general partner in a travel agency has the right to participate in management of the agency, to inspect the books and records of the agency at any time, and to have a predetermined share of the profit and/or loss. A written partnership agreement setting forth the specific rights and obliga-tions of each partner should exist in any agency partnership.

Limited Partnership

A limited partnership generally consists of one or more general partners with powers to conduct ordinary business and any number of limited, or special, partners. In typical limited partnership agreements, limited part-ners are silent in management decisions, including those decisions affecting their investment. Their liability, however, is limited to the amount of their investment. The general partners, on the other hand, retain management power but have unlimited liability for debts.[3]

Corporation

The corporate form of a travel agency is the most formal and the most com-mon. Today, approximately two-thirds of travel agencies are organized as corporations. A corporation is a distinct and separate legal entity from the stockholders and operates under the laws of the state where is it incorpo-rated. It has almost all the rights and powers of an individual, such as the right to sue and be sued and to issue stock, make contracts, and perform other business-related tasks. If this option is selected, a board of directors must be elected and officers of the corporation chosen to carry out the policies and business of the company. Advantages of the corporate form of ownership include

- Limited liability for stockholders (stockholders can only lose the amount of their investment)
- Perpetual existence (death of owners does not affect the corporation)
- Separate legal entity
- Attraction of additional capital through sale of stock
- Quick transfer of ownership without dissolving the corporation
- More tax options

Disadvantages of the corporate form of ownership include

- Higher organizing expenses
- Requirement to file two tax returns (individual and corporate)
- Additional record keeping (tax returns, corporate registration, annual reports, minutes, and so on)
- Strict adherence to the state requirements with respect to corporate practices

Another option for owners wanting to incorporate is to elect the S corporation status. The S status allows the profit or losses of the corporation to flow through the individual stockholders but does not affect the limited liability for those persons. The form to declare an S corporation status must be filled in within 75 days of the initial incorporation.[4]

Before deciding on the best business form, it is critical for prospective owners of new travel agencies to consult with an experienced attorney who can make all necessary arrangements for the legal establishment.

FINANCIAL POTENTIAL

The bottom line of any business is profit or loss. Potential profits should be the primary reason anyone establishes a travel agency and should exceed the amount of income an individual could otherwise achieve through other forms of employment. In the case of a travel agency, however, it may take three to four years to reach this level.

The management of any business requires risk, stress, long hours, and personal sacrifices. The owner will want to be compensated eventually, if not immediately, for his or her efforts and investment consistent with the demands of the enterprise. To assure that there will be profits and return on investment, financial projections, also termed "pro forma," are essential before the business is formed. Realistic projections over a period of one to five years of business performance will give owners and vendors an idea of the possible revenues, costs, and profit margins for measuring the potential return on both operations and investment. (See Chapters 8 and 9, which cover accounting and financial management, including pro forma.)

Assistance in constructing financial projections may be obtained from a variety of sources. Workbooks are available to assist prospective entrepreneurs and may be purchased in an office supply store or borrowed from a public library. Professional accounting firms and independent CPAs commonly provide consulting and pro forma services for a fee. Banks may offer assistance by providing forms and referrals to qualified individuals who can help. The Service Corps of Retired Executives (SCORE) may also be called upon for help with the assignment of a retired business executive to offer guidance.

A few general guidelines should be observed in developing financial projections.

1. Figures should always be realistic and laid out on a spread sheet for the desired period of time. Costs should not be underestimated or potential revenue overstated; conservative thinking applies. It is better to err with higher cost and lower revenue estimates than vice versa. Cost and revenue estimates can be obtained from business people who know the industry.

2. All cost and revenue estimates should be used, including important variables such as a salary for the manager, even when the owner is the manager. Exclusion of important variables, such as taxes, depreciation, and interest, can spell the difference between profit or loss. The services of a professional accountant can be invaluable in this area.

3. Monthly fluctuations, or seasonal variations, should be shown. In the travel agency industry, certain months are likely to have higher costs and/or revenues than others.

4. Figures should be double checked; it is easy to make errors that can affect projections by thousands of dollars. First-draft financial projections are unlikely to be usable, as generally this task requires at least one revision.

5. While entrepreneurs are often very sensitive to questions concerning their financial projections, they should seriously consider the review critique of others. Projections might even be submitted for review to an owner-operator of a noncompeting, successful travel agency.

Well-prepared financial projections offer the prospective travel agency an opportunity to understand the following:

- Amount of invested capital required
- Timing of investment capital—when it will be needed
- Cash flow projections
- Seasonal fluctuations and possible need for seasonal input of capital
- Budgeting requirements
- Likely returns (profits)

Investors and bankers are impressed with well-prepared financial projections. Indeed, it is not likely that either a loan or an outside investment for a new agency can be attracted in the absence of a realisticlaly developed pro forma.

New owners tend to underestimate operating expenses drastically and consequently do not obtain sufficient financial backing, which is a major cause of business failure. One guideline is that a new agency should have sufficient working capital to carry it one full year without revenue.

REGULATORY ASSOCIATIONS

As discussed earlier in the chapter, travel agencies need to obtain appointments from associations representing international and domestic airlines, authorizing them to serve as sales agents and allowing them to write tickets and collect commissions from the carriers. Travel agents must also abide by the various regulations established by these associations. This section will discuss how the two primary regulatory associations (ARC and IATAN) operate and explain their various requirements. A diagram illustrating the relationship between ARC and IATAN and travel agencies is shown in Figure 2.2

The Airlines Reporting Corporation

Within the United States, the Airlines Reporting Corporation (ARC) serves the domestic airline industry. Its stockholders are the passenger carriers of the Air Transport Association (ATA), but many additional airlines, both domestic and foreign, participate in ARC.

ARC's purpose is "to provide a method of approving authorized agency locations for the sale of transportation and cost-effective procedures for processing records and funds of such sales to carrier customers."[5]

Consequently, ARC establishes several agency requirements that must be met as well as basic ticketing and reporting procedures to be followed. Since the majority of income for most travel agencies is derived from commissions on airline ticket sales and the ARC represents the various airline carriers, it is mandatory that a prospective travel agency obtain ARC appointment.

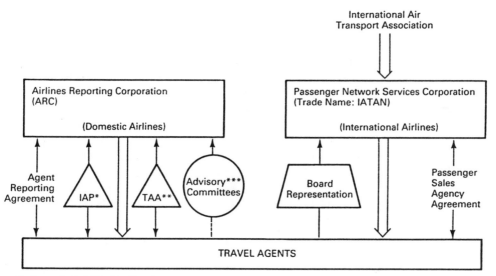

* Independent Arbitration Panel
** Travel Agent Arbiter
*** Travel agents work with ARC through advisory committees; there is no agent representation
on the ARC board.

FIGURE 2.2   Regulatory relationships

Area settlement plan.   All ARC travel agents report and settle ticketing transactions with the carrier participants by means of ARC's Standard Ticket and Area Settlement Plan (ASP).

The essential elements of the plan provide

1. Standard traffic documents instead of individual carrier documents
2. One-step imprinting on documents of the issuing carrier's name and the agent's validation at the time the document is issued
3. A consolidated sales report and single-sum remittance for all carriers to a designated area bank (an example of an agent sales summary report provided in Appendix A)
4. An area bank, acting as a clearinghouse, to determine the amount due each carrier and to transmit such amount to the carrier
5. Computer-generated sales summaries to each agent and carrier for their respective sales activity

ARC requirements.   To qualify for participation as an ARC travel agent, several criteria must be met, after which an appointment designation is not difficult to obtain, as ARC generally approves the majority of accreditation applications received. Any applicant may be denied accreditation if the applicant includes any material misrepresentations or inaccuracies in the application.

For new agencies, an application in the format specified by ARC must be submitted that will require up to 90 days to process. While the new agencies may apply for appointment prior to opening, ARC accreditation will be granted only when the agency is in full operation at a suitable location and with a qualified manager at the time of ARC's onsite inspection conducted during the application processing period. An agency conducting business during the processing period, must obtain tickets directly from the individual carriers on a strict cash basis at the city ticket offices or airport. Normally, commissions are paid retroactively after approval is granted to the agency. These decisions are made entirely by the carriers, not ARC. This can create cash flow problems for a new agency.

Requirements to become an ARC Industry Agent are listed in the ARC *Industry Agents' Handbook* (which is usually updated three times annually). The major requirements are

1. *Financial.* The ARC requires a bond or an irrevocable letter of credit. The bond is a performance or financial guaranty type of bond. The irrevocable letter of credit is a guarantee of payment issued by a federally insured lending institution. The minimum amount required of the ARC bond or irrevocable letter of credit is $20,000. An ARC bond is obtained through a surety or bonding company, while an irrevocable letter of credit is obtained through a bank. An attorney can provide advice concerning these procedures, and a bank may also provide advice with respect to the irrevocable letter of credit.

2. *Personnel.* The ARC requires that the location shall have at least one person who is a full-time employee and on the payroll of the applicant. This person must have had, within the past three years, one year's full-time experience in airline passenger ticketing, and possess each of the following qualifications:
   (a) Exercises daily supervision of and responsibility for the operations of that agency location and has the authority to make management decisions
   (b) Demonstrates a working knowledge of the *Industry Agents' Handbook* by completing a written questionnaire
   (c) Has had at least two full years' experience in either selling general travel services to the public or supervising the operations of a business offering such services

3. *Location.* The location of the travel agency must be freely accessible and clearly identified to the public. The office must be primarily engaged in the sale of passenger transportation. There are exceptions to accessiblilty requirements for restricted access and customer premises/locations.

4. *Other Requirements.* Other ARC requirements for inclusion cover
   • Identification of the agency to the general public

- Name of agency—cannot be misleading
- Citizenship of the applicant
- Financial integrity
- Criminal background
- Change of agency ownership
- Change of agency bank accounts

These requirements are, however, subject to change. Anyone desiring to open a travel agency should write to the ARC for current information.

Airlines Reporting Corporation
1709 New York Avenue, NW
Washington, D.C. 20006

Agent reporting agreement.   Before an application is approved by the ARC, the agent is required to enter into an Agent Reporting Agreement, which specifies the rights and obligations of both parties. The complete text of the Agent Reporting Agreement is contained in the ARC's *Industry Agents' Handbook*. Covered in the *Handbook* are the following elements:

- Locations covered by this agreement
- Qualifications for retention on the agency list
- Appointment of agent by carrier
- Change of ownership
- Change of name or location
- Reports and settlements, defaults, and other financial irregularities under ASP
- Refund or exchange of ARC traffic documents
- Liability and waiver of claim
- Delivery and withdrawal of ARC traffic documents and airline identification plates
- Custody and security of ARC traffic documents and airline identification plates
- Inspection and retention of agent records
- Review of qualifications of and breaches by agent
- Application and annual fees
- Special location exemptions
- Notices
- Central collection service
- Transfer or assignment of agreement, deaths affecting ownership
- Reduced rate transportation
- Remuneration of agent

- Arbitration
- Interpretive opinion procedures
- Memorandum of agreement
- Amendment of agreement
- Effectiveness
- Termination

The Agent Reporting Agreement has generally been viewed by the travel agency industry as an "adhesion contract," meaning that terms are unilaterally dictated by the carriers to the agency on a "take it or leave it" basis.

ARC audits.   ARC maintains a staff of full-time auditors based in various cities. The auditors' role is to inspect the books and records of travel agencies to determine compliance with the Agent Reporting Agreement, such as

- Proper reporting of air transportation sales
- Accountability of ticket forms
- Security of traffic documents and airline identification plates
- Reduced rate travel eligibility
- Adequate bond coverage
- Ownership verification

Travel agent arbiter.   Between 1977 and 1987 a Travel Agent Commissioner program existed within ARC to settle disputes between a carrier and a travel agent when an agent had breached a provision of the Agent Reporting Agreement. Following an out-of-court settlement of a suit brought by the Association of Retail Travel Agents (ARTA) against the ARC, in 1987 the Travel Agent Commissioner program was replaced with the Travel Agent Arbiter (TAA) program. While the two programs are similar in some ways, the TAA is neutral—that is, financed by both agents and airlines—whereas the Travel Agent Commissioner program was funded solely by the airlines. The Arbiter retains the Commissioner's functions of ruling on ARC complaints against individual agents and in addition has the role of hearing individual agents' complaints against ARC.

The Arbiter also has much wider discretion and flexibility in deciding cases. For travel agents, the new program represents a step in the right direction toward establishing a fair and equitable means to settle disputes between agents and airlines. Disputes commonly center around late remittances, rejected applications, ticket security, failure to maintain required bonding, and reporting violations.

Independent arbitration panel.   As part of the same 1987 settlement between ARTA and ARC, an Independent Arbitration Panel (IAP) was established. The IAP is a panel of three persons (non-ARC employees) with the authority to hear appeals brought by agency organizations that feel that ARC has adopted unreasonable rules or fee changes. The formation of the IAP represents an end to the airlines' absolute power to set rules governing agents.

International Airlines Travel Agent Network (IATAN)

The International Air Transport Association (IATA) was founded in 1945 to promote safe, regular, and economical international air service; to study the problems of air commerce; and to provide a means of collaboration among international air transport enterprises. Members of IATA are scheduled international airline operators; associate members are scheduled airlines in domestic service. The Passenger Network Services Corporation (PNSC) is a subsidiary of IATA that trades under the name International Airlines Travel Agent Network (IATAN).

The IATAN serves a similar function as that of the ARC but for international air carriers. Appointed agencies enter into the IATAN Agency Agreement, which incorporates the procedures set forth in the IATAN *Travel Agent Handbook* and IATAN *Ticketing Handbook*. Some U.S. travel agents find they do not need to hold appointments by both organizations as they can write tickets on most international airlines through the ARC. Others believe it is important to belong to both groups.

The PNSC has agent representation with full voting rights on their board of directors, unlike ARC, whose board comprises solely air carriers. PNSC's control over travel agents is somewhat less strict than prior to deregulation. Still, applicants seeking endorsement and appointment by IATAN are required to meet the minimum standards set out in the "Standards for Endorsement as an International Airlines Travel Agent," many of which are similar to ARC requirements. A complete and current listing of IATAN requirements can be obtained by writing IATAN.

A new travel agency must be open for business before applying for IATAN accreditation. IATAN requirements are also subject to change. Further information should be obtained directly from this organization.

> International Airlines Travel Agent Network
> 2000 Peel Street, Suite 4060
> Montreal, Quebec, Canada H3A2W5

> International Airlines Travel Agent Network
> P.O. Box 93
> Essex Junction, VT 05452

Other Regulatory Associations

Each area of transportation is governed by its own association rulings. In addition to ARC and IATAN, travel agents may also work with the International Passenger Ships Association (IPSA), the Pacific Cruise Conference (PCC), and the National Railroad Passenger Corporation (NRPC).

SUMMARY

The careful development of a business plan prior to opening a travel agency can be invaluable to the success of the enterprise. A business plan allows a manager to understand potential problems and pitfalls and serves as a road map to profitability.

A thorough and well-thought-out business plan requires considerable time and patience. Unfortunately, managers often elect to shortcut this process for the sake of expediency in opening the business, which can prove a serious error. It is safer and easier to anticipate and prepare for problems in a business plan than to attempt to correct them once the business is in full operation. The process of developing the plan, moreover, can serve as a valuable learning tool for ownership and management.

In order for travel agencies to serve as sales agents for air carriers and other transportation suppliers, they must receive appointments from the relevant associations and abide by their requirements and procedures. New owners must be fully cognizant of the responsibilities and relationship that ensue from this regulatory function and the legal restrictions it places on the operator's freedom to run the travel agency.

DISCUSSION QUESTIONS

1. Why have travel agencies historically been easy to establish?
2. What are the major purposes of a business plan? Define some of the key elements of the business plan.
3. Discuss problems associated with having multiple owners of a travel agency.
4. Discuss the advantages and disadvantages of the following types of organizational forms of travel agencies: proprietorship, partnership, limited partnership, and corporation.
5. What is a pro forma? How is a pro forma developed?
6. What are Conference Appointments? Discuss some of the requirements to obtain an appointment.
7. What are the primary functions of the Airlines Reporting Corporation (ARC) and the International Airlines Travel Agent Network (IATAN)?

ENDNOTES

[1]James Langston, "Travel Agency Strategic Planning," *ICTA Journal*, n.d., pp. 41–43.

[2]Laurence Stevens, *Guide to Starting and Operating a Successful Travel Agency*, (Wheaton, IL: Merton House Travel and Tourism Publishers, 1983), p. 99.

[3]Jeffrey Miller and Laura Ochs, "Partnership Form of Ownership," *Travel Marketing and Agency Management Guidelines*, March/April, 1988, pp. XVI–13.

[4]Internal Revenue Service, phone consultation.

[5]*Industry Agents' Handbook*, Section 1.0, (Airlines Reporting Corporation, 1709 New York Avenue, NW, Washington, DC 20006, 1986), p.1.

SUPPLEMENTAL READING

ANOLIK, ALEXANDER, *The Law and the Travel Industry*, vol. II. San Francisco: Alchemy Books, 1987.

DILTS, JEFFREY, AND GEORGE PROUGH, "Travel Agent Strategies for Managing Today's Dynamic Environment," *Tourism Service Marketing: Advances in Theory and Practice*, vol. II. Special Conference Series, 1986.

FREMONT, PAMELA, *How to Open and Run a Money-Making Travel Agency*. New York: John Wiley & Sons, Inc., 1983.

appendix a

Example of agent sales summary

```
RPT ID FNARC-1        AIRLINES REPORTING CORPORATION        REF NBR 03-05-1-2
PAGE - 1                   AGENT SALES SUMMARY               RPT PED  05/05/85

00 12345-6 ABC Travel

        TICKET    ERR  I   TOTAL                COMMISSION       TAX          NET
A/L     NUMBER    CDS  C   SALE    FARE     AMT      CODE     AMT    CD      REMIT
006   8010129128         174.00C 174.00   17.40    10.00     .00    NC      17.40-
001   8010129129         217.00  217.00   21.70    10.00     .00    NC     195.30
016   7070104945         272.00- 251.85- 25.19-    10.00   20.15-   08     246.81-
              RFND - 3 - 7070104945
              RFND - 4 - 7070104945
006   7100105013         181.00  167.59   16.76    10.00   13.41    08     164.24
015   7100105014    Q      8.00    7.41     .74    10.00     .59    08       7.26
              EXCH - 3 - 015-7100105001
              EXCH - 4 - 015-7100105001
001   7100105015         174.00C 161.11   16.11    10.00   12.89    08      16.11-
016   7100105016         346.00C 320.37   32.04    10.00   25.63    08      32.04-
007   7100105017         252.00C 233.33   23.33    10.00   18.67    08      23.33-
016   7100105018         412.00  381.48   38.15    10.00   30.52    08     373.85
015   7100105019    X   1613.00 1600.00  128.00    08.00   13.00    NC    1480.00
007   7100105021         275.00C 254.63   25.46    10.00   20.37    08      25.46-
015   7100105022         412.00  381.48   38.15    10.00   30.52    08     373.85
037   7100105023         269.00  249.07   24.91    10.00   19.93    08     244.09
001   7100105024    L    206.00  190.74   19.07    10.00   15.26    08     186.93
007   7100105025         136.00  125.93   12.59    10.00   10.07    08     123.41
016   7100105026         233.00C 215.74   21.57    10.00   17.26    08      21.57-
006   8207482048    0    190.00  175.93   17.59    10.00   14.07    08      17.59-
037   8227284124         304.00C 281.48   28.15    10.00   22.52    08      28.15-
037   8227284125         CONJ
001   8227284127    X    299.00  286.00   31.46    11.00   13.00    NC     262.54
007   8227284128         307.00  284.26   28.43    10.00   22.74    08     278.57
015   8524919335         305.00  282.41   29.24    09.66D  22.59    08D    275.76
006   8524919336         357.00  330.56   34.06    09.71D  26.44    08D    322.94
037   8964363124         ADJ                                               18.30
007   8977001468                            7.37   09.99D                   7.37-
              AAD - 007 - 8207482120     ORIG RPTD 03-03-4-2
037   8994101841         598.00- 553.70- 55.37-    10.00   44.30-   08      55.37
              RFND - 1 - 037 8207482115
              RFND - 2 - 037 8207482115
006   8994101842    E     50.00-  46.30-  4.63-    10.00    3.70-   08       4.63
006   7100105028
              EXCH - 4 - 006-7100105010
006   8227284129    Z    128.00  INVALID CC ACCT NBR 3700123456789012       .00
                    A    100.00                                             .00
--------------------------------------------------------------------------------
NET CASH          4450.00   NET CASH     4450.00   CASH SALES       4722.00
LESS COMMISSION    526.20   NET CREDIT   1300.00   CASH REFUNDS      272.00-
NET ADJUSTMENTS     18.30   TOTAL        5750.00   NET ADJUSTMENTS    18.30
NET REMITTANCE    3942.10                          AAD'S               7.37-
MAX AUTH AMOUNT   3995.60   FARES        5439.71   ARC TOTAL        4460.93
ADDTL AMOUNT DUE     0.00   TAXES         310.29   AGENT CASH TAPE  4354.93
                            TOTAL        5750.00
                                                   CREDIT SALES     1948.00
                                                   CREDIT REFUNDS    648.00-
AUTH NBR 850501                                    NET CREDIT       1300.00
AVG COMMISSION PCT  10.00                          AGENT CREDIT TAPE 1634.00
```

Source: Industry Agents' Handbook, Section 1.0, (Airlines Reporting Corporation, 1709 New York Avenue, NW, Washington, DC 20006, 1986), p. 1. Information from the *Industry Agent's Handbook* is used by permission of Airlines Reporting Corporation; however, since the handbook is revised frequently, the material included in *Professional Travel Agency Management* should be verified by comparison with the current edition of the handbook. The handbook is available from ARC for $35.

```
RPT ID FNARC-1          AIRLINES REPORTING CORPORATION        REF NBR 03-05-1-2
PAGE - 2                    AGENT SALES SUMMARY                RPT PED 05/05/85

00 12345-6

NUMBER OR AUDITOR'S COUPONS REPORTED BY DOCUMENT TYPE

TAT - 14  2-CPN - 05  MCO - 02  TOUR - 00   TELE - 00   TOTAL - 023
ATB - 00  4-CPN - 00  PTA - 02             OTHER- 00

COMMISSION AND FARES BY CARRIER ID PLATE

A/L  TOTAL COMM  TOTAL FARES  NET REMIT   A/L  TOTAL COMM  TOTAL FARES   NET REMIT
001     88.74       838.78      623.26    015    196.13      2271.30      2131.87
006     79.29       787.57      458.71    016     66.57       665.74        73.43
007     89.81       898.15      353.19    037      2.31-       23.15-      266.67

FARES BY COMMISSION - CURRENT PERIOD

         CASH FARES   PCT.   CR-CD FARES  PCT.   ALL FARES  TOT COMM  PCT.   TRANS
DOM
   10.00   2149.08    51.0     1202.38   100.0    3351.46    336.67   65.0     21
   11.00    200.93     4.0        .00      .0      200.93     22.10    4.0      1
TOTAL     2349.01    55.0     1202.38   100.0    3552.39    358.77   69.0     22

INTL X
   08.00   1600.00    38.0        .00      .0     1600.00    128.00   25.0      1
   11.00    286.00     7.0        .00      .0      286.00     31.46    6.0      1
TOTAL     1886.00    45.0        .00      .0     1886.00    159.46   31.0      2

TOTAL     4236.01   100.0     1202.38   100.0    5438.39    518.23  100.0     24

QTD FARES BY COMMISSION - 005 REPORTS

         CASH FARES   PCT.   CR-CD FARES  PCT.   ALL FARES  TOT COMM  PCT.   TRANS
DOM       6696.88 .   55.8     3324.79    62.8   10021.67   1008.07   62.4     94
INTL X    5306.72    44.2     1971.00    37.2    7277.72    607.09   37.6     12

TOTAL    12003.60   100.0     5295.79   100.0   17299.39   1615.16  100.0    106

DISCREPANCIES
**********     A - AMOUNT ON TAPE, BUT DOCUMENT MISSING OR RETURNED.....SEC-12.0
7100105014     Q - REFUND OR EXCHANGE - NO FLIGHT COUPONS PRESENT.......SEC- 6.0
7100105024     L - ITEM LISTED ON INCORRECT TAPE........................SEC-12.0
8207482048     O - AUDITOR'S COUPON REPORTED OUT OF PERIOD..............SEC-12.0
8227284129     Z - CREDIT SALE BEING RETURNED - CORRECT AND RESUBMIT....SEC- 8.0
8994101842     E - COMMISSION CODE/AMOUNT MISSING......................SEC- 5.2
```

chapter 3

Types of Travel Operations

LEARNING OBJECTIVES

- To understand the different types of operations involved in selling and providing travel services
- To be able to differentiate between these operations
- To be able to explain how these different operations are interrelated
- To understand the operational issues and trends facing travel companies today

KEY TERMS

- Consolidator
- Full-Service National Tour Wholesaler
- General Sales Agent (GSA)
- Ground Operator
- Inbound
- In-House National Tour Wholesaler
- Outbound
- Principal
- Profit Centers
- Regional Tour Wholesaler
- Specialty Channeler
- Specialty Tour Operator
- Standard Costs
- Tour Operator
- Tour Wholesaler
- Wholesaler

INTRODUCTION

The basic functions of a retail travel agency, as described in Chapter 1, have not changed significantly over the years. Other types of travel operations, however, have developed in response to changes in the marketplace. During the early post-war years, tour operators in the United States served mostly independent travelers rather than group travelers. It was not until 1966 with CAB Approval of Inclusive Tour Charters that low-cost charter travel was available in the United States to the general public without any affinity restrictions.[1] Subsequent approval of Group Inclusive Tour fares on scheduled flights and less restrictive charter requirements during the early 1970s brought about mass travel on low-cost group packages.

With deregulation, the market has shifted back to independent travelers since it is no longer necessary to travel in an organized tour group to gain the benefit of low airfares. Companies involved with group travel have thus had to adjust to the changes in travelers as well as face increased competition.

Although this text focuses mainly on retail travel agency operations, it is nonetheless important for students to understand the differences among the other types of intermediary operations involved in the selling and providing of travel services. A retail agency must deal with wholesalers, tour operators, consolidators, general sales agents, and specialty channelers either as business associates or competitors. As shown in Figure 3.1, suppliers can sell their services directly to travelers or through any one or more

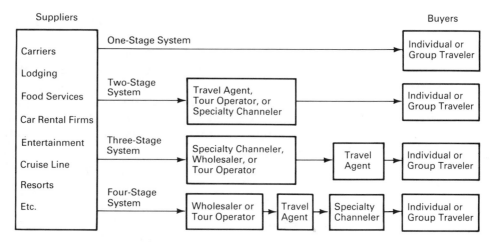

FIGURE 3.1 Travel sales distribution system
Source: Chuck Y. Gee, James C. Makens, and Dexter J. L. Choy, *The Travel Industry,* 2nd ed. (New York: Van Nostrand Reinhold, 1989,) p. 178.

stages in the sales distribution system. Understanding these operations and how they interrelate will facilitate business dealings and assist in uncovering new opportunities for increasing revenues—for instance, expanding the agency's business from retail to wholesale to special-interest travel.

RETAIL TRAVEL AGENCIES

We discussed earlier that retail travel agents act as agents for travel suppliers such as airlines, cruise ship lines, hotels, car rentals, and railroads. The retail agency receives a commission from suppliers for selling their respective services. Like other retail businesses, retail travel agencies sell directly to the consumer, but the analogy ends here. Retail agencies do not take ownership or have any advance commitment to purchase travel services from suppliers. A retail agency will usually not purchase services from an airline, hotel, or any other supplier until a client already has paid for the travel services he or she has requested.

When the need for travel services comes to mind, most people think of the retail travel agency, which routinely makes reservations for airline flights, hotels, and car rentals; sells package tours, travel insurance, and travelers cheques; develops travel itineraries; and provides one-stop convenience in planning and collecting payment for all services associated with a trip.

Retail operators are usually outbound oriented. Their operations involve making reservations and providing services for people who are leaving home for a vacation or for business. This is the opposite of an inbound tour wholesaler, who is mainly concerned with incoming passengers arriving at a particular destination. In many parts of the world, "outbound" and "inbound" are used to further describe an agency's business and interrelationships with other operations.

A retail agency may occasionally develop tours on an ad hoc basis for a specific client or group. However, developing a tour upon a client's request does not mean that an agency is engaging in wholesale operations, although some travel agencies do operate both retail and wholesale divisions. As the success of retail travel agencies and tour wholesalers depends on different factors, readers should know how these two types of operations differ.

TOUR WHOLESALERS

Tour wholesalers specialize in designing tour offerings that are marketed through retail travel agencies, not dealing directly with consumers unless they also operate a retail division (which many do). Wholesalers may specialize in developing tours for outbound travel, inbound travel, or both. A key distinction between wholesalers and retail agencies is that a wholesaler will contract for services from suppliers such as airlines and hotels in large volume in order to achieve lower cost per unit, then repackage the services for resale through retail travel agents. The success of a wholesale operator is dependent upon its ability to design and market tour packages that meet the needs of the traveling public.

In the case of outbound travel, wholesalers develop package tours that are offered with predetermined departure dates. Inbound packages comprise ground services, which may include any one or all of the following: reception, baggage handling, transportation, accommodations, food and beverage, entertainment, and sightseeing tours. Wholesalers also understand the growing preference of consumers for independent rather than group travel and in setting their rates have provided retail travel agents with maximum flexibility in combining or modifying components of a tour to satisfy individual client needs. Having such flexibility allows a retail travel agency to use the services and lower cost advantages of a wholesaler for both its group and individual clients.

A wholesaler can contract for services at substantially lower costs than a retailer not only due to sheer volume but also by providing suppliers with stable business throughout the year. A retail agent, on the other hand, may be willing to commit to suppliers during peak travel periods but not during off peaks when suppliers need assistance in selling their available capacity. In this instance, wholesalers, who provide steady volume throughout the year, will have greater leverage with suppliers.

Wholesale agencies may operate the tours they offer or they may contract with tour operators for the whole tour or only certain land arrangements. Wholesalers are often referred to as tour operators, but these two terms should not be confused. The following distinctions apply: (1) A wholesaler presumably sells nothing at retail, while a tour operator often does. (2) A wholesaler usually combines and contracts for existing services to produce a new package, whereas a tour operator usually creates new products, for example, sightseeing tours, and offers services of its own. (3) A wholesaler is less inclined than a tour operator to perform local ground services.

Classification of Tour Wholesalers

Tour wholesalers can be categorized into several classes: (1) national full-service wholesaler, (2) limited product or in-house national wholesaler, (3) specialty tour operator, and (4) regional or limited wholesaler.[2] A national full-service wholesaler typically offers the largest range of products and covers more markets than the other classes of wholesalers. In-house national wholesalers are operations created by suppliers such as airlines, hotel chains, and rental cars to sell their own products by including them as part of tour packages. A specialty tour operator usually offers only one product, designed to suit the tastes of a specific market segment, such as bicycle tours, garden tours, or skin diving tours. A regional or limited wholesaler usually operates in only a few cities and offers only a few products.

Another key characteristic of wholesalers that distinguishes them from retailers is that they usually must commit large deposits to block and secure space from suppliers.[3] The investment of wholesalers also includes research to design tour programs, development of tour brochures and other sales tools, and advance marketing of the tour programs to retail travel agents. In addition, new tour programs must usually be promoted directly to consumers as well. The time lag from inception of a tour program to actual sales may be 12 to 18 months or longer. Retail travel agencies in most cases do not have the capital and/or are unwilling to risk the upfront investment necessary to develop a regular series of tour programs. While the financial risks of wholesalers are higher than those of retailers who do not have to invest large sums of money in advance of any sales, the returns are also higher for the wholesaler.

TOUR OPERATORS

Tour operators may sell directly to travelers upon arrival at their destination or market their tours through retail travel agencies as wholesalers. As suppliers of ground services, tour operators may also supply wholesale travel agencies with ground packages on a contractual basis. Tour operators are primarily responsible for delivering and performing the services specified in a given, advertised tour package. They can provide these services themselves, as some own buses, hotels, and other facilities, or they can obtain them from travel suppliers—hotels, bus companies, car rental companies, restaurants—or even other tour operators.

Tour operators referred to as "ground operators" provide services at the destination only and usually do not package or market transportation to or from the destination. Outbound tour operators and outbound wholesalers are the ones who package the transportation to and from a destination, complete with ground services. Prior to deregulation, a popular type of tour developed by tour operators was the charter tour package, where tour operators chartered entire flights from airlines at substantially reduced fares and assumed responsibility for the payment of the flights, whether or not all seats were sold.

A tour operator typically offers a variety of packages in a single season, for individuals or groups, either escorted or unescorted. With predetermined departure gateways and itineraries, common departure points such as Los Angeles or New York were used in the past to "collect and stage" individual travelers to take advantage of lower group airfares. However, with today's low discount fares and bulk fare contracts, individuals can travel inexpensively by themselves. Wholesale travel agencies and tour operators have met this challenge by offering flexible packages that can be varied to suit the individual needs of the travel agency's clients.

CONSOLIDATORS

In the past, a consolidator was a person or company that specialized in forming groups to travel on airline charters. The term today refers to travel companies that receive maximum overrides in return for an annual volume of substantial size or lower contracted rates. A consolidator is a wholesaler and is usually not set up to sell directly to the public.[4] Unlike tour wholesalers, a consolidator wholesales only one of the components, such as airline seats or hotel rooms. The term in practice is often associated with airline seats but conceptually can be applied to other components as well.

Airline consolidators usually sell through retail travel agents and other travel intermediaries. They may make reservations, confirm bookings, and issue tickets. Depending upon the contract with the airline, consolidators may waive some of the restrictions associated with discounted tickets. A consolidator may even sell directly to individuals by establishing a separate retail operation, but this may not be desirable since its own retail operations would come into direct competition with outside travel agencies that may be customers.

GENERAL SALES AGENTS

A general sales agent (GSA) is the exclusive representative of a principal for a given area. The principal may be a supplier of an off-line airline, a car rental company, or a hotel that does not have its own sales office in the area. A general sales agent may also be the representative for government tourism bureaus and other destination organizations that want to develop a market in the area where the agent is located.

The principal normally contracts a GSA and specifies the terms and conditions of the representation. With regard to travel suppliers, GSAs may be authorized to act on behalf of the principal in taking reservations, completing sales transactions, and making sales calls. In essence, the GSA may function as the local sales and reservations office for the principal.

SPECIALTY CHANNELERS

Specialty channelers include incentive travel firms, meeting planners, and professional conference organizers. Unlike retail travel agents, they usually do not receive commissions or act as middlemen in reselling travel services, but instead they act as intermediaries in contracting for travel services at efficient costs on behalf of the organizations they represent. Incentive travel firms, as specialty channelers, do not fit the normal pattern because they may either sell their professional services of designing and implementing an incentive travel program for a buyer or act as middlemen for both buyers and suppliers. Other types of special-interest travel such as student tours, company educational programs, and clubs often involve specialty channelers, which may be independent companies or part of a travel agency.

INTERRELATIONSHIPS OF TRAVEL OPERATIONS

If companies specialized in only one type of operation, business policy and management direction would be greatly simplified. Under this condition, a retail travel agency would only sell available tours and travel services to the public, and a wholesaler would sell its tours only through retail travel agencies or specialty channelers. Suppliers would have the largest degree of latitude in selling directly to consumers and also through travel agents, wholesalers, GSAs, tour operators, and so on. However, the very lack of restrictions for entering into these varying types of travel operations makes it relatively easy for a travel company to offer multiple services to the public. In realistic terms, few travel agencies today can afford to limit their operations to one or two product lines or services. Rising fixed costs as well as labor costs require new sources of revenues to keep travel sellers in business.

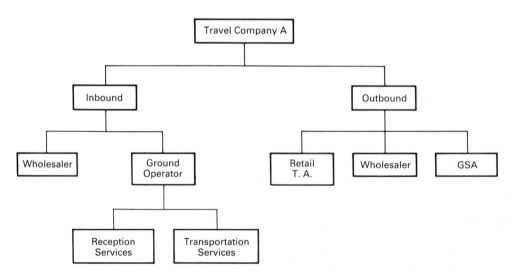

FIGURE 3.2 Example of multi-operations under one ocmpany in same city or local area

Vertical Integration Option

Vertical integration can be an attractive avenue for business growth. For example, a ground operator might decide to enter the wholesale package tour business and eventually sell directly to customers. Even though more than one type of service activity, or operation, can be incorporated into a single agency, each operation within the agency should be kept separate, except for the sharing of common facilities and activities where there are gains from economies of scale. The interrelationships between divisions should be understood. For instance, success in one type of operation may conflict with another type, and that should be known before any diversification or expansion decisions are made. To clarify the interrelationships, two situations are illustrated below: (1) multi-operations company structure in the same city or geographic area, and (2) multi-operations company structure with branch offics in different areas or countries.

Multi-Operations Company Structure in One Geographical Area

Figure 3.2 illustrates the divisions of a hypothetical company (Travel Company A) with multiple operations in one geographical area. The types of operations included are not meant to be exhaustive but illustrative of certain problems that may arise in undertaking different operations within the same company. Each division could be a separate company in itself. For example, there are companies that offer only transportation services or reception services. Management should treat each division as a separate profit center that requires a different strategy for success.

In assessing the outbound divisions in Travel Company A, the retail agency would sell travel services directly to consumers. The wholesale division would package outbound tours and market them through other retail agents in the area. The GSA division would service both wholesale and retail agents and might also sell to consumers in the area.

The success of the outbound wholesale division is dependent upon support from other retail travel agents in the area. In selling its own tours through its retail division, the company is in effect competing with other agents, which, in turn, may discourage them from supporting Travel Company A's wholesale division. A similar conflict can exist for the GSA operations if it sells directly to consumers.

No universal solutions exist for these conflicting activities. A workable compromise may be for the GSA operations to keep direct sales to a minimum and to primarily service other agencies. The retail travel agency operations might focus on commercial accounts with the wholesale division packaging pleasure tours. Other configurations are also feasible, depending upon the company's marketing power, each operation's revenue potential, and the extent to which profitable market segments can be isolated.

Underlying conflicts are also found in the inbound divisions of Travel Company A. The inbound wholesale division is organized to sell its tours through retail agents and to outbound wholesale agencies that send clients to the inbound destinations. The ground operations division is organized as a supplier to market its servivces (1) through outbound wholesalers and retail agents in origin areas; (2) through other inbound wholesalers located in the same area as the company; and (3) directly to visitors through company-operated sales desks situated in such convenient and heavily trafficked locations as hotel lobbies and airport terminals.

Instead of competing with other inbound wholesalers for the general visitor market, the inbound wholesale division could develop itself as a specialty channeler, focusing on incentives and other special-interest groups. It could also contract for transportation services instead of running its own transportation operation in direct competition with other ground companies.

Two final points should be made. Local market conditions and laws of different countries may require a well-defined organizational structure that would minimize conflicts of interest between activities. Alternatively, the avoidance of conflict—and expanded market outreach—could be achieved by opening branch offices in different areas or countries. This approach can provide opportunities for designing a network of complementary operations for each branch office that would not be possible otherwise.

Multi-Operations Travel Company with Branch Offices

To illustrate the advantages of expanding through branch offices, assume that Company B has one office with multiple operations in the United States and a second office in Japan. Both offices are involved in inbound and outbound operations, as shown in Figure 3.3. Again, the operations included are not meant to be exhaustive. Alternative configurations are feasible depending upon local market conditions and available resources.

The Company B office in Japan consists of an inbound wholesale division, an outbound wholesale division, and GSA representation. The common thread linking the three types of operations is that they all provide services to retail travel agents and do not attempt to compete with them. Assuming that both the inbound and outbound wholesale divisions use common suppliers, such as the same hotel chain or air carrier, the combined volume would strengthen the company's position with suppliers in contracting for lower rates. The GSA representation provides travel agencies in the area with additional services from suppliers that do not have their own local sales offices. Another complementary operation that may be

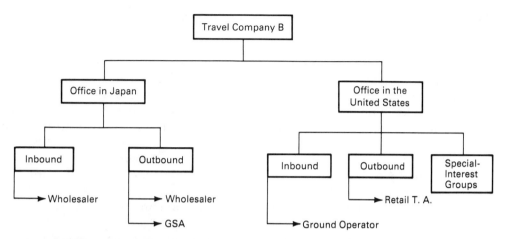

FIGURE 3.3 **Example of multi-operations under branch offices in different countries**

added to the existing divisions is an airline consolidator or bulk fare operator to provide retailers with competitive fares for their clients.

The inbound ground operations of the U.S. office are designed to be complementary to the outbound wholesale operations in Japan by providing the ground services for tours to the United States, also giving direct quality control over the tours. The U.S. retail operations would sell all outbound travel, not only travel to Japan. The special-interest group division could handle such things as inbound and outbound incentives, meetings, and conventions.

In principle it is not difficult to understand how the opening of branch offices to develop a regional or even world-wide network allows each branch to capitalize on local market conditions and to benefit from the working interrelationships between branches and their activities. In fact, the network of offices is worth more than the sum of the individual branches. Each branch can sell the services of the entire network, and the combined volume provides substantial leverage in contracting with suppliers. From a client's standpoint, the network provides the advantages of size, quality assurance, multiple offices to render assistance when he or she is away from home, and perhaps a sense of confidence that the company will have staying power.

In addition to branch offices, travel agency franchises and consortiums have evolved to attain the benefits of a network, but individual ownership of local outlets and independent management make it difficult at times for franchises or consortiums to achieve the maximum benefits of complementary relationships among outlets. Understandably, each owner in the franchise or consortium is more interested in generating revenues for his or her outlet than in promoting the common objectives and relationships among other franchise or consortium outlets.

DEVELOPMENT OF TRAVEL INTERMEDIARY
INSTITUTIONS

In today's travel distribution system, there are a variety of middleman institutions that offer travel products and services to the general public. Their development has reflected the realities of shifting market conditions, the economic climate, consumer preferences, and regulatory changes. These environmental factors have imposed Darwinian law to effect institutional change in how travel intermediaries operate. As mentioned in the preceding section, many travel agencies find themseles engaging in both retail and outbound wholesale operations by necessity; but there are also companies in Europe, the United States, and Japan that still profitably specialize in only one type of operation, for instance, wholesaling, incentives, or representation.

Large companies with strong reputations tend to be involved in multiple activities or travel operations. The perennial strength and reputation of American Express (AMEX) makes it possible for its branch offices to sell AMEX tours even when they are also sold through competing retail agencies. AMEX travel offices in different cities may be retailers, wholesalers, and/or tour operators. To some extent, the reputation of AMEX tours is assisted and promoted by the image of the AMEX card and travelers cheques. AMEX offices typically provide services for both inbound and outbound travelers. Moreover, AMEX has developed special services directed at the business traveler, even providing in-house corporate services for large commercial accounts.

For example, take the case of a vacation package to Hawaii. As a national wholesaler, AMEX designed and packaged the Hawaiian tour for distribution through American Express Vacations located in Norcross, Georgia. The Hawaii AMEX office contracts with hotels, sightseeing tours, and ground transportation operators to provide the actual services to travelers upon their arrival in Hawaii. AMEX also sells tours to Europe, Latin America, Asia, and other parts of the world so that Hawaii tour packages make up only one of the product lines offered.

The trend toward larger agencies noted in Chapter 1 reflects the fact that companies with a strong reputation and large volume can leverage their market power into multiple operations. The entry of large travel companies and suppliers, such as airlines and hotels, also has made it very difficult for small agencies to compete. United Airlines recently opened its own tour wholesaling division, United Vacations, and other U.S. airlines are now following suit. Outside of the United States, foreign airlines have already developed their own tour wholesaling divisions.

Nontravel companies such as banks operate some of the largest travel agencies in Australia. It is not unusual to find countries where government tourism ministries operate tours, ground services, and government-owned hotels in competition with the private sector. Due to deregulation, nontravel companies can now easily enter agency operations in the United States. Financial institutions such as credit unions and loan companies may also enter the travel agency business. The number of commercial accounts at independent travel agencies has been limited due to the increasing number of corporate in-house travel departments.

The development of today's travel distribution system and intermediary institutions has followed a tortuous path, especially in the United States in the years after airline deregulation. The business is so competitive that profit margins are slim, and agencies are competing not only with each other but also with suppliers and large corporations entering the field. This requires agencies to be even more marketing oriented (this will be discussed in Chapter 5) and to study operations for ways to improve profit margins.

PROFIT CENTERS

The concept of profit centers is not new. However, an agency's activities are usually developed on an ad hoc basis and, if successful, are continued as part of the agency's existing structure. This makes it hard to ascertain the activities that are truly profitable versus those that are marginal or operating at a loss. Within a company, profit centers are units that have distinct activities and responsibilities for generating revenues. For large agencies, the different types of operations, such as retail, wholesale, and GSA, provide a basis for identifying profit centers. Small agencies with a few staff doing multiple assignments may instead use productivity analysis, discussed later in Chapter 6. As the name implies, the purpose of organizing profit centers is to evaluate the profitability of each type of operation separately. Temporary losses in some operations may be acceptable in order to provide a service mix to clients; it may be more profitable in the long run to discontinue those operations that are marginal or consistently losing money.

An appropriate accounting system is necessary to track revenues and costs by each operation, and systems are available that do this. The difficult management issues relate to interdivisional transfer of services and allocation of common costs. For example, a wholesaler with ground operations should separate the performance of the wholesaling activities from the ground operations. Determining divisional profits is difficult when facilities and services are jointly used, for instance, the allocation of administrative overhead and marketing services that may cover multiple units, or the situation where one unit such as ground operations provides services for a wholesaling division.

Established market prices can serve as a guide in determining how much the ground operations should charge the wholesaling division for its services. In many cases, the internal or transfer price between the two divisions is negotiated to reflect qualitative factors such as local market conditions and internal efficiencies. Using cost as a basis for the transfer price is not simple when common costs exist, since the allocation of common costs tends to be arbitrary. The development of "standard costs" is one way to partially resolve these issues. A general approach is to establish in advance budgeted performance for the divisions and compare actual with planned or budgeted performance.

SUMMARY

Developing travel operations today requires the application of formal management techniques due to the increased complexity and competition in the marketplace. The average agency must compete against large companies with vast resources. The use of computers, covered in Chapter 10, provides a technical means to enhance staff productivity and, in turn, agency profits. The initial key decisions still relate to which types of operations, such as retail, wholesale, inbound, and outbound, are profitable to undertake and how to integrate the different operations. Agency management must then develop service delivery systems to ensure consistent quality, which is discussed in the next chapter focusing on internal operations for retail agencies.

DISCUSSION QUESTIONS

1. What are the key differences between retail and wholesale travel operations?
2. How do tour wholesalers differ from tour operators?
3. What conflicts may arise from integrating all the different types of operations under a single office? How would branch offices alleviate some of the problems?
4. What problems arise in evaluating the performance of profit centers?

ENDNOTES

[1]Dexter J. L. Choy, "Airline Pricing of Domestic Passenger Charters," (unpublished Ph.D. dissertation, University of Hawaii, 1978, pp. 11–14).

[2]Paul Hall, "Travel Marketing: The Role of the Tour Operators," *Travel & Tourism,* January, 1987, pp. 3 and 6.

[3]Alistair Ballatine, "Who's a Middleman?" *The Travel Agent,* January 28, 1982, pp. 22 and

[4]Allen McQuaid, "Consolidators and Bucket Shops: When Will We Get the Point?" *ASTA Agency Management,* March, 1988, pp. 153–154.

SUPPLEMENTAL READING

MARTI, ANDREW, "Coping with the Future," *The Travel Agent,* December 10, 1984, pp. 20, 23, 24, and 60.

chapter 4

Retail Travel Agency Operations

LEARNING OBJECTIVES

- To understand the range of services offered by retail travel agencies
- To be familiar with the elements involved in defining the service concept for an agency
- To understand the major principles involved in designing a service delivery system for an agency
- To be familiar with the stages of personal selling
- To understand the importance of documentation and post-sale services

KEY TERMS

- Automated Ticketing Machines (ATMs)
- Buyer Decision Process
- Customer-Oriented Approach
- Design Quality
- Fam Trips
- Fitness of Design
- Full-Service Travel Agency
- Limited-Service Travel Agency
- Overrides
- Post-Sale Services
- Prospecting
- Quality of Services
- Sales-Oriented Approach
- Service Concept
- Service Delivery Process

- Standard Operating
  Procedures

- Travel Advisory
- Travel Documentation

INTRODUCTION

Although retail travel agencies are classified under a single industry group-ing, there can be significant differences in the range of services and prod-ucts offered by individual agencies. A quick look at travel advertisements in any major newspaper will confirm the existence of a variety of retail agen-cies by the products and services offered. This situation is similar to that of retail stores, which also differentiate themselves according to their competi-tive advantages.

There are full-service travel agencies that offer all services and products related to international and domestic travel, such as air, rail, or motorcoach transportation, rental cars, airport transfers, accommodations, cruises, tour packages, travel insurance, and travelers cheques. At the other extreme, there are limited-service agencies that may do only airline ticketing and of-fer discounted airfares as the primary basis for attracting clients.

Travel agencies also can specialize according to market segments and product lines. Besides commercial agencies specializing in business and in-centive travel and corporate accounts, there are agencies serving holiday travelers, agencies for handicapped travelers, student travel agencies, eth-nic agencies, and many others that provide services and products to select market segments. In addition, some agencies specialize only by product line such as cruises, adventure tours, single destination travel (for example, Las Vegas junkets), Oriental tours, or European tours.

The range and level of services offered by retail travel agencies thus will be dependent upon their client mix, product lines, and the level of ser-vice they intend to provide. Rather than attempting to cover all of the possi-ble variations in agency services, this chapter will discuss the basic services offered by retail agencies to meet travelers' needs, the major principles in-volved in providing quality services, and personal selling of travel products to clients.

SERVICES TO MEET TRAVELERS' NEEDS

Three of the basic needs common to all travelers are safety, reliability, and accurate information. Even frequent travelers cannot keep abreast of all changes related to their travel, such as recent outbreaks of communicable diseases, financial failure of inbound tour operators or local carriers, or ma-jor construction underway at the receiving destination. These factors are more important when travel to foreign destinations is involved, since current information from abroad is harder to obtain than information on domestic conditions. While the U.S. Department of State issues "travel advisories" warning U.S. travelers of potential problems or safety hazards, in particular overseas destinations, even these are not always up to the minute.

Besides information, travelers' concerns may include time and money constraints and the desire for convenience, comfort, novelty, status, and variety. A person's past travel experiences and his or her individuality will also determine specific needs. Corporate accounts may require twenty-four-hour availability for reservations and changes, mailing or door-to-door delivery of travel documents, and controls to manage their travel costs.[1] At the same time, corporations expect airline and hotel discounts commensurate with their volume of travel.

In today's deregulated environment, not only is competition among agencies intense but travelers have the option of dealing directly with suppliers. A buyer can now obtain his or her own airline ticket through self-service ticketing machines, otherwise known as automated ticketing machines (ATMs), such as American Airlines Travel Teller. (See Figure 4.1.) Instead of calling a travel agent, one can use an airline reservationist not only to purchase air transportation but also to book hotels, car rentals, and other available travel services on the airline's computerized reservation system. Consequently, the success of a retail travel agency is dependent upon its ability to provide services that meet travelers' needs better than the services already available directly from suppliers and other travel agencies.

In order to design the operations, agency management must first define the agency's service concept in terms of tangible features, range of services, and intangible features.[2] Items to consider in defining an agency's service concept include

1. Tangible Features
   - Physical location and accessibility
   - Size of facilities
   - State of technology in equipment
   - Size of professional staff
   - Product offerings and brochures
   - Agency information and/or promotional materials
   - Hours of operation
2. Range of Services
   - Reservations capabilities
   - Travel counseling, itinerary development
   - Travel documents, visas, certifications
   - Mailing or delivery of travel documents
   - Billing and analysis of travel costs
   - Special services related to travel (for example, tickets for entertainment shows, transfers, giveaways, complimentary services)

FIGURE 4.1 American Airlines Travel Teller
Source: Courtesy of American Airlines

- Individual client services
- Post-sale follow-ups

3. Intangible Features
   - Image of agency
   - Atmosphere created by physical facilities, for example, lighting, comfort, colors
   - Service atmosphere created by agency staff, for example, appearance, attitude, friendliness, professional qualifications (competence), and promptness of service

- Degree of personalization
- Reputation of and client confidence in agency

An agency's service concept also must be consistent with its overall marketing mix in regard to pricing, promotion, and distribution (as discussed in Chapter 5). Once decided upon, the service concept must be implemented through a service delivery system comprising physical materials and facilities, agency personnel, and operating procedures that define how the services are delivered to agency clients.

STANDARDIZATION OF OPERATIONAL PROCEDURES

The production of services as opposed to physical goods presents many problems due to the qualitative apsects associated with services and the personal interaction involved with the delivery of services. In addition, travel agencies must deal with numerous details in arranging travel itineraries, packaging tours, and performing ground services. Mistakes in any of the arrangements can result in dissatisfied clients. The technical aspects of making reservations, issuing airline tickets, and other booking procedures are well documented by respective suppliers. The delivery of travel services also involves behavioral standards that are important to successful agent-client relations. These include timeliness of service, sequencing of services, anticipating clients' needs, positive attitudes, suggestive selling, and problem solving. To ensure that services are delivered in the quantity and manner intended, agencies need to develop policies and standard operating procedures (discussed further in Chapter 6) that incorporate both physical and behavioral standards.

Procedures may differ by type of client, and sufficient flexibilty should be allowed to individualize services. Nevertheless, minimum standards are necessary to ensure that consistent quality of services is delivered to each customer. In addition, operational procedures provide the basis for training new staff and improving staff efficiency. Agencies too often rely upon on-the-job training for new staff rather than having operational procedures. Although valuable, on-the-job training varies from staff to staff and can produce inconsistencies and incomplete training.

While documenting service procedures, even minor revisions can improve efficiency, making the process worthwhile. Unfortunately, it may take as many as ten man-years to develop appropriate standard operating procedures. Most agencies are small and do not feel that they have the time or resources to invest in developing their own procedures. Increased competition, however, will force agencies to be more concerned about the level and quality of the services they are providing.

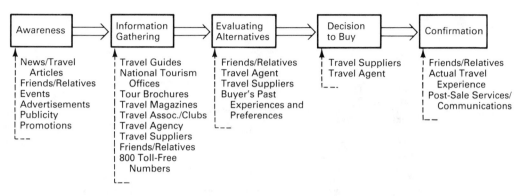

FIGURE 4.2 Buyer decision process

SERVICE DELIVERY PROCESS

A good starting point for developing standard procedures is an analysis of the agency's service delivery process, which requires documenting the sequence of activities involved in producing services for agency clients. A useful method for visualizing the service delivery process is to design a flow chart of the intended activities.[3] Before designing the flow chart, it is useful to first understand the buyer decision process, since the agency's ultimate objective is to sell travel services.

Figure 4.2 shows how an individual progresses through various stages of problem solving to reach a purchase decision for travel products and services. There is a variety of information sources that are listed below each stage. Factors such as time, cost, distance, mode of travel, availability, and so on will, of course, ultimately influence the buyer's decision. The main point is that travelers today are more sophisticated and desire to make informed decisions about their trips. Since travel products involve services that are intangible and cannot be pretested, travelers will seek the advice of friends and relatives who have already taken similar trips. They will also utilize unbiased sources such as travel guides and travel clubs to obtain reliable information.

Retail travel agencies may play a role in each of the buying stages. In the instance of vacation travel, this role can be significant. An agency's advertisements, especially those that appear in travel editorial sections of newspapers reaching the general public, can help to create awareness of new tours, special packages, and lower airfares. Agents will provide information and assist clients in evaluating alternatives. In their role as professional travel counselors, agents are viewed as being less biased in their recommendations, say, than travel suppliers who only sell their respective products.

One of the 75 Ask Mr. Foster Travel Service offices in 1940 was this one at Strawbridge & Clothier department store in Philadelphia, Pa.

At the evaluation stage, travel agents can help clients weigh the various travel alternatives and choose the most advantageous option in the purchase of travel products. After purchasing, travelers will seek confirmation that they made the right decision. Post-sale services are important for reassuring clients, follow up on any complaints or changes, and developing a long-term agent-client relationship. It is through the counseling and post-sale services to ensure satisfied clients that the image and overall confidence in an agency are established.

The sequence of activities to service clients should be designed to correspond with the buyer decision process. For illustrative purposes, Figure 4.3 provides a flow chart of activities involved in servicing walk-in clients. It should be noted that the actual performance of each activity is more complex than it appears in the chart because of customer communication and interaction at each step. Moreover, an agency may have to vary the sequence of activities depending on the type of customer or limit the activities in conformance with organizational design and the level of service intended.

Recognizing that the time spent by agency staff represents money, walk-in customers must be screened in some manner to ensure the produc-

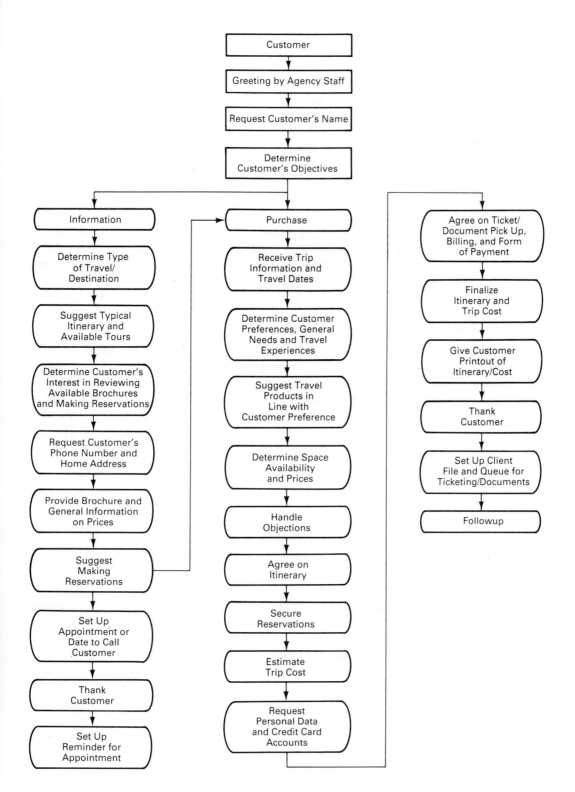

FIGURE 4.3   Flow chart for servicing walk-in customers

tive use of agents' time. Requesting a customer's name early in the sequence can deter those who are only window shopping. In large agencies, receptionists can be trained to screen walk-in customers and provide brochures before referring them to an agent.

Complete itineraries may require several visits or discussions in order to give an agent sufficient time to evaluate alternative routings and secure reservations. Requesting personal data, credit card accounts, form of payment, and billing data can indirectly cinch a sale and limit the probability of cancellation. Until travel has actually taken place, a customer can cancel a trip at any time, resulting in use of a significant amount of agency staff time without producing sales. Payment deadlines and so on should therefore be based upon the date of reservations input rather than dates of travel. Cancellation fees are also becoming more common to help recover the costs of staff time and agency overhead.

QUALITY OF AGENCY SERVICES

The term *quality* is often confused with levels of service or standards. For example, people often think that quality means more services (quantity) or deluxe service (class). In reality, quality simply means conformance to a predetermined standard based on price and value to intended market(s). There are three components underlying quality that managers should understand. The first component is design quality, that is, the intended level of services to be delivered to specific groups of customers.[4] An agency should determine whether such services as extensive counseling, twenty-four-hour service, passport and visa services, ticket delivery, and so on are desired and in some instances required for specific customers.

The second component of quality is consistent performance. That is, the intended services should be delivered in the same manner consistently over time. Standard operating procedures and staff training are critical in achieving consistent performance. Figure 4.3 illustrates the design of service procedures.

The third component is fitness of design, or, in practical terms, whether the intended services continue to meet customer needs. Management must periodically review an agency's service delivery process to identify shortcomings in meeting customer needs as well as recommend appropriate improvements to maintain an agency's competitiveness.

There are countless ways for mistakes to be made in a travel itinerary. Once a client embarks on a trip, lost time cannot be replaced; incorrect bookings, the failure to send in payments, and other mistakes made by agency staff cannot be easily rectified to the satisfaction of the traveler. It is all too well documented that one dissatisfied customer will tell as many as seven or more other people about his or her bad experiences. It is even more dangerous to cross people who are considered influential travel leaders and trend setters. Since travelers depend upon friends and relatives as a valuable source of information in evaluating alternatives, complaints of dissatisfied customers will impair an agency's reputation.

When one considers the full consequences of mistakes, it becomes apparent that the cost of providing quality services may be minimal compared to the potential loss in revenue. Correcting the mistakes will cost money; providing customers with some type of compensation for the mistakes is also costly; and the money spent initially to attract customers has been wasted when mistakes result in dissatisfied customers who will be negative word-of-mouth advertisers for the agency. Correcting a negative image is for a fact more expensive than creating a positive one in the first place.

SELLING TRAVEL

The bottom line of a travel agency is to sell travel products. Agents are salespeople, but they often perform only as reservationists; that is, they handle customers' requests for travel instead of selling travel to customers. A comparable analogy is that of a professional waiter or waitress who is not only an order taker but is expected to increase the average check by selling the extras—a bottle of wine, a dessert, and so on. Part of the confusion is due to the fact that there are different types of sales positions. Retail agencies may have inside sales agents who handle walk-in clients and telephone sales, as well as outside sales agents who call on corporations, group accounts, and high-frequency travelers.

While an inside sales agent, or the waiter or waitress, does not have to prospect for new clients, as in the case of outside sales agents, they have ample opportunity for upselling by following simple personal selling procedures (see Figure 4.4).

To make prospecting (that is, finding and cultivating new clients) more productive, outside sales agents also should identify in advance those who are more likely to purchase from the agency and obtain general knowledge about a prospective client before approaching him or her. Inside sales agents perform similar activities as part of their approach to customers. How to greet and meet customers is very important since it establishes the service atmosphere and tone for customer interaction.

There are two basic approaches to personal selling. The first approach is sales-oriented or high-pressure selling, and the second is customer oriented. Combinations of the two basic approaches are also possible. An agency offering a limited range or only a single product such as discounted airfares will probably generate more sales through a sales-oriented approach. A production mentality may be required to generate adequate sales to meet the agency's overhead costs and provide minimal profit margins,

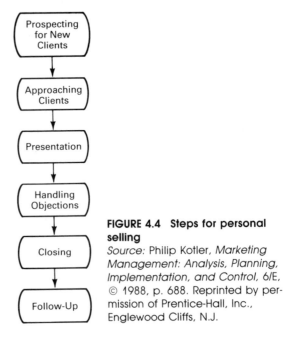

FIGURE 4.4 Steps for personal selling
Source: Philip Kotler, *Marketing Management: Analysis, Planning, Implementation, and Control, 6/E,* © 1988, p. 688. Reprinted by permission of Prentice-Hall, Inc., Englewood Cliffs, N.J.

especially in the instance of low-cost discounted products. Efficiency with courtesy may be appropriate for this situation.

A customer-oriented or a combined approach will likely be necessary for corporations, group accounts, frequent travelers, and special-interest travelers. Some of the reasons for failing to gain these types of clients are

1. Not preparing for the sales call
2. Not being professional
3. Failing to communicate in terms of the client's frame of reference
4. Overpromising
5. Not asking for the sale
6. Not calling back[5]

In order to be effective salespersons, agents must have knowledge about travel and the workings of the travel industry. General knowledge of geography, time zones, equipment differences such as aircraft types, differences in service standards by country or supplier, routings, travel regulations, and so on are prerequisites with which agents must be familiar. Agents must also acquire a specific knowledge of reservation procedures, fare construction, fare regulations, ticketing procedures, supplier rules such as those regarding baggage and denied boarding, reputation of travel suppliers, and conditions at destinations. Reference materials are available to assist agents on the latter aspects. These materials would include

- *Travel Planner,* European, North American, and Pacific Asia
- *Industry Agent's Handbook* (ARC)
- *Travel Agent Handbook* (IATAN)
- *Hotel and Travel Index* (HTI)
- *Official Hotel and Resort Guide* (OHRG)

All the knowledge of world travel, however, will not guarantee sales. Agents must be creative in meeting clients' needs and develop the interpersonal skills to deal with clients of differing personalities and persuasions. Rather than waiting for orders, it is important that agents, both inside and outside, create and capitalize on opportunities for selling travel.

DOCUMENTATION

The generation of travel documents appears to be perfunctory, but it serves several purposes. For clients, travel documents typically include an itinerary, itemized billing, tickets, and vouchers. Copies of these documents, in turn, are necessary for financial accounting and control purposes (this will be discussed again in Chapter 9). From a management perspective, the information on the documents is necessary for analyzing agency accounts, evaluating agents' productivity, and assessing product line performance. Consequently, agency documents and forms must be designed to contain the relevant data in such a way that it can be easily retrieved.

Separate procedures for generating the documents are necessary to ensure their completion on a timely basis and for entry into their respective files. In smaller agencies, each agent may be responsible for generating the clients' itineraries, billings, tickets, and vouchers. Increased volume of sales may allow for specialization, in which agents handle the selling and inputting of itineraries and clerical staff are trained to generate the documents. This allows agents to focus their time on selling activities instead of clerical duties that can be handled by clerical staff.

Specialization may also produce other economies. With specialization, using evening and weekend shift work to complete documentation is possible, resulting in higher utilization of equipment and office space. Specialization can also help to reduce the number of errors caused by numerous copies of documents and the ensuing paper chase.

Each document item, for instance, is produced at least in triplicate. One copy is for the client, a second copy is for the permanent numerical file, and a third copy is for accounting. A trip involving one client flying to three

destinations with rental car and hotel vouchers for each destination will
generate

Airline ticket	3 copies
Rental car (3 × 3)	9 copies
Hotel (3 × 3)	9 copies
Total	21 copies

The potential for mistakes in filing and inputting is multiplicative, that is,
$3 \times 9 \times 9 = 243$ possible combinations for mistakes. This also illustrates
the need for computerization (discussed in Chapter 10).

POST-SALE SERVICES

The selling and service delivery process does not rest with the transmission
of travel documents to the client. Quality-minded agents should follow up
with clients upon their return from a trip to determine the client's overall
satisfaction with the trip and the services provided by specific travel suppliers. Feedback from clients provides up-to-date information on the performance of suppliers that may not be available otherwise. A follow-up call also
serves as a means to ensure that a client is satisfied; if not satisfied, the agent
has an opportunity to rectify the situation and at the same time inquire
about the client's possible future travel plans. A satisfied client is one of the
easiest customers to sell again.

In cultivating a long-term agent-client relationship, travel agents must
recognize that clients' needs change over time. Clients initially may seek
more counseling and information, but they become more knowledgeable
and sophisticated with increased travel experiences. Some frequent travelers may become price oriented; others may seek newer facilities at destinations for excitement and change. Agents must attune themselves to the
changing needs of their clients or they risk losing them to competitors.

Other post-sale services relate to maintaining a presence in clients'
minds and marketing new products through direct mailing techniques such
as newsletters and special sales promotions (discussed in Chapter 5 on marketing). Nonetheless, it should be emphasized that gaining an initial sale is
not an end in itself but a beginning for developing agent-client relationships
as a source for repeat business and new business over time.

WORKING WITH SUPPLIERS

In assessing operational elements, travel agency management must consider
relationships with suppliers. Careful planning in this area can assist an
agency in lowering costs and increasing revenues. Two agencies with identi-

cal bookings could have different net earnings, depending on whether or not planning was involved.

Overrides and incentives. Many suppliers, including airlines, hotels, auto rental firms, tour wholesalers, and cruise ships, offer overrides and special incentives to travel agents, amounting to extra income of up to several thousand dollars per year. An override is an extra commission paid for frequent bookings with a particular company. Percentages vary widely and can be quite complicated. Overrides become available after the agency has written a required level of business with a supplier, and some are retroactive to include all bookings with a supplier during a set period of time.

If a travel agency has the flexibility to place clients with a particular tour operator, hotel, airline, or other travel supplier, the agency can benefit by accruing bookings that lead to these extra commissions. Other special incentives given to travel agencies by suppliers include trading stamps, personal merchandise, and free bookings that the agency can sell to clients at a profit. Nonmonetary forms of reward include preference in securing space when availability is tight and a generally more responsive and supportive relationship with the supplier. Incentives can have significant economic value and add directly to agency profits; in some cases they are used as motivational tools for the agency's salesforce.

Familiarization trips. Familiarization trips, or "fam trips," provided by suppliers or destinations are commonly used as a motivational tool by travel agencies and are viewed by some travel agents as part of their compensation package. When fam trips become commonplace or are viewed as a sales agent's right, they lose much of their value. A fam trip should serve not only as a motivational tool but also as an educational tool for travel agents. Upon returning from a fam trip, agents should be prepared to present the information gained about destinations and travel suppliers to others in the office. The travel agency can obtain valuable sales promotional items or services free of charge from suppliers, which can be instrumental in increasing total bookings. (Fam trips are discussed further in Chapter 6.)

Agent training programs. Managers of travel agencies should encourage supplier representatives to attend agent meetings, present their information, and answer questions. In addition, many suppliers and destinations offer free educational programs for travel agents. Some suppliers, principally airlines, sponsor professional training seminars; attendance at these seminars should be viewed as an educational opportunity.

Premiums and prizes. Travel suppliers are often willing to furnish free services for use in contests, open houses, and other public relations activities by travel agents. An open house, for instance, might include a drawing for a free weekend at a luxury resort, provided by a travel supplier.

Client and prospect promotions.   Suppliers are happy to work with travel agencies in developing and offering travel films, travel nights, and other programs with the purpose of educating and enticing clients and prospects. Suppliers spend millions of dollars each year for brochures, films, specialty products, and trained sales representatives. Travel agencies usually can obtain or borrow material or book speakers either free or at a slight charge. Unfortunately, many travel agents do not use these supplies and services to their best advantage and may throw away boxes of promotional material that should have been given to the public.

Equipment.   The relationship between suppliers and a travel agency regarding computers is covered extensively in Chapter 10.

Travel discounts.   Most suppliers offer special discounts, for example, 75% Agency Discount and upgrade, to travel agents to encourage them to use their services whenever they travel. Some suppliers, however, have questioned this practice since they feel that travel agents take it for granted and often abuse the privilege.

Sources of information.   Travel suppliers represent the best source of information concerning current developments within the travel industry. They have information concerning pending legislation and technological change, and they may have marketing studies that can assist an agency in developing its marketing plan. Agencies where the managers do not have the time or interest to meet supplier representatives tend to adopt a myopic and self-destructive attitude. Supplier reps have a dual allegiance to the travel agencies and their employers and can provide a new dimension to the travel agency and innovative ideas for marketing. By helping improve professionalism and marketing within the agency, the supplier rep makes the agency a stronger marketing arm of the suplier. After all, suppliers are the lifeline for a travel agency, with supplier reps providing the vital link between agent and supplier.

SUMMARY

The management of retail travel agency operations is more complex today. Agency management has the option to focus on certain market segments or product lines. In turn, the agency's service concept must be developed to give the clients what they want in a consistent manner over time. Standardization of operational procedures and analysis of the service delivery system are prerequisites to producing quality services. The end product of a satisfied customer must be achieved in line with the agency's financial goals in selling travel. After all is said and done, agents are salespeople and must generate sufficient sales to cover the costs of operations, including returns to owners. Cultivating long-term agent-client relationships is beneficial to both as an agency develops new services or products to meet changing client needs.

DISCUSSION QUESTIONS

1. How do retail travel agencies specialize?
2. What elements are important to consider in defining an agency's service concept?
3. What factors must be considered in standardizing operations?
4. What progressive stages does an individual go through in making travel purchase decisions?
5. What is quality? Identify the components of quality and how management achieves quality services.
6. What are the purposes of travel documentation?
7. Identify the steps in the personal selling of travel. Why are post-sale services important?

ENDNOTES

¹Dennis W. Day, "Eight Steps to Win Today's Corporate Accounts," *ASTA Travel News*, November 1, 1986, pp. 3–5.

² W. E., Sasser, R. P. Olsen, and D. D. Wyckoff, *Management of Service Operations: Text Cases and Readings* (Boston: Allyn and Bacon, Inc., 1978), pp. 8–14.

³Ibid., pp. 74–81.

⁴D. Daryl Wyckoff, "New Tools in Achieving Service Quality," *The Cornell Hotel and Restaurant Administration Quarterly*, November, 1984, pp. 78–91.

⁵Bradford Burns, "Trouble Getting Commercial Accounts?" *The Travel Agent*, May 21, 1984, p. 32.

SUPPLEMENTAL READINGS

HESKETT, JAMES L., *Managing in the Service Economy*. Cambridge, MA: Harvard Business School Press, 1986.

HOOSON, CHRISTOPHER, AND NONA STARR, *Travel Career Development*, 2nd ed., Wellesley, MA: Institute of Certified Travel Agents, 1985.

LEHMANN, ARMIN D., "Improving Agency Operations," *Travel Agency Marketing/Operations*, February 28, 1983, pp. 18–27.

chapter 5

Travel Agency Marketing

LEARNING OBJECTIVES

- To know the importance of marketing in today's consumer-driven environment and why it is necessary to develop and follow a specific marketing plan
- To understand that a marketing plan follows an agency's overall objectives, involving many steps in applying the five Ps, and to be able to describe the five Ps as they relate to travel agencies
- To be able to explain factors that affect the anticipated travel experience
- To state the different ways agencies can classify clients and why target marketing is effective
- To be aware of the different types of media available to travel agencies and the advantages and disadvantages of each

KEY TERMS

- Advertising
- Advertising Budgets
- Agency Audit
- Anticipated Travel Experience
- Audience Reach
- Budget
- Client Mix Analysis
- Dealership
- Demographic Characteristics
- Destination Management Services
- Discount versus Full-Margin Agencies

- Distribution
- Diversification
- 80/20 Rule
- Environmental Audit
- Five Ps
- Frequent Traveler Program
- Gantt Chart
- Group Handling Agents
- Inbound Agents
- Incoming Tour Operators
- Key Clients
- Marketing
- Marketing Objectives
- Marketing Plan
- Marketing Potential
- Market Share
- Mission
- Positioning
- Preferred Supplier Program
- Price-Value
- Product Line Mix
- Psychographic Characteristics
- Publicity
- Public Relations
- Reciprocal Arrangements
- Satellite Ticket Printers (STPs)
- Self-Liquidating Premiums
- Situational Analysis
- Specialization
- Specialty Advertising

INTRODUCTION

Retail stores in the industrialized free world offer consumers an endless variety of merchandise and services, using highly sophisticated merchandising techniques. Travel agencies in the prederegulation era were often content to take whatever business that came along and to sell on a straight commission basis without the bother of merchandising or having to do extensive marketing. Today, travel agents are not only in competition with retailers but with every other sophisticated marketer for the discretionary income of the pleasure traveler.

As discussed in previous chapters, competition in selling travel products and services increasingly comes from nontraditional vendors of travel services, such as financial institutions, home computers, supermarkets, department stores, and direct selling by travel suppliers. Even teleconferencing competes to a degree with travel agencies in the business travelers market. While new forms of competition are making inroads into the travel agents' market, the heaviest competition continues to come from fellow travel agents. Despite the competitive environment, an average of over 2200 new agency locations have entered the industry in each year over the past decade. (See Figure 5.1.) And the trends seem clear: Travel agencies are becoming larger, more automated, and more sophisticated in management; travelers are also becoming more experienced and sophisticated, demanding more from the travel agent.

In this competitive environment, while product knowledge and enthusiasm were enough to generate travel sales in the past, marketing skills are necessary ingredients for a travel agency's survival and growth today. Successful agencies today perceive themselves as retail merchants as well as

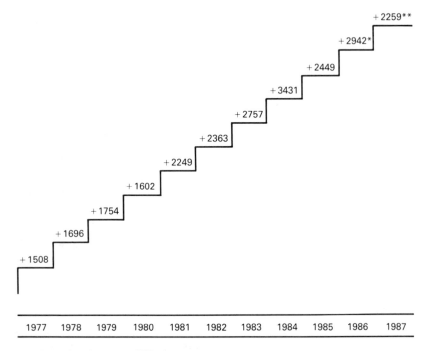

*315 new locations were STPs
**643 new locations were STPs

FIGURE 5.1   New travel agency entrants
Source: Airlines Reporting Corporation. Information from the *Industry Agents' Handbook* is used by permission of Airlines Reporting Corporation; however, since the handbook is revised frequently, the material included in *Professional Travel Agency Management* should be verified by comparison with the current edition of the handbook.

service professionals. They place much greater emphasis on finding new prospects and convincing them to use the agency's services to purchase travel products. Travel products are, nevertheless, still products, which must be brought to the attention of potential buyers and promoted like any other consumer goods.

THE TRAVEL EXPERIENCE

Unlike other retailers, travel agents do not sell a tangible product that can be seen, touched, packaged, and carried home. Travel agents sell *anticipated travel experience*; the client cannot "test" the product or be guaranteed that the travel experience will always be positive. Travel intangibles are difficult to market because they involve so many variables. Whether anticipated travel experiences are positive or negative depends upon many factors, including the following.

Past experiences.   Past experience with the service from travel agencies, hotels, airlines, automobile rental agencies, and others creates expectations regarding future travel. The more recent the travel experience, the more vivid.

Successful marketing efforts to build repeat clientele depend upon feedback from the client concerning positive and negative aspects of recent trips. This information also fulfills a quality control function for the agency by ensuring that meals, accommodations, and other services were delivered as promised and that shortcomings will be corrected on future trips. It pays for the agency to carefully record the preferences of their clients and match these with appropriate travel products. Agents must build upon the positive experiences of clients and eliminate or reduce negative ones. A client who has had an unhappy experience is seldom appeased by being told that the travel agent or other clients have never experienced those problems.

Advertising and promotion.   While the influence of brochures, posters, and advertisements cannot be measured, they undoubtedly affect perceptions of future travel experiences. A poster of a smiling couple on a moonlit beach, for example, is designed to create an anticipation of romance in the travel experience. Travel videos on specific destinations can greatly influence the anticipated travel experience. Videos are used by approximately 25 percent of all travel agencies.

News events.   Within seconds, an anticipated travel experience can change from positive to negative as news stories break. News of a fire in a Las Vegas hotel, an earthquake in Mexico, or a terrorist incident in Europe have had dramatic effects upon perceptions of future travel experiences. Bad news of dramatic events having dire consequences on life and safety leave impressions that remain with the public and are difficult to overcome, and travel agencies are the first to feel the effect as clients call to cancel reservations.

Travel writers.   Travel writers play an important role in the dissemination of information concerning travel destinations, attractions, events, and travel suppliers. Other reporters and editors, such as those who cover sports, dining, and outdoor gardening, also create travel impressions when they describe places where events are held.

Entertainment media.   The influence of cinema and popular novels on travel cannot be overlooked. For example, after the showing of such films as *Crocodile Dundee, Gandhi, Passage to India,* and *Out of Africa,* interest in travel to Australia, India, and East Africa peaked. And novels such as *Shogun* and *Noble House,* followed by television productions with massive viewerships, stirred the American imagination and interest in travel to Japan and Hong Kong.

Word of mouth.   Next to a client's own personal experiences, the most important force that molds anticipated travel experiences is "word of mouth." This is true for every element of travel, whether it is a destination, a carrier, a hotel, shopping, sightseeing, or limousine service. Managers who sell services of any kind, including travel, know that word-of-mouth advertising is the single most powerful factor influencing purchase decisions of a low-risk nature, that is, all products not falling under the high-risk category—a new automobile, real estate, and other high-value items. Because travel is by and large a highly personalized experience, in the absence of one's own experience with a new destination or service, it is not surprising to find that the opinions and experiences of family, friends, neighbors, co-workers, and experts will have a significant influence over most buyers.

Travel agents.   Advertising, news events, entertainment media, and so on are the fuel that feeds the urge to travel (or not travel). Within this environment of information bombardment, travel agents play an important part in creating anticipated travel experiences. Clients look to the travel agent as a professional to provide objective counseling and realistic expectations.

STRATEGIC MARKETING AND THE MARKETING PLANNING PROCESS

The term *marketing* is often used interchangeably with advertising, promotion, or even public relations, but, while these activities are part of the marketing process, they are not marketing per se. Marketing is the performance of all business activities that direct the flow of goods and services to consumers in order to satisfy customers and accomplish company objectives. In other words, marketing is the creation of a demand that results in an exchange of consumer dollars for products. A marketing plan serves as a road map and timetable for directing all the agency's marketing activities. To be effective, a marketing plan must be tailored to the objectives of the seller or producer of goods and services by interpreting conditions in the marketplace and then effectively meeting market needs.

Marketing may be viewed as an umbrella that is supported by a strong central core, which in turn is supported by radial spokes. (See Figure 5.2.) Sales represents the central support structure for marketing. The sales function for a travel agency is normally accomplished by person-to-person contact between travel agent and client, as discussed in the previous chapter. But nontraditional sales techniques, such as direct mail, machines, computers, and even point-of-purchase packaged displays in retail outlets, may be on the rise. The spokes of the umbrella, which support the sales function, consist of advertising (sales promotion), product packaging, publicity, and marketing research.

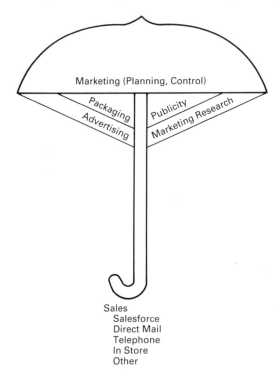

Marketing (Planning, Control)

Packaging
Advertising
Publicity
Marketing Research

Sales
Salesforce
Direct Mail
Telephone
In Store
Other

FIGURE 5.2   What is marketing?

Marketing planning is the process by which all marketing activities are coordinated. The flow chart in Figure 5.3 illustrates how the marketing planning process should work and ensure that marketing activities match the resources, time requirements, and objectives of the firm. Marketing planning forces an agency to make its objectives explicit, improves communication within the agency, and minimizes irrational responses or activities. In a large agency, marketing planning is generally the responsibility of an individual with a title such as director or vice-president of marketing or sales. In a smaller agency, it is generally the direct responsibility of the manager.

The following sections will discuss the various marketing activities a travel agency should undertake, as illustrated in the flow chart of the marketing process.

Agency Objectives

Since marketing plans must be custom designed to fit the needs of individual agencies, it is important to have a clear understanding of what the owners and/or managers desire for their agency. Included in this analysis is determining the "mission" or what the owner wants out of the agency. The owners and managers of a travel agency must also decide what type of agency they wish to operate: full-service versus specialty agency; discount

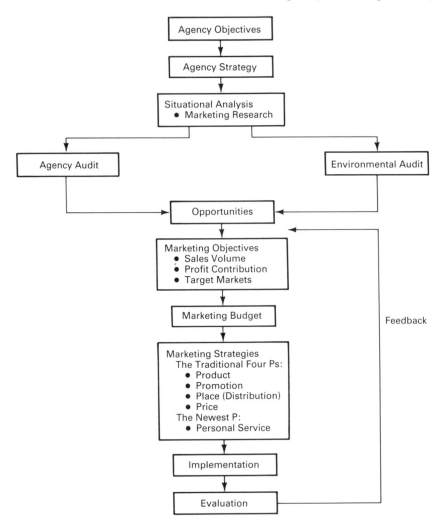

FIGURE 5.3 The marketing process

versus full-margin agency. The development of a marketing plan depends upon this critical step.

Agency Strategy

In terms of a growth strategy, the manager or owner of a travel agency is faced with three growth alternatives (as indicated in Table 5.1): status quo, retrenchment, or planned growth.

Status quo.   This strategy is used by the many agencies that operate without the benefit of a marketing plan and drift along with a status quo

TABLE 5.1 STRATEGIC GROWTH ALTERNATIVES—TRAVEL AGENCIES

Do nothing—status quo

Retrench
  Cut product offering
  Cut number of clients—remove marginal accounts, specialize
  Cut locations
  Cut costs
  Cut employees

Planned growth

	Rapid		Slow—sustained	
	>	>		>
Specialized	>	>		>
	>	>		>
	>	>		>
Full-service	>	>		>
	>	>		>

attitude. Due to the many changes affecting the travel agency environment, however, it is becoming increasingly difficult to survive with a status quo mentality.

Retrenchment. A strategy of retrenchment may be appropriate for a small or mid-size agency with an elderly owner or manager or one suffering from poor health. These individuals often lack family members who want to take on the agency's operations and consequently decide that they wish to remain active but prefer to operate on a reduced scale.

Planned growth. Growth can come in many forms, including an increase in sales, profits, or number of locations. It may entail selling existing products to new market segments, expanding the product line for existing markets, or even vertical integration—for example, a decision to package tours. The type of growth will determine the direction of the marketing plan.

Situational Analysis

In the situational analysis phase of the marketing process, management examines the various factors that affect the agency's marketing objectives and strategies. The agency audit (internal) and the environmental audit (external) are the two primary parts of this analysis. As part of the situational analysis, research should be conducted to gain a better understanding of the agency's clientele.

Internal audit.   The agency audit is primarily an assessment of internal strengths and weaknesses. The evaluation contains objective and subjective appraisals of variables that directly determine the type of marketing plan an agency is able to implement.

Table 5.2 provides a partial listing of the types of variables to be considered in an audit. These variables include financial resources available, office location, specific expertise or travel experiences of personnel, special destination knowledge, the physical condition of the office, available equipment, existing clientele and potential contacts with new prospects, and supplier

TABLE 5.2   EXAMPLES OF VARIABLES TO EXAMINE IN AN AGENCY AUDIT

Variable	Assessment	
	Objective measures	Subjective measures
Advertising	Current budget Media used Message used	Effectiveness in helping to increase sales Effectiveness in promoting corporate image
Corporate image	Results of research studies Letters from clients	Effectiveness in correctly positioning the agency Effectiveness in aiding sales
Distribution	Branches and other forms of outlets. Example—machines.	Effectiveness of distribution system Correctness of locations
Equipment	Type Number Age Value	Effectiveness in aiding productivity Effectiveness in helping to obtain greater sales volume Effectiveness in helping to obtain more profitable sales
Human resource development	Type Number Cost	Value to personnel Value to company
Personnel—sales	Number Years experience Training Education Sales record	Interest in work Ability to sell Desire to sell and excel Willingness to learn and use new techniques Ability to become member of management Level of product knowledge
Relationship with suppliers	Billings Record of payment Complaints	Suppliers' interest in working with and helping the agency Suppliers' desire to see the agency prosper

relationships. The agency audit analyzes recent sales performance, including the "mix" of traffic handled and a determination of the profitability of different types of sales. The audit will result in a composite of strengths and weaknesses and a determination of a comparative advantage.

External audit.   The environmental audit should be performed concurrently with the agency audit. This audit calls for a comprehensive analysis of factors external to the agency: demographics, psychographics, trends in the travel industry, trends in the economy—local and general—the strength of the competition, and the impact of changing government legislation. Assumptions about the future should also be made. Sources of information for the environmental audit include the Chamber of Commerce, the State Department of Economic Development, banks, investment firms, airlines, the local newspaper, surveys by travel industry magazines, and in-house surveys.

Market Potential.   As part of the external analysis it is important to determine the agency's market share and the market potential for the specific area. *Market potential* refers to the total market available for travel agency services within a selected geographical area. The portion held by an individual agency is referred to as *market share.*

Although market potential is difficult to measure, agencies need to be aware of changes in market size before deciding upon a marketing program. In some geographic areas, the market potential may be declining due to an aging population, the disappearance of industry, or other economic and social factors. In others, market potential may be expanding rapidly. Agencies not prepared for the challenge of obtaining a greater percentage of market share in an expanding market will be left behind.

Market potential can be determined by (1) the total sales volume of all agencies in an area (added to this should be a percentage for available business that is not obtained by any agency but could be through aggressive marketing); (2) deriving a ratio of market potential through demographic segmentation, buying power index, economic activity, or other variables; and (3) using industry statistics when available. A study of market potential should also contain an analysis of the different travel segments in the area.

The Competition.   Until recently, it was relatively easy to keep track of the competition. Today, travel agents must keep abreast not only of the activities of their fellow travel agents but also national trends such as franchising and competition from nontraditional vendors. Information concerning competitors in the immediate area can be obtained from an agency's personnel, suppliers, clients, job applicants, meetings with other agents, travel trade periodicals, and publicity and advertising by competitors. The analysis of the competition should include an objective appraisal of the strengths and weaknesses of each competitor.

Market research.   Complementary to the internal and external audits of the situational analysis is market research—the lifeblood of new information for marketing strategy and operational decisions. It is through research that the agency will know who its clients are, which ones are profitable, which are unprofitable, and which markets are untapped. In the final analysis, a successful marketing effort will be the result of an agency's efforts to understand customers or potential customers, how they fit into the marketplace, and how the specific travel services that are sold match and fulfill the needs of customers. Research and a thorough analysis of the agency's existing client mix is, therefore, required. The client analysis should consist of the following:

1. Classification of clients by purpose of travel—commercial, pleasure, incentive, and so on
2. Determination of key clients
3. Determination of demographic and psychographic characteristics

Client Information File.   Agencies should develop an information file for each client. A computer can be invaluable in this task as it permits information to be updated, retrieved using different specifications, and further analyzed. Many agencies obtain information from new clients through the use of a questionnaire. Two examples of client questionnaires are provided in Figure 5.4; one solicits specific information on travel preferences and credit card information and the other solicits general information on vacation habits. Additional information that may be useful for commercial clients might include such corporate travel policies as who may travel first class or business class and special corporate rates with hotels, car rental firms, and so on. New information should be added to the customer's information file as it is obtained, such as change of address, change in employment, change in preferences for airlines, or other data. All travel taken by the client should be recorded as well.

Classification by Commercial or Pleasure.   Clients can be classified basically as commercial or pleasure travelers, although other classifications are also possible. Occasional overlapping of the two is desirable since it indicates that an agency is performing well for the client.

A travel agency sometimes finds it advantageous to subgroup commercial clients into the following categories so it can select appropriate target markets:

Commercial independent
    Professional
    Sales—distribution
    Manufacturing
    Other

    Commercial corporate
      Individual
      Groups
        Conventions, meetings
        Incentive
    Commercial nonprofit
      Schools
        Individual
        Group
      Government
        Individual
        Group
      Quasi-public
        Independent
        Group

For example, if an agency sees that it has been particularly successful in attracting small manufacturing companies, it can obtain a directory of small manuafcturing firms in its market area and promote to them.

Agencies can similarly categorize pleasure travel clients into various subgroupings. Once groups, or segments, have been identified and individuals' common characteristics have been determined, the agency can match product sales information with client segment information to determine which products are appealing to which segments. If a product appeals to a particular client segment and meets the needs of that segment's individuals who share certain traits, it can be assumed that it is likely to appeal to others with similar traits. Marketing activities can then be directed toward matching available products to customers inclined to prefer these products.

Determination of Key Clients. Most businesses have discovered that a majority of their sales and profits are derived from a minority of their customers. This is often referred to as the 80/20 rule, meaning that 80 percent of the business is generated by 20 percent of the clients. An analysis of client sales will reveal which clients provide the majority of sales and profits for an agency. Once identified, these key clients should receive special consideration as appropriate.

The determination of key clients will also reveal unprofitable customers, clients who demand a great deal of service, absorb large tracts of time, and yet purchase very little. Travel agencies lend themselves to this type of customer since they historically have provided free information. For some people, calling travel agencies for "dream vacation" information fulfills fantasies. Then there are people who cannot make up their minds and will change their travel plans more than once after tickets are written. Clients who continuously require ticket reissues are probably costing the agency

NOTE: This is not a credit card application. To apply for the credit card please fill out enclosed form. Thank you.

TRAVELER PROFILE

Make photocopies of Profile if more than one person is enrolling. Information in the Profile is confidential and is used only for making personalized travel arrangements.

Name of traveler _____

Address _____

City _____ State _____ ZIP _____

Work phone ( ) _____ Home phone ( ) _____

CREDIT CARDS

All purchases will be charged to your Working Assets Visa Card unless otherwise indicated.

Other major credit card: ☐ Visa ☐ MasterCard ☐ American Express
Card no. _____ Expires _____

TRAVEL PREFERENCES

Seating: ☐ Aisle ☐ Window ☐ Non-smoking ☐ Smoking ☐ First class ☐ Business ☐ Economy

Meals: ☐ Regular ☐ Vegetarian ☐ Other (specify) _____

Airline _____ Frequent flyer no. _____

Airline _____ Frequent flyer no. _____

Car rental _____ Special reservation no. _____

Hotels: ☐ Twin bed ☐ Double ☐ Queen/King
Arrival at hotels will be guaranteed with your Working Assets Visa Card unless otherwise requested.

I am interested in receiving information on the following types of trips:

☐ Environmental outings such as river rafting, whale watching, mountaineering or (specify)_____
☐ Tours with political and social components to Central America, China, USSR or (specify)_____
☐ Complete package vacations in Hawaii, Caribbean, Greece or (specify)_____

Signature _____

(a)

THE QUESTIONNAIRE

In my next vacation, I will be away for:
[A] less than one week
[B] one week
[C] one to two weeks
[D] two weeks
[E] more than two weeks

I'd like to visit:
[A] a tropical paradise
[B] the mysterious Orient
[C] the Alaskan frontier
[D] historic Europe

By day, I want to:
[A] just plain relax
[B] sightsee
[C] shop
[D] go to the beach
[E] golf
[F] play tennis

By night, I want to:
[A] go nightclubbing
[B] visit a casino
[C] see a show
[D] disco
[E] just watch the stars

During the trip, I'd like to be with:
[A] people my own age
[B] people younger than myself
[C] people older than myself

And I'd rather be:
[A] with couples
[B] with singles
[C] with families
[D] alone

I like a:
[A] fast-paced resort atmosphere, lots to do
[B] relaxed atmosphere
[C] fully escorted package, everything taken care of
[D] more independent self-paced vacation

I prefer service that's:
[A] posh, pampering, white-gloved
[B] pampering, but a bit more casual
[C] close enough to call, but out of sight
[D] minimal—I'll wait on myself most times

My idea of good food is:
[A] just basic meat and potatoes
[B] haute cuisine—dishes I don't normally eat
[C] healthy—low fat, low cholesterol
[D] yummy—who cares about diet on vacation

For my next vacation I'll travel:
[A] by myself
[B] with friends
[C] with family
[D] with friends and family

I usually take a vacation:
[A] twice a year or more often
[B] once a year
[C] every other year
[D] rarely

My preferred vacation months are:
[A] winter
[B] spring
[C] summer
[D] fall

My vacation budget:
[A] is usually ample
[B] sometimes seems stretched
[C] often limits what I can do

(b)

FIGURE 5.4 Simple questionnaires can provide agencies with useful and time-saving information on clients.

Source: Travel Agent Magazine, June 20, 1988, p. 17.

more than their business is worth. Corporate clients who demand rebates should also be evaluated in terms of profit potential.

The days are gone when agents could shrug off marginal profit situations by claiming that "any business is good business." It makes no sense to continue serving unprofitable customers: Every sale should justify itself either as a cost-effective transaction or as a necessary service to retain profitable clients. Travel agencies may eventually be forced to alter their long-held policies and begin charging per transaction as some agencies have already done.

Most agencies continuously seek new business, sometimes at the expense of overlooking business opportunities within their existing client base. Existing commercial clients, for example, can often be induced to book their pleasure travel through the same agency. In addition, commercial clients also offer opportunities for new services such as convention and meeting planning or motivational programs (incentives) with travel as the reward. Expanded opportunities also exist with pleasure travelers who belong to social, professional, or religious organizations such as alumni clubs or church groups that may have an interest in a group tour. A satisfied and loyal business or pleasure client is also likely to introduce new clients to a travel agency.

Demographic Characteristics. *Demographics* refers to easily quantified statistics or facts concerning the local population and/or the agency's clientele. The travel agency manager must decide what types of demographic data are needed to describe pleasure and commercial clients. A system of gathering, tabulating, updating, and using this information can then be implemented.

The following is an example of potentially useful demographic information:

Pleasure Travelers	Commercial Travelers
Name	Company name
Address	Address
Business phone	Zip code
Home phone	Division
Zip code	Type of company
Occupation	Number of employees
Income	Number of branches
Education	in market area
Marital status	Location (Urban,
Sex	Suburban, Rural)
Number and ages of children	Names of commercial
	travelers
	a. Title
	b. Address
	c. Business phone
	d. Home phone
	e. Name of secretary

Other demographic data, for example, home ownership, could also be included if it is significant to the agency. Agencies sometimes ask for data such as age or education without understanding how it can be used, so before asking for demographic information, they should have a plan for using the data. Clients may regard a request for personal data such as age, ethnic origin, religion, or marital status as an invasion of privacy and may react by seeking a less inquisitive agency unless they understand the reasoning behind the data collection.

The most common uses of demographic data are to determine the degree of penetration that an agency has made in a particular market segment and to target new prospects. Zip code information may be the most useful demographic variable and is usually given freely by a client. Based on the assumption that people prefer to reside in locations where their neighbors share similar characteristics, zip code analysis can be useful in indicating the economic level and sometimes occupational levels of clients and in planning a mail or phone campaign.

Psychographic Characteristics.   *Psychographics* refers to the role of attitudes, opinions, interests, values, personality, and lifestyle in consumer consumptive behavior. These attributes affect travel habits, preferences, and purchasing behavior, which can be of substantial value to travel agencies. The following is an example of psychographic information:

- Number of trips per year
- Seasonality of travel
- Individual who makes reservations
- Method used to pay for travel
- Types of airlines, hotels, rental cars, and so on preferred
- Departure hours preferred
- Attributes important in destination selection
- Prime motivators to travel

Psychographic data permit the agent to custom design a travel package that meets with the client's lifestyle. Generally, clients are quite willing to provide this information since they can immediately see its usefulness.

Focus Groups.   Use of focus groups is becoming increasingly important as a marketing research method. Focus group research involves holding a series of informal discussions with eight to ten present (or potential) customers. The purpose of focus group research is to delve into the attitudes and behavior of specific groups and to gain an understanding of the group's experiences—their prejudices and preferences and their perceptions about travel. Focus groups can be helpful for agencies by providing feedback about tour packages and individual travel products; giving information about the group's willingness to spend more for higher-quality travel; and revealing what their expectations are regarding certain travel products or destinations. An agency can better choose its product line and other marketing strategies with the aid of such information.

Opportunities

Utilizing the information derived from marketing research and linking the results of the agency audit with the results of the environmental audit provide the agency with the best marketing plan. This process should identify the agency's prime prospects and the best possible use of the available resources. An assessment of available opportunities should assist the agency in deciding upon the most appropriate marketing objectives and strategies.

Marketing Objectives

The primary marketing objective consists of three important parts: It must have a quantifiable sales objective, a specific deadline, and a profit and loss statement. An objective could read: to reach total bookings of $10 million by the end of the year at a net profit of 5 percent. An objective can also be broken down into subobjectives that describe the source of the $10 million, such as reaching billings of $2 million in hotel bookings, $3 million in cruise ship bookings, and so on. Other examples of marketing objectives could be to sell 30 percent more traveler insurance, to increase sales to a particular destination by 20 percent, or to develop twenty new corporate accounts.

Marketing objectives serve as the basis for sales quotas and for determining the number of personnel and level of expenditures needed to obtain the stated objectives. Solid marketing objectives should be challenging yet realistic, verifiable, and taken seriously by all individuals within the agency. All staff must be made to feel responsible for the fulfillment or failure in reaching the stated objectives.

One of the most important marketing objectives is the selection of target markets. Because being all things to all people is difficult, agencies are finding that some form of specialization is often needed.

The market potential available to an agency in any geographic area is a composite of several different market segments. An agency must decide which segments offer the greatest opportunity and which segments cannot realistically or profitably be serviced. The new business generated from selected market segments should replace the less desirable accounts with more profitable ones. Once these segments are identified and the best options selected, they become target markets and products and services are then specifically designed to serve them. The peculiar characteristics of the targeted market segments will determine the most appropriate marketing strategies.

Marketing Budget

A marketing plan must be guided by a budget. This budget should clearly show (1) total annual marketing expenditures; (2) annual expenditures for each marketing element (for example, advertising, direct mail, and so on); (3) expenditures per month for each marketing element; (4) the relationship of each marketing cost area as a percentage of the total marketing budget; and (5) the percentage relationship of the marketing budget to the total budget for the agency. While a budget can help to direct marketing activities over some time period, a certain degree of flexibility is also required so that marketing programs can be responsive to changing environments.

Marketing Strategies

Marketing strategy entails decisions on how best to utilize the agency's resources to meet objectives and maximize profits. Strategies in any organization are traditionally designed around "The Four Ps": Product, Promotion, Place (distribution), and Price. (See Figure 5.5.) Given the service nature of

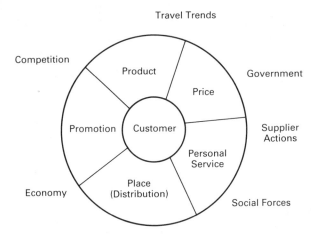

FIGURE 5.5   The marketing mix

the industry, travel agencies are concerned with an additional P, which is Personal Service. These five elements will be discussed in the following sections. It should be recognized that specific marketing strategies cannot properly be established until the previously described steps have been taken. A common mistake is to begin planning promotional campaigns or other marketing strategies before selecting target markets, analyzing the competition, or setting objectives. Only by chance will strategies designed in this manner allow an agency to accomplish its objectives.

	Outbound														Inbound			
	Commercial Independent				Comm. Corp.		Commercial Nonprofit						Pleasure/ Personal		Group			
	Professional	Sales-Distribution	Manufacturing	Other	Individual	Group	Schools: Indiv.	Schools: Group	Gov't.: Indiv.	Gov't.: Group	Quasi-Public: Indiv.	Quasi-Public: Group	FIT	GIT	Conf. Business	Pleasure	International	Domestic
Air Transportation	Present		Planned										Present	Planned				
Train													Present	Planned				
Auto Rental	Present		Planned										Present					
Hotel	Present												Present	Planned				
Package Tours													Present	Present				
Own Tours																		
Cruise													Present					
Travel Insurance														Planned				
Financial Services																		
Recreation																		
Incentive																		
Group Planning																		

■ Present   ▨ Planned

FIGURE 5.6   Product-market matrix

THE FIVE Ps OF STRATEGIC AGENCY MARKETING

Product—the First "P"

All product decisions revolve around the filling of need or creation of demand. The use of a customer/product line matrix (See Figure 5.6) can assist management in developing the product aspect of a marketing plan. Projections of the dollar sales volume expected for each customer segment for various product lines enable management to determine probable sources of income for the next year and to plan marketing activities. Travel agents will find it increasingly necessary to plan the next year's product mix to maximize income.

Specialization: Business and Pleasure

Some agency analysts see specialization as being inevitable, particularly for the small agency. Even in the instance of a full-service agency, specialization may occur by offering expertise in a specific product category. The most common specialization practiced by agencies is to opt for either commercial or pleasure travelers. Firms that concentrate on business travelers may further specialize into corporate travel or professional travel (medical doctors, lawyers, and so on.) Agencies that specialize in pleasure travel, on the other hand, have the chance to serve a market segment providing high-yielding vacation travel that may include various other components besides airline, hotel, and car rental bookings, not to mention cruises and specialty travel.

Inbound—Domestic

A minority of agencies have decided to specialize as inbound agencies (as discussed earlier in Chapter 3). These firms handle group tours, incentive groups, or meetings and convention planning. These types of firms may be variously known by such names as Congress Handling Agents, Meeting Planners, Ground Handling Agents, Incoming Tour Operators, Destination Management Servicers, or Professional Conference Organizers. Inbound agencies generally work closely with local corporations, the Chamber of Commerce, local visitor attractions, hotels, ground transportation organizations, and others who have an interest in attracting visitors.

Diversifying into the inbound market represents one way to develop a competitive edge and to improve an agency's bottom line, but it is an area only briefly explored by U.S. travel agents thus far.

Inbound—Foreign. Specializing in inbound services for the millions of foreign visitors who come to the United States each year provides another option for diversification. The United States Travel and Tourism Association (USTTA) has been encouraging agents to follow this route and has developed an international network to help domestic agents develop inbound business.

Product line specialization. Agencies may also specialize by product line or by type of client. Specialization by product line offers market niche opportunities for a firm. Particularly in large metropolitan areas, agencies can specialize by product line such as motorcoach or cruise ship or by handling travel to a particular destination. These firms develop an expertise with one or two product lines and a strong client base generally composed of groups. For example, an agency specializing in cruise ships will be knowledgeable about a wide product range, appealing to all tastes and pocketbooks. Because of the high volume of cruise ticket sales, the agency may be able to offer attractive discounts to customers. Specializing in group sales makes it possible to make the right match of cruise to client and to capitalize on the agency's experience and detailed product knowledge.

Client-specific specialization. Specialization in customers with a specific lifestyle or hobby can provide another opportunity for travel agents. Figure 5.7 illustrates that the most popular special-interest vacations are for skiers, golfers, and honeymooners. Agents report that over 20 percent of their clients booked special-interest vacations in 1985.[1] Specialization in these vacations can lead to high-volume expansion if the agency is able to handle all the details.

One of the most common forms of agency specialization is by ethnic or social characteristics. Market niches have been found by concentrating upon Black, Jewish, Asian, Hispanic, or other ethnic groups and handicapped communities. In recent years more agencies are specializing in such markets as family travel, the gay community, and singles. A recent study,

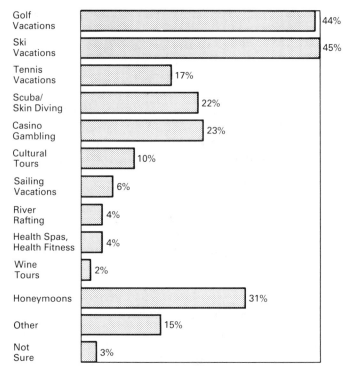

FIGURE 5.7 Most popular types of special interest vacations—1985
Source: Travel Weekly's Louis Harris Survey June, 1986, p. 100.

for example, indicates that 77 million singles reside in the United States today and that this market accounts for more than 15 percent of total vacation expenditures.[2]

A market that continues to be pursued by many travel agents is the expanding senior citizens market. With longer life expectancies and more senior citizens having the time, money, and inclination to travel, this market is slated for future growth, as many older people take several trips per year.

A market niche philosophy can be beneficial as the agency does not have to worry about the total travel industry since it has a specific focus. The agency becomes less concerned with the overall size of the market and more concerned with its ability to compete in the niche. The danger with this form of specialization is that the agency may limit its growth potential. Agencies that specialize in this manner are more likely to be found in large metropolitan areas.

Diversification.   Given an environment of high competition and vulnerability to external forces, diversification is a strategy worth considering. Ways for the agency to diversify include putting together its own tours or packages, becoming a wholesaler, or increasing the number of specialty areas. Diversifying into areas peripheral to travel also provides additional options. The process of analyzing potentially profitable product lines and customers forces management to carefully analyze the current resources of the agency.

Travel related merchandise.   Agencies may also find that they need to offer nontraditional products such as luggage or recreational vehicles as part of their product line. Other travel-related merchandise sold by agents include passport photos, suntan lotion, calculators programmed with foreign exchange rates, tickets to sporting events, and travel guidebooks—items that can earn a respectable profit. Certain product lines such as travel insurance, travelers cheques, and other financial services offer profit-making opportunities and may become more important to agencies. The commission for travel insurance, for instance, can sometimes amount to close to 50 percent of the purchase price. Some agencies have begun selling information via computer output; an example of this would be guidelines for travel budget management sold to corporate clients.

Perceptions of the agency product.   Because of the intangible nature of the travel agency industry, the product aspect of the agency also entails the consumer's *perception* of what the agency has to offer, including the skill and knowledge of the agency personnel, the office environment, location, appearance, facilities such as automation, and services performed. Services are becoming an increasingly important aspect of the travel agency product line and consist of consultation, processing of papers, convenience, and the overall management of travel arrangements. To gain a competitive edge and to ensure repeat business, travel agents have begun to offer a myriad of extra services, ranging from overnight ticket delivery and 800 numbers to corporate reports and one-day passport arrangements.

Promotion—The Second "P"

The second P in the marketing mix is *promotion.* A wide variety of advertising, publicity, public relations, and other promotional opportunities exists for travel agencies. Before committing to any program activity, marketing objectives should be clearly understood and stated. Promotional activities will vary depending on marketing objectives and product decisions.

Overall, a travel agency has two reasons to provide the public with a message: (1) to form and enhance a strategic market position and image and (2) to promote the services of the agency.

Strategic positioning and image building. In marketing, the term *position* is not simply another buzzword, for it means everything in the marketplace. Avis Auto Rentals, for example, built a successful company by positioning itself strongly as a number two with an image of a firm trying harder to succeed. The art of positioning is not confined to any industry or type of company. Today, the consumer is bombarded with thousands of advertising messages and cannot be expected to remember all the companies or products. Therefore, management needs to devise a strategy that clearly positions the travel agency in a particular status or characteristic in the mind of the target customer.

An agency might wish to be positioned as the largest full-service agency in town or as a quality professional agency specializing in commercial travel. The task of successfully implementing a positioning strategy depends upon developing a clear, positive, and easily remembered image that sticks in the mind of the consumer. The corporate name and logo, stationery, location and appearance of the office, and even the appearance and telephone manners of the travel agents all combine to create an image, intentional or unintentional, of the agency.

Window displays can also enhance the image of a travel agency and are a valuable selling tool. A bright and appealing window display is relatively easy and inexpensive to design using maps, posters, and other free material from various travel suppliers and destinations.

Advertising. Advertising refers to paid messages delivered through a variety of media including radio broadcast, yellow pages, TV, print, specialty, outdoor, and others such as in shopping malls, on transit lines, and at shelters (bus stops). Advertising messages attempt to persuade the prospective customer to buy from a particular agency and can appeal to a number of different needs or desires, including snob appeal, money savings, health, physical comfort, family togetherness, and cultural exposure. In all cases

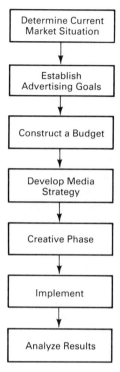

FIGURE 5.8 The planning process for advertising campaigns

the advertising message should be interesting, compelling, and creative, focusing on the prospective client. Figure 5.8 illustrates the steps to follow in planning an advertising campaign.

Agency managers should be aware of the number of restraints imposed by statutes, regulations, and court decisions regarding deceptive advertising. A travel agency's advertising, therefore, should not make any false or misleading statements. Agencies involved with legal battles over these issues are often faced with court sanctions, civil damages, and substantial legal fees.

Advertising Budgets.   Advertising budgets are determined by various methods, including (1) allocating a percentage of sales; (2) spending what the agency can afford; (3) looking at what the competition is spending and doing likewise; or (4) spending to meet the objective or task at hand. One guideline is that the advertising budget must balance the incremental cost of advertising with incremental returns. Moreover, advertising should be planned in terms of campaigns rather than isolated activities. The advertising activities selected should complement each other, producing a synergistic effect and consistently reflecting the desired image and positioning statement.

Advertising Media.   The following sections discuss some of the more common advertising activities undertaken by travel agencies.

1. *Television.* With the exception of large travel agencies, most have a limited advertising budget and do not invest heavily in mass media such as TV. Although TV advertising has its advantages, the high cost generally does not justify its use. Also, the "reach" or audience covered by mass media is certain to contain too many individuals who cannot be considered as good prospects.

2. *Newspapers.* Many newspapers (and magazines as well) offer regional issues that reach only a portion of a city or other geographical area. The advantages of newspaper advertising are (a) its relatively low cost and (b) its ability to reach a wide range of households. Additionally, people who are making travel decisions often use newspapers as a reference source. The disadvantage of newspaper advertising is the amount of wasted circulation.

3. *Magazines.* Magazines have several strong points, including the possible use of color reproduction, long life, and efficiency in reaching a target audience. The difficulty with magazine advertising is that it requires a long lead time and costs can be prohibitive.

4. *Radio.* Many radio stations reach selective audiences such as "ethnic," "easy listening," and "classical." Selective radio advertising often offers the right combination of price and audience to be attractive to a travel agency, can reach the market quickly, and messages can be easily changed. One disadvantage of radio is that it provides no hard copy or reference for customers.

5. *Yellow Pages.* Advertising in the yellow pages is a must for almost all agencies, often the only continuous form of advertising done by the travel agency. Yellow pages advertising can be effective if the ad draws the attention of the reader and quickly provides the necessary information.

6. *Specialty Advertising.* Travel agencies often use specialty advertising, which means providing clients with an endless variety of agency brand souvenir items such as calendars, pens, plastic rulers, luggage tags, shoe horns, and matches. Many travel agency managers feel that these items, which are designed for frequent use in travel and work, serve as a constant reminder of the agency. Specialty advertising is most effective when the items are useful or clever, have a long life, and are distributed efficiently.

7. *Direct Mail.* Direct mail advertising is an effective method for travel agencies to sell well-defined products to a specific audience, but the cost of printing and postage dictates that this medium be well planned and professional. Professional assistance in designing a direct mail campaign may be well worth the expense. The response rate for direct mail varies markedly depending upon many variables, including the time of year, the impact of the message, and the method of selecting the recipients. Direct mail is only as good as the mailing list; therefore, since direct mail costs more per person than any other form of promotion, the direct mailing list should be reviewed and updated frequently. One of the major advantages of direct mail is that the vehicle can be personalized. The trick to effective direct mail

campaigns is to pinpoint the right audience, tailor a perfect message, and give the audience a means of responding.

8. *Newsletters.* Newsletters are becoming popular with travel agencies, performing two important functions: (a) keeping in touch with the agency's clients and (b) informing them of any special offers. A good newsletter will feature one lead story such as a specific vacation destination, a new Frequent Flyer program, or new air-fares. Other supporting features might include seasonal stories, timely news on exchange rates, customs requirements, or contributions from satisfied customers. The newsletter's strength is that, it is personalized like other direct mail, and provides a means of communicating directly with the agency's clients. Figure 5.9 is the first page of a newsletter used by Zenith Travel Inc. in New York City.

9. *Self-Liquidating Premiums.* The use of self-liquidating premiums or advertising that pays for itself offers potential for travel agencies. The sale of t-shirts and other apparel with the agency's distinctive logo and travel or tote bags with the name of the agency imprinted on the side are examples. Creative individuals can design many other forms of such advertising. Ideas can come from employees, clients, and those involved in selling specialty advertising items. Managers should consider and encourage these ideas.

Cooperative Advertising. Cooperative advertising within the travel industry is becoming increasingly common. Agents can double advertising space at no extra cost by identifying leading suppliers and participating in available co-op advertising programs. Generally, a supplier will allow a certain amount of cooperative advertising funds based on the volume of sales produced by the agency. Co-op monies should be integrated with an agency's regular advertising plan.

Assessing Advertising Results. Advertising programs should be pretested (with a pilot test) before they are implemented and evaluated for effectiveness after implementation. A pilot test can be as simple as getting the opinions of several unbiased readers with questions: Did the ad get your attention and keep it? Is it attractive and eye appealing? Did it say something of worth? Did it give viewers a reason to respond? Did it make it easy for viewers to find the agency?

The result of advertising programs should also be tracked by asking clients, using coupons, and so on. Newspapers ads, for example, should increase business, or at least calls from readers, 10 to 15 percent if they are to be considered effective. If the ads are not bringing in new business, the advertising program should be reevaluated and ads redesigned.[3]

Publicity. Publicity generally refers to unpaid messages about a travel agency or its services. Because publicity is unpaid, it often has more credibility in the eyes of consumers. The managers of some companies seem to have a talent for gaining favorable publicity through news stories or sim-

Around The World with Bonnie Kogos

A serendipitous, discerning travel compendium—what's noteworthy, valuable, different, exciting and fun in attractions, locale, transportation, accommodations and packaging for you.

Kogos Publications Co.
at Zenith Travel Inc.

Volume 9, No. 1
Summer-Fall 1988

404 Fifth Avenue, New York, NY 10018
212 947-6969

GREAT ADVENTURES AWAIT YOU...

INSATIABLE TRAVELER: IS THAT YOU?

Did you drop in for tea last season at the Gan Dan Monastery in Ulan Bator, Mongolia, and wonder what you will do this year? For some travelers, seeking the arcane, offbeat and unusual is a continuous quest.

Adventure travel, from the dusty roads of Borneo to the enchanted islands of the Galapagos, is much easier these days with about 20 companies specializing in the offbeat, and unusual tours. They "carry" you, whether your stamina is high or low, to destinations you've not yet imagined. Visit Australia, Bhutan, Burma, Rwanda's gorillas, the Andes, the Himalayas, Zaire's Mountain of the Moon, the Nile River, the Sahara Desert, Easter Island, Greenland, Upper Volta or the Arctic. One company I particularly like, called Wilderness Travel, organizes over 80 adventure trips a year---from the Amazon to visiting archeological digs. Call me for nifty ideas.

SPECIAL SUMMER TAHITI AND MEDITERRANEAN CRUISES

The three ships, WIND STAR, WIND SONG and WIND SPIRIT are the most luxurious sailing ships! As an ex-Caribbean Yachtie, I'd love a sail on one of these big babies. Windstar Sail Cruises offers 3 elegant, upscale motorized sailing vessels that are more yachtlike than mass market cruise ships. There are 75 cabins for 150 people and it is very expensive and elite. EXCEPT FOR THIS SUMMER!

With savings of almost 50% off regular rates, these cruises represent special value. You can spend your vacation in the Mediterrean, the Bahamas, Tahiti or the Caribbean on a Windstar cruise.

WIND SPIRIT, from June 12 through August 7, offers special rates of $2895, plus $34 port charges, for a complete 10 day Mediterranean trip. Fly to Monte Carlo on Air France, stay at Loew's Monte Carlo Hotel for 3 nights, sail for 7 days. All prices mentioned here are based on per person double occupancy.

WIND SONG leaves from Papeete, Tahiti, on one week cruises through French Polynesia from May 20 through September 2. Special cruise rate is $1995 plus $32 port charge. Or choose a 9 day Tahiti Cruise Package, including the 7 day yacht voyage, roundtrip air on UTA between San Francisco and Tahiti, and two days/one night accommodations at Hotel Tahara in Papeete prior to the cruise. All of this costs only $2495 per person. They want you to get addicted. And you will...

WIND STAR is based in Miami, with special new 9 and 10 day summer cruises between Miami and Martinique offered at savings up to 48% vs. normal summer rates. The Bahamas cruises range from 4, 5 to 7 days where you explore private and uninhabited islands. A 4 day sail departing Miami on September 3 is a low $1,050 per person. I have other sailing dates and rates. You get the best in enjoying the high seas, the lovely evenings, the romance of sailing, delicious cuisine, comfort and congeniality. Do call for a brochure.

FIGURE 5.9
Source: Kogos Publications Co. at Zenith Travel Inc., vol. 9, no. 1 (Summer-Fall 1988).

ply a mention of the company's name by journalists, news reporters, commentators, or editors. Serving in civic, professional, philanthropic, and other organizations helps managers cultivate good press relations.

Publicity is also an end product of *public relations,* a catchall term used to refer to all public promotional activities of a firm other than paid advertising. While large agencies can hire the services of a professional public relations firm, most travel agencies conduct these activities without professional assistance.

Public relations programs for travel agencies often require a budget. Such a program might include talks before community groups, open houses, film or slide showings, theme parties on a specific destination, major prize giveaways, seminars, public travel shows, sponsoring a Little League team, or sponsoring a free trip for a handicapped child to visit Disney World. Public relations tactics often result in favorable publicity for the agency; however, these activities take time and money and require judgment on the part of the agency manager. The agency must guard against spreading itself too thin. Public relations activities should be based on the firm's marketing objectives. A public relations program is particularly beneficial when an agency is growing and plans to open new branches and add new personnel.

Place (Distribution)—The Third "P"

The distribution of a travel agency's product entails all the factors—human, physical, and electronic—that can bring its services to the attention of prospects who are remote from the office. The manager must consider means of reaching potential customers within a geographical range where the delivery of services is both possible and practical. Personal selling, telephone calls, directories, trade shows, travel displays, and parties in shopping malls are all proven ways of distributing the travel product.

Word of mouth is the single most effective marketing distribution tool. Friends of the staff, satisfied clients, suppliers, and other firms that bring in referral business either directly or indirectly are important factors in the distribution system for travel agencies.

Clearly, the importance of referrals and contacts should not be underestimated.

In the larger scheme of the travel sales distribution system, travel agents are intermediaries between suppliers and end users and are themselves the key distributors. But as previously discussed, agents' loss of exclusivity and several other factors have combined to threaten this longstanding relationship.

Managers of travel agencies cannot remain blind to the emergence of new distribution channels, including direct selling by suppliers. Sears' and K-Mart's attempts to enter the travel sales distribution system are indicative of this new trend toward new and innovative distribution systems.

The ability to add millions of dollars worth of travel expertise to your company—without cost—is now in your hands.

Whether or not your company has a corporate travel department, you can put over 200 travel professionals and a state-of-the-art computerized travel information bank to work for you. Without spending a cent.

This book is designed to help you tap those resources and ultimately save you time, trouble and money when making corporate travel arrangements for your company.

We're Garber Travel. And we wrote the book on corporate travel.

As one of the largest travel agencies in the nation, Garber Travel has the experience, expertise, manpower, and computer and telecommunications capabilities to expedite all your travel needs. And since our resources are available to you without cost, there's simply no reason not to take advantage of them.

So acquaint yourself with the travel resources available to you. Then rest assured that putting those resources to work for you is only a phone call away.

FIGURE 5.10
Garber Travel Service Inc. in Boston Mass. specializes in corporate travel and provides potential customers with this brochure.

Travel agencies may eventually want to establish travel booths in supermarkets or department stores. They may also need to develop a system for interfacing with computers in the offices and homes of clients and to establish and operate ticketing machines in shopping malls and other public areas. Satellite ticket printers (STPs) have been granted accreditation from the Airlines Reporting Corporation and are becoming increasingly common. Over 1500 STPs were granted accreditation from ARC between 1986 and '88.[4]

Travel agency in-plant offices on the premises of large corporations and out-plant travel operations may also be viable options.

Dealerships. Dealerships represent another distribution option for the agency-supplier relationship. A dealership relationship would most likely take the form of a "preferred supplier" arrangement; however, these are not exclusive dealerships. In a preferred supplier agreement an agent, working in concert with a supplier, agrees to push (prefer) that supplier. In turn, the agent gets incremental commissions or overrides above the ordinary 10 percent. Airline overrides in the domestic market have traditionally run up to 5 percent (a 50 percent increase) and international overrides are generally much higher.

Reciprocal agreements. Another distribution option that can dramatically increase an agency's sales and profits is to form reciprocal arrangements with other retailers in the community. For example, a reciprocal arrangement between a travel agency and a luggage shop would include advertisements for the luggage shop on all agency ticket jackets and luggage purchasers receiving promotional flyers for the travel agency. These techniques are fairly easy to devise because travel agents are selling one of the most desirable products in the world.

These and other innovations may require capital and outside expertise. Managers of travel agencies must remain flexible in their thinking and be willing to consider new channels of distribution. One thing is certain—if they don't, someone else will.

Price—the Fourth "P"

The fourth variable within the five Ps is *price*. Until recently, there was little that travel agencies could do about price since both prices and commissions were determined for the agencies. Today, travel agencies must consider price and how it will be used in their strategic marketing plans.

Rebates. The practice of rebating is, in effect, a price discounting strategy whereby a travel agency shares part of its commission with the client. Earlier it was mentioned that suppliers frequently seek to increase their sales volume at travel agencies by offering either discounts or price commission overrides. Some agents pass along part of this override to their clients. While this practice may produce large total billings for the agency, whether it provides the essential net income is not clear. Most travel agencies have been confronted with requests for discounts or rebates, especially from commercial clients, practices that have been prevalent for years in other nations, particularly those of Southeast Asia. The experience in some countries has demonstrated, however, that many agencies cannot survive in such an environment.

Rebating is no longer prohibited within the United States, although the Federal Aviation Act still prohibits rebating in international air transportation. In the domestic arena, this matter is settled between travel agent and air carrier. Only a few airlines have stated that travel agents are free to rebate, but the practice is generally tolerated by most carriers. There are no restrictions on rebating with commissions earned from hotels, car rentals, cruises, and tour packages. Agents can, therefore, develop creative ways of rebating to customers without using the air carrier portion of the commission. Most agents oppose rebating in principle, but it is likely to continue, nonetheless. For many agencies, rebating is the only way to retain market share. Some see it as part of the outgrowth of being pulled into the mainstream of U.S. retail merchandising via deregulation. Rebating does attract corporate customers and raise volume, thereby enhancing the agency's ability to earn overrides.

Service charges.   On the other extreme, another option in terms of travel agency pricing is to charge clients a fee for services performed, a service charge concept supported by many airlines. While some agencies already charge a fee, the idea has not yet been adopted on a large-scale basis because the first travel agency in a competitive neighborhood to charge a fee is likely to see its customers walk down the street to a competitor. From the agency's perspective, the service charge may not make a great contribution to net profits, but it can discourage unprofitable transactions and help clients realize that an agent's time is valuable.

Purchase of supplier products.   The day may come when travel agents will need to purchase and resell stocks of tickets for travel products, which would change the entire relationship between travel suppliers, travel agents, and consumers. Historically, the retail travel agent has served as an "agent" for the supplier. The contract ensuing from the sales transaction has been binding on the supplier and the consumer. If agents were to start buying their own products for resale, they might no longer be viewed as agents of the supplier.

Price-value concepts.   Another aspect of pricing concerns creating consumer price-value consciousness. Travel shoppers are becoming increasingly value conscious, so agencies must learn to use pricing intelligently and creatively in their merchandising.

One way to improve pricing techniques involves showing the agency's prospective customers that the agency is price conscious by advertising the various special offers available from travel suppliers. Some of these special rates are widely advertised by suppliers, but others are not. Agency employees also need to keep well informed of these special offers so they can assist clients in making low-cost travel arrangements.

Another pricing technique deals with the person who requests "the cheapest airfare available." Instead of just quoting the lowest figure, a more effective technique might be to quote the lowest unrestricted airfare and then state the special discounted fare. Here, the agent has placed a higher fare in the client's mind, and anything lower will be perceived as a good value. The agent has also demonstrated a willingness to find bargain rates. These merchandising techniques will become increasingly important to the travel agent.

Personal Service—the Recent Fifth "P"

When aptitude and effciency are more or less equal between agencies, personal service, the fifth "P" in the marketing mix, becomes an extremely important factor. Especially given the threat of direct sale by suppliers and increased competition from nontraditional sources, an agency's quality of personal service can make the difference between survival and failure. Agencies may go the extra mile for clients, such as obtaining visas, delivering tickets, furnishing prepared baggage tags, airport pickup and delivery of clients, and assistance in clearing immigration.

In addition to specialized services, personal service also entails staff attitude in dealing with clients. Staff should treat all clients with courtesy and respect and counsel and provide professional advice as appropriate. For travelers with special needs, such as the handicapped or elderly, agents should make every effort to ensure that travel plans go smoothly and special arrangements are made when necessary.

Another aspect of personal service can come in the form of recognition of valued customers. Some agencies have established frequent traveler programs, similar to airline-sponsored frequent flyer programs, providing clients with a selection of awards for their loyalty to the agency. Gifts and travel are the most common incentives, and awards are generally made by virtue of a point system, with x amount of travel sales generating so many points.

Implementation of Marketing Strategies and Checkpoints

The marketing plan should describe when marketing activities will occur. If an advertising program is planned for the summer, the plan should indicate what activities are to be scheduled each month, such as radio advertising in June and July and newspaper advertising in August. Yellow page advertising should be determined in anticipation of the press date of each new edition.

The plan should also specify what tasks need to be accomplished before the scheduled marketing activity. A checkpoint system is helpful to ensure completion of each of the marketing actions and to provide guidance when alternatives must be adopted when a situation changes. A checklist or Gantt Chart to track the progress of the planned schedule is a useful management tool.

Final Review and Evaluation

Marketing plans should be reviewed and revised every year, with the results evaluated against the objectives of the marketing plan, such as an increase in sales volume, profitability, or market share. A marketing plan is never perfect, and changes will often need to be made in the format or the procedure. Subordinates should be involved in the review of a current marketing plan to help revise areas that were not well understood or did not lend themselves to efficient handling.

SUMMARY

Success for a travel agency will increasingly require strategic marketing. Marketing encompasses sales, advertising, public relations, and other functions. The basis for all successful marketing is understanding client needs and matching these with appropriate products. A written marketing plan serves as a road map for a travel agent to ensure that changing client needs are satisfied.

All travel agencies must establish objectives, which are met through strategies. In the case of marketing, the five Ps serve as the basis for establishing marketing strategies.

It is critical for a travel agency to determine what it wishes to be, reflecting the philosophy of the owners and managers of the agency. A successful marketing plan depends upon clearly understanding precisely what kind of an agency is desired. In the absence of this kind of direction, an agency finds itself trying to be all things to all people. The process of marketing planning is essential and will become even more important as competition becomes more intense.

DISCUSSION QUESTIONS

1. Of what significance is the concept of an "Anticipated Travel Experience" to travel agents?
2. How can travel agents benefit by classifying some clients into a group of key clients?
3. What is the purpose of a marketing plan?
4. What are the essential parts of an objective?

5. What is the relationship between marketing objectives and marketing strategies?

6. Discuss the role of the five Ps in designing a marketing plan. How important is the fifth P in providing a competitive edge in marketing?

ENDNOTES

[1]*Travel Weekly's Louis Harris Survey,* June, 1986, p. 98.

[2]Rosemarie Clancy, "Desperately Seeking Singles," *Travel Weekly's Guide to Group Travel,* March 30, 1986, p. 43.

[3]Gloria J. Pierce, "Making Your Ad Mean Business," *The Travel Agent,* November 27, 1986, p. 55.

[4]Airlines Reporting Corporation (ARC), phone consultation.

SUPPLEMENTAL READINGS

American Society of Travel Agents. *Marketing Research: Gateway to Profits.* Pan American World Airways. N.D.

REILLY, ROBERT T., *Travel and Tourism Marketing Techniques.* Wheaton, IL: Merton House Publishing Company, 1980.

chapter 6

Agency Organization and Office Management

LEARNING OBJECTIVES

- To know the principles of organizational structure for travel agencies
- To understand general management concepts as they apply to travel agencies
- To be able to explain some of the components that a professional agency comprises.

KEY TERMS

- Conflict Management
- Cruise Only Market
- Departmentation by Function
- Departmentation by Territory
- Employee Turnover
- Full-Service Branch
- In-plant Branch
- MBWA
- Motivation
- Organizational Climate
- Organizational Structure
- Out-plant Operation
- Policies and Procedures Manual
- Professionalism

INTRODUCTION

The organization of a typical travel agency is generally simple, being limited in terms of scope of business purpose, division of labor, span of control, and financial control. Except for multi-unit and very high-volume operations, the typical travel agency has only one or two tiers of management. This fairly basic structure is due to the nature of the product and the fact that most employees are front-line people who deal directly with the public. Although there is an apparent trend toward larger agencies, the organizational chart remains relatively simple, and increased layers of management are usually not required.

Many management theories are developed around the larger service or industrial organizations, but few are applicable to the typical travel agency, which employs only a small number of workers. Despite the emerging trend toward larger agencies and consortia, a recent study found that 56 percent of agencies employ from three to six full-time employees, 28 percent employ two or fewer employees, while only 16 percent employ seven or more.[1] Management theories touching on such aspects as motivation, division of work, leadership, competition, and organizing, therefore, must generally be considered from a small individual agency unit viewpoint rather than from a complex, highly evolved organizational structure perspective.

The fundamental role of the travel agency can be summarized in a few words: information, distribution, reservation, and service. Although some have also become suppliers of travel products, the traditional business of the travel agency is to provide expert advice and one-step access to all types of travel services. That is, travel agencies traditionally provide clients with information on flights, hotels, cruises, and other travel products with regard to availability, schedules, routing, prices, and so on. In day-to-day business, the typical functions of the travel agency include

making sales calls
advising clients
booking space
transmitting information
writing tickets
bookkeeping and accounting
billing
filing
ordering
maintaining and controlling
 airline ticket stock

keeping tariffs up to date
maintaining correspondence
planning and carrying out promotional campaigns
budgeting
analyzing clients and maintaining Passenger Name Records
 (PNRs)
acquiring as much information
 as possible about the available
 travel products

collecting and reviewing brochures and other literature
from travel product suppliers
and ascertaining the currency
of information

delivering tickets to commercial
clients

DIVISION OF WORK

Like other businesses, the travel agency will operate most effectively and
efficiently if an explicit organizational structure exists. This formal structure
should specify the role that each member in the organization plays and how
each role relates to others through a reporting and decision-making com-
munciation network. This network will support the agency's goals and
objectives and give each member an understanding of his or her responsibilities toward achieving those goals and objectives.

Agency Job Classification

Based on the business functions to be handled within the agency, the number
of possible job classifications needed to do the work would soon surpass the
modest number of staff employed in the average-sized travel agency. In all
agencies but the smallest, staff must available to assume duties and responsibilities for such specialized activities or functions as:

- Managing the enterprise and making business decisions and policies
- Marketing the agency
- Selling the products represented by the agency
- Accounting for the profitability of the agency
- Bookkeeping daily transactions
- Providing travel counselling to retail clients
- Handling commercial clients
- Dealing with specialized products and services
- Handling automation and clerical functions

For the average agency with fewer than seven employees, it is not possible to create a title and position to fit every specialized function. The reality is that employees must be flexible and willing to perform a wide variety
of tasks ranging from those that require a great deal of experience or skill
to those that are routine in nature.

Some of the more common job classifications and titles identified to
the travel agency business include the following examples:

- Agency manager: Responsible for day to day business management of
the agency and representing the agency in the community.

- Accountant: Handles the financial transactions of the agency and prepares budgets and financial statements as needed for timely management decisions.
- Commercial agent: Handles the travel arrangements of corporate customers and looks after commercial accounts.
- Domestic agent: Works with retail clients and sells domestic travel products and services within the continental United States, Hawaii, Alaska, plus North America destinations such as Canada and Mexico; also Central America and the Carribean which are popular destinations for domestic travellers.
- International agent: Handles international travel products and services requiring specialized knowledge of foreign destinations; passport, visa and health regulations; currency and customs restrictions; travel conditions and contingencies.
- Marketing manager: Prepares and implements a strategic marketing plan to increase the agency's competitive position and increased market share.
- Sales agent or representative: Responsible for planning and making sales to increase the profitability of a specific territory, branch, or market segment that has been targeted by the agency.
- Ticketing clerk: Performs routine tasks in processing travel paperwork, ticket writing, make reservations on the CRT, filing, updating travel literature, tracking, ticket inventories, and so on.
- Travel consultant: Works with retail clients mainly to advise and sell holiday travel. One who has specialized knowledge of vacation destinations, attractions, tour packages, itinerary planning.
- Travel counselor: Performs the general work of a travel agent and also has knowledge of agency management; a title established by ICTA, especially with reference to an agent who has met ICTA certification.

Agency Size

No scientific method exists for designing the optimal organizational chart. The most effective structure will be contingent upon such variables as size and age of the agency, business concentration (commercial, vacation, incentive travel, group travel, and so on), span of management control, delegation of authority, and quality of personnel presently employed. A recent survey revealed that on the basis of sales productivity per agent for agencies selling more than $1 million in travel annually, it is the mid-size agency that has the highest output efficiency. While the smallest category of agency ($1 million to $5 million in annual sales) reported a per-agent volume of $549,991, and the largest agencies ($10 million + in annual sales) averaged $523,055 per counselor, agencies in the $5 million to $10 million group reported an average sales otuput of $608,770—a gain of more than 10 percent over the second highest category.[2] The consulting firm performing the survey concluded that the higher productivity of mid-size agencies reflects tighter management, while the larger agency has a tendency toward higher overhead and administrative costs and the smaller agency lacks the economy-of-scale advantages.

As discussed in the introductory chapter, however, it is the mid-size travel agency that is currently experiencing a decline in numbers as well as in the percentage of business handled. Smaller agencies survive on the basis of low overhead, personalized service, and specialization, but deregulation tends to favor the larger agencies with adequate staffing and other resources to produce volume business. As expected, mega-agencies continue to acquire smaller independent agencies to increase their overall efficiency through economies of scale and an enlarged distribution network.

Increased efficiency, however, has not always been realized by these expanded agencies, due to poor internal organizational development and management and heavy administrative costs. While many agencies grow rapidly, management is often unprepared for the economic and organizational problems of larger corporations that must deal with the delivery of personalized services. With the vastly increased competition and constant state of change of the travel industry itself and airline tariffs, it becomes more difficult to find knowledgeable, professional staff and to manage and control a large office effectively.

Smaller agencies have responded to the problem of size by joining co-ops, consortiums, or franchise chains in an effort to achieve some of the benefits of the larger agencies. By doing so, agencies are able to pool their resources to support educational programs, computer and telecommunication systems, advertising and promotions, and joint marketing programs. Today, nearly half of the smaller agencies in the United States belong to some type of co-op, consortium, or franchise to meet the new business challenges imposed by deregulation and increasing competition.

In designing the organizational structure, a travel agency is free to use any means of departmentation that is appropriate to its volume of business, the types of clients it serves, or the specific functions it must carry out to conduct agency business. The following methods of departmentation have their basis in general principles of organizational design.

Departmentation by Time

One uncommon method of departmentation, at least for a travel agency, is to organize on the basis of time—appropriate only for the travel agency operating twenty-four hours a day on a shift schedule. In this situation, each shift manager, taking on a generalist role, is responsible for covering all necessary functions of the travel agency's operations, from accounting to ticket printing, for that shift.

Certain agencies are offering twenty-four-hour-a-day service to fill a special niche in the industry to serve customers who wish to make travel arrangements at their own convenience, regardless of the time of day. The 24 Hour Travel Agency in Santa Monica, California, for example, finds that approximately 25 to 30 percent of its business comes from the off-hours of operation. Business clients are offered the convenience of being able to call from anywhere in the country at any hour using the agency's national WATS line, and nonbusiness callers are able to request immediate assistance with travel problems involving family crises. With twenty-four-hour service available, clients can handle changes, problems, or emergencies any time, and the agency makes maximum use of its office facilities and terminals.[3] The twenty-four-hour service is an innovative way to attract and retain commercial travel business, but the organization must then have its service delivery system designed to handle this demand.

Departmentation by Function or Occupational Specialization

With the travel agency business becoming increasingly complicated, one effective way of organizing for the mid- or larger-size agency is to have three distinctly separate, functional departments: administration and accounting, sales, and operations. (See Figure 6.1.)[4]

With this type of organizational structure, routine sales, such as travel requiring only standard air, lodging, or car rental arrangements, are as-

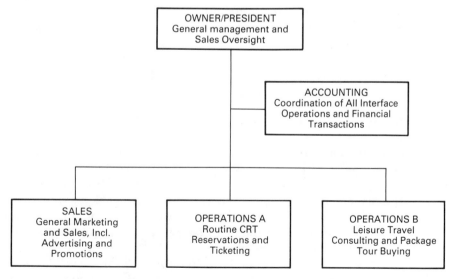

FIGURE 6.1 Travel agency departmentation by function or specialization
Source: Mort Kauffman, ''Getting Down to Basics: Who Should Be Doing What in Your Agency,'' *Travel Trade,* December 17, 1984, pp. 32–33.

signed to the operations department, leaving the more complex requests and nonroutine sales to the sales department. The operations department handles ordinary requests through CRT operators who can quickly process travel reservations for clients systematically. With operations staff working strictly on the CRT, their productivity can reach as high as $1 million in sales per employee each year. Depending upon volume and the size of the agency, there may be a CRT operator handling international air, car rentals, and lodging while another operator handles domestic air, car rentals, and lodging. Other operators or specialists may be added as dictated by volume and markets. For example, a group specialist and package tour buyer may work within the operations function. The theory behind this type of organizational design is that profits are more likely to be increased by expert buying and ordinary selling than by ordinary buying and expert selling. This is how departmentation by function makes proper use of staff expertise.

After the reservation work is completed, all remaining work, such as credit, collections, tearing tickets, invoicing, and quality control, is channeled to the administration department, and bookkeeping completes these transactions, displacing much of the work formerly done by reservationists. Assuming that the business has adequate volume, efficiency can be increased with this "production line" method.

Besides overseeing general operations and sales, the owner or manager handles all nontravel activities such as finance, hiring, maintenance, and community relations.

The advantages to this functional method of organizing are that it follows the principle of occupational specialization and simplifies training. Table 6.1 provides an alphabetical index showing how the various responsibilities are assigned to each of three departments: operations, sales, and administration. In analyzing the numerous tasks to be accomplished, the efficiencies to be gained with departmentation by function are obvious. This index may also be used in the development of a policies and procedures manual for the travel agency.

Departmentation by Territory

While the majority of travel agencies in the United States remain one-office operations, it is no longer uncommon for agencies to establish *full-service branches* in different locations. Most full-service branches are able to offer services similar to a regular travel agency and are accredited to earn full commissions from travel suppliers. Other forms of the "extended" travel agency may include an *out-plant operation* and an *in-plant branch* to serve commercial or corporate clients.

The out-plant operation is one where the corporate client performs most of its own itinerary work, then transmits the information to the agency, which does the actual ticketing. The commission is paid to the travel agency by the

TABLE 6.1 FUNCTIONAL AREAS OF AGENCY RESPONSIBILITY

Administration	Sales & Marketing	Operations
Accounting	Advertising	Air travel
Annual/Quarterly/Monthly	Commercial accounts	Bartering
statements	Group sales	Car rental
Balance sheet	Incentive sales	Charters
P & L statements	Marketing	Cruises
ARC Reports	New products development	CRT operations
Automation	Promotions	Delivery
Bonding	Public relations	Destination
Budgeting	Publicity	Documentation
Cash flow analysis	Sales training	Familiarization travel
Collections	Sales servicing	Fares/tariff
Consortium	Travel sales growth	Ground transport
Consulting		Operations training
Contracts		Package tours
Dues & subscriptions		Quality control
Employee benefits		Reports
Equipment		Specialized travel
Finance		Ticketing
Insurance		Tour escorting
Investment		Visas
Legal matters		Wholesale tour buying
Office expenses		
Organization		
Payroll		
Rebating		
Security		
Yield analysis		

various suppliers and is split according to a negotiated arrangement between the client and the agency.

An in-plant branch operation is one that is established by the travel agency to serve the client at its own location, using the client's own employees to do the agency work with, again, a split-commission arrangement to help defray the client's overhead cost. In the instances of a full-service branch or in-plant branch, a decentralized organizational design will be necessary to put management as close as possible to local conditions and service delivery requirements.

Departmentation by Types of Markets and Customers Served

By far the most common organizational structure for the typical travel agency is to have an office manager in charge of three or four travel agents or account executives, with possibly one file clerk or reservation clerk. (See

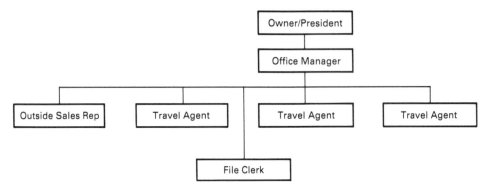

FIGURE 6.2   Organizational structure of the typical travel agency

Figure 6.2.) With this type of structure, the travel agency generally handles each transaction from beginning to end, taking responsibility for all the necessary paperwork relating to the client's request. While this ensures personalized service for the client and an element of follow-through, it can be time consuming for the agent to perform all the tedious tasks required and may make inefficient use of his or her travel product expertise. With this type of organizational arrangement, travel agents are frequently assigned according to specific customer markets such as commercial (business) travel, vacation and cruise (pleasure) travel, and package tours. (See Figure 6.3.) They may also be assigned on the basis of domestic or international travel, with the international counselor requiring far more expertise. An extension of this example would be agents specializing in specific destinations or serving particular market segments such as the elderly, the handicapped, or the youth market.

In contrast to the office that has all travel agents doing virtually identical work, the specialist approach in organizing employees reduces intraof-

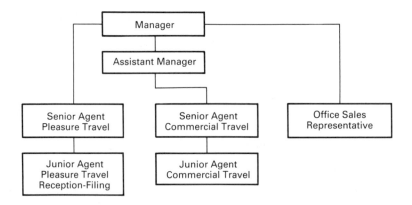

FIGURE 6.3   Structure of an agency organized by customer markets

fice competition and allows the agent to become an expert in a certain type of travel. This may be the key to survival for the agency operating in the post-deregulation era. The travel agency of the future must increasingly be able to provide expertise, counseling, and service that other parts of the travel distribution systems do not offer if it is to remain a viable part of and necessary intermediary within the distribution system. Most analysts, therefore, predict that the trend toward specialization will continue. And while agents specializing in commercial traffic will be primarily concerned with the technical aspects of their service, leisure-oriented counselors will be concerned with product knowledge, counseling, and selling tools.

Repeat customers provide the majority of bookings for both commercial and pleasure travel, making professional service and product knowledge a necessity. Organizational departmentation by market segments and/or product lines allows travel agents to get back to the basics of applying their special knowledge and skills to serve people, according to their individualized desires and needs. Departmentation by type of markets, however, is not without problems. The seasonal patterns of certain types of travel, uneven demands, trends and fashions in travel, and other factors may create disparities in work distribution for the travel agency.

ORGANIZATIONAL GROWTH

Under the economy-of-scale premise that larger agencies can operate more efficiently, an owner of a smaller agency may at some point over the life cycle of his or her business plan for expansion and growth or consider joining one of the many co-ops or consortiums. It bears repeating that a larger agency does not necessarily ensure more efficient operations or improvements to the bottom line. Growth, if desired, requires a strategy on the part of management. The effects of growth must be planned and monitored closely, with the necessary organizational and operational changes made, if there is to be any benefit from expansion. In planning for growth, the strategy may include any of the following options either singly or in combination:

- Restructuring the organization with specialized staff
- Expanding the current operation with additional products and/or staff
- Setting up branch operations
- Merging with other agencies
- Acquiring existing agencies
- Setting up a form of partnership or joint venture with one or more agencies
- Joining or forming a cooperative or consortium
- Joining a franchise

The advantages and disadvantages of all options should obviously be carefully analyzed before a decision is made. The option selected should take
into consideration available resources in terms of money and personnel.
While some industry analysts predict that small retailers will be nonexistent
in a few years, others assert that the travel agency industry is in a transi-
tional stage and the smaller agency may yet prosper because the service it
provides is more personalized. Although bigger agencies can operate more
skillfully and economically, bigness will not solve all problems. The key to
survival for all travel agencies will be in the quality of service matched to
the right clients, the training and experience of the staff, efficient operations, and, most of all, the ability to adjust to rapidly changing conditions.

POLICIES AND PROCEDURES MANUAL

Rationale for Developing the Manual

A policies and procedures manual establishes standards for handling all activities of the travel agency and provides guidelines for making consistent
decisions. The "policies" portion covers the agency's policies on such matters as annual leave, fam tours, and fringe benefits, while the "procedures"
portion establishes standards for handling phone calls, filing brochures,
handling personal checks, and so on. The larger the agency the greater the
need for such a manual, but agencies of any size stand to benefit from its
use. For an agency that is expanding or diversifying, a manual can greatly
alleviate some of the aforementioned problems relating to that growth. The
manual can be as simple or as elaborate as agency needs dictate.

A policies and procedures manual helps to develop professionalism
within the agency and also serves to reduce conflict and misunderstanding
that frequently ensue from verbal explanations alone. When the obligations
of both management and staff are clearly spelled out in such a manual, the
agency is likely to have an atmosphere that is both more harmonious and
more businesslike. From a legal standpoint, a policy manual that clearly
spells out employment terms and practices may provide protection to the
agency in the case of labor disputes.

Determining the Manual Contents

Policies are usually an outgrowth of practices and exist whether they are
written down or not. The best way for a manager to make the policies understandable, fair, and acceptable, however, is to formalize them, that is,
put them in writing. The four principal sources for determining the content
and meaning of policies are

   1. Past practice in the agency

2. Prevailing practice among other agencies

3. Management perspectives

4. Employee perspectives

Well-written policies and procedures in a manual increase efficiency by freeing management from the need to constantly make routine decisions or answer repetitive questions. Included in the manual should be an explanation of the agency's organizational structure, job responsibilities, and work-flow patterns. It should contain standardized formats to follow, professional practices to observe, and the rewards and benefits offered by the agency, as well as performance criteria and disciplinary procedures. Table 6.2 provides a more detailed list of possible topics for inclusion in such a manual. A sample employee policy manual, which covers primarily policies and not operational considerations, is provided in Appendix A at the end of this chapter. Advising employees about how they fit into the agency's operations, which can be made explicit in a manual, is an integral part of motivating them to do the best job possible. As a rule, all agency practices relating to client services and personnel policies covered in the manual should be checked with an attorney to ensure full compliance with federal and state laws.

The manual should include the assignment of personnel backups so that in the absence of managers or other key personnel operations will continue to run smoothly. And although the purpose of the manual is to establish standardized practices, policies should also allow for some discretion on the part of managers, depending on the policy in question.

The policies and procedures manual should be given to and signed by each new staff member. Many agencies have prospective employees read the manual prior to being hired to allay any misconceptions about the job itself or the agency. The manual should be updated periodically with input from both staff and management. Either as part of the manual or separately, it is a good idea to have a written job description for each position, discussed further in Personnel Administration, Chapter 7.

Other Useful References

In addition to the individual agency's policies and procedures manual, the Airline Reporting Corporation (ARC) provides an *Industry Agents' Handbook* to cover the agent's procedures and activities with respect to domestic airlines. IATAN publishes a *Travel Agent Handbook* and a *Ticketing Handbook*. Employees should be familiar with these handbooks and refer to them as necessary. The table of contents from ARC's *Industry Agents' Handbook*, specifying the various procedures and topics covered, is provided in Appendix B of this chapter.

TABLE 6.2   TOPICS FOR INCLUSION IN EMPLOYEE POLICIES AND PROCEDURES MANUAL

Letter of welcome
Company history
Purpose of manual
Organization of agency
Job responsibilities and work-flow patterns
Compensation
Control functions, as applicable
Usage of preferred suppliers
Professional practices to be observed
Credit procedures
Service charge policy
Explanation of how phone is to be answered
Hours of work
Policy on time cards, wages, overtime and fringe benefits
Policy on absences, tardiness
Office coverage
Policy on fam trips, cocktail parties, and educational seminars
Conduct of agency representative, including dress code
Use of company vehicles
Policy against conflicting employment
Policy on resignation
Grievance procedures
Dismissal
Policy on gifts to clients
Policy on gifts from clients or suppliers
Worker's compensation
Accident reporting
Solicitation on premises
Employee evaluations and bonuses
Promotion policies
Staff meetings
Employee training and development
Policy on reduced-rate travel
Policy on smoking
Confidentiality of travel plans
Reservation procedures, reservation cards and files
Invoicing and credit policies
Procedure on handling consumer complaints
Correspondence
Sample forms and documents

MANAGEMENT OF AGENCY EMPLOYEES

For any travel agency, the professional staff is an extremely important asset—second only to the agency's clients. The significance of the staff is obvious, as travel agencies generally offer no other product than service. Salaries and benefits together also make up the agency's largest expense, usually in excess of 50 percent of total operating costs, further emphasizing the importance of staff.

The management of employees is consequently the most important function of the agency manager. Figure 6.4 outlines the fundamental responsibilities of travel agency management. While these responsibilities apply in general to all types of organizations, in the instance of travel agencies emphasis is placed on those aspects that deal with people and human relation skills—organizing, leading, staffing, organizational climate, and motivation. In the travel business, the competitive edge comes from the way business and particularly people are managed.

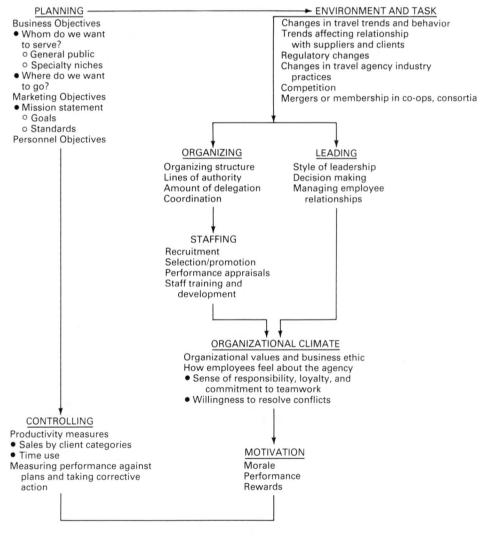

FIGURE 6.4 The Fundamental responsibilities in travel agency management

Organizational Conflicts

The maintenance of good working relations on the job and the reduction of internal conflicts between employees and management and among employees themselves contribute greatly toward increasing productivity and improving professionalism.

As discussed earlier, the organizational chart and well-written job descriptions can help to reduce staff conflict by clarifying relationships and authority lines. However, these do not cover the many informal relationships that inevitably develop within an agency to satisfy other human needs and, at times, to accomplish tasks outside of formal channels.

Agency managers should accept the fact that it is not possible to eliminate all conflicts from the working environment. Often the pressures and stress of agency work itself invite conflict. However, in the healthy organization occasional conflict draws attention to the problem areas, and better ideas are often formulated from friction. Staff members are also forced to clarify their views on issues when they have to argue for them. A certain amount of conflict may even serve to keep the agency from being complacent. It is the unhealthy type of conflicts—those based on an unfair reward and punishment system and other inequalities—that management should seek to avoid. In general, the most productive agency will foster a team attitude among its employees. Prolonged conflict for any reason will have negative consequences on employee morale, leading to stress, frustration, and anxiety.

A sense of teamwork or group spirit within the agency is contingent upon satisfactory relationships among peers and can help employees survive occasional work slumps, air-conditioning breakdowns, and complaining customers. A manager can help to maintain good employee relations by avoiding favoritism, providing the opportunity for social gatherings, reducing the number of situations in which employees compete with each other, and handling employee conflicts with tact and diplomacy.

Employee Turnover and Retention

Historically, the major organizational problem faced by the travel agency industry has been employee turnover. This is due in part to the transferable-skill nature of the industry but also to relatively poor compensation, spouse transfers, and the ease of entry into the field, so that employees will frequently quit to open up or manage new locations. The turnover problem may be worsening. Full-time staff members in 1985 averaged 3.9 years with an agency, down from 4.7 years in 1983—a significant difference of nearly ten months in average length of tenure.[5]

Organizational climate and job satisfaction. In order to instill employee loyalty and avoid the high costs of selecting and training new employees, managers should try to provide employees with good working conditions and logical or efficient work flows, looking for ways to enhance job satisfaction. A positive organizational climate is critical and managers should be accessible and approachable to all employees. When communication between managers and their subordinates is open and multi-directional, managers are able to anticipate problems and potential dissatisfaction. While jobs should be designed to maximize the productive efficiency of the agency and to make proper use of skills and knowledge, satisfaction of workers should also be taken into consideration.

Competitive pay and the amount of challenge and interest in the work itself are among the most important determinants of job satisfaction. Because the travel agency industry is not known for high salaries, managers need to develop a good understanding of nonmonetary rewards, including a pleasant work environment, job security, recognition, industry benefits, and an opportunity to grow personally and professionally. Travel education and destination familiarization, as an example, offer an unending source of opportunity for employee professional development in terms of acquiring product knowledge.

Employees are much more likely to stay with an agency that provides them with a chance for advancement. By adhering to promote-from-within policies and taking a direct role in the continuing education of employees, managers can do a great deal to allay turnover problems. Managers should also ensure that there is minimal discrepancy between what an individual expects to get out of a job and what the job actually offers. During the hiring stage, the agency manager should explain to prospective employees that working in the travel business is not always as glamorous and exciting as it may first appear. It entails detailed work in hundreds of low-yield, time-consuming transactions, conscientious follow-ups to suppliers and clients, and awareness that small mistakes can have monumental consequences for the client and the agency. Travel benefits, when they do come, are usually a few years down the line, and participating in fam tours can sometimes entail family sacrifices.

Motivation and Morale

Motivation, that is, the inner drive that makes an individual willing to perform to the best of his or her ability, is an equally important factor to those of skills and ability in determining the quantity and quality of work performance. Poor morale and indifferent attitudes can seriously afect the sales and profitability of an agency. A motivated staff, on the other hand, will pick up ringing phones quickly, attend to walk-in prospects as soon as they enter, develop effective sales techniques to be good producers, take some of the workload off each other when necessary, handle complaints judiciously, and take the initiative to follow up on clients who have returned from trips.

There are many different theories as to what actually motivates workers, most of them based on studies of large production-based organizations. For the travel agency business, which is wholely service based, motivation must be approached on an individualistic, relational basis to be effective. In essence, managers must take care of their employees as individuals so that employees will take care of clients as individuals. Managers should always treat employees as professional colleagues and not as workers on an assembly line. A work environment that enables employees to feel good about themselves, take satisfaction from their jobs, and feel important to the agency and its clients becomes an important factor in motivation as well as in prevention of turnover.

Vroom's expectancy theory.   V. H. Vroom offers a simple "expectancy" theory for understanding the concept of motivation.[6] According to this theory, motivation will take place only if (1) there is an incentive important to the employee, (2) the employee has the necessary skills, resources, and instructions to do the job, and (3) the employee feels that effort on his or her behalf will lead to obtaining the incentive.

With respect to point 1, travel agency managers have many possible motivational incentives to offer employees that need not always involve money. Table 6.3 lists a variety of reinforcement or motivation options separated into six categories: tokens, social reinforcements, privileges, food-

TABLE 6.3 REINFORCEMENT OPTIONS

Tokens	Social	Privileges
Money	Friendly greetings	Job with more
Stocks	Informal recognition	responsibility
Stock Options	Formal acknowledgment	Job rotation
Discounted vacation	of achievement	Early time off
trips	Invitations to social	with pay
Coupons redeemable	gatherings	Extend breaks
at local stores	Solicitations of	Personal time off
Profit sharing	suggestions/advice	with pay
Supplier discounts	Compliments on work	Fam trips
	progress	
	Pat on the back	
	Smile	
Food Related	Prestige	Visual/Auditory
Coffee-break treats	Wall plaques	Office with a window
Company picnics	Commendations	Pleasant work environment
Employee birthday cake	Rings/tiepins	Company literature
Recognition lunches	Special assignments	Private office
Celebration dinners	Recognition in	Popular speakers
Christmas food gifts	house organ	or lecturers
		Feedback about
		performance

related reinforcements, prestige, and visual and auditory motivations. Recognition, appreciation, and being consulted and kept informed on office matters, for instance, can be powerful motivators for many employees.

Herzberg's hygienic factors.   Herzberg's theory on motivation suggests that there are certain job factors that lead to job satisfaction and self-fulfillment, while others are related to job dissatisfiers he calls the "hygienic factors." When people are satisfied with their jobs, they most often credit factors related to their tasks and to events that indicate successful work performance and professional growth. On the other hand, when there is dissatisfaction, it is not usually related to the work itself but to the conditions (hygienic factors) that surround the doing of the work. For the travel agency these hygienic factors would include

1. Agency policies and administration
2. Manager-employee relations
3. Peer relations
4. Working conditions
5. Compensation
6. Quality of supervision

Job satisfiers come from within the job itself and can lead to changed behavior in a positive direction. These satisfiers leading to motivation are

1. Achievement
2. Recognition
3. Work itself
4. Responsibility
5. Advancement
6. Growth and learning

The motivation challenge.   Maintaining a high morale can sometimes be difficult in a travel agency where salaries are relatively low and frustrations are frequent. Deregulation, which resulted in a multiplicity of fares that are constantly changing, has caused the agent's job to become much more complicated and frustrating. Deadlines are constant and even small errors can be disastrous. Agents must also put up with complaints from clients regarding a supplier's failure to meet the client's expectations, overbooked hotels, missed flights, and so on. Sitting behind the CRT for a full day is tiring for the eyes, and agents must deal with the additional frustration of coping with heavy traffic during seasonal peaks and some callers with endless questions who may not have any intention of booking a trip. Communication—consulting with staff members on an individual basis to discuss problems and on a group basis to keep staff up to date on new developments within the industry and agency—can be a critical factor in maintaining morale. The successful agency manager will therefore be a good leader, a teacher, and a person able to keep the company running efficiently and effectively. He or she will make good use of the agency's most important resources—clients, staff, and capital.

AGENCY PRODUCTIVITY

The old saying that "time is money" is particularly applicable to travel agencies since the amount of time spent servicing clients encompasses personnel and administrative costs. Agency managers frequently concentrate most of their time and effort on increasing sales with little thought given to productivity improvement. Productivity involves reaching the highest level of performance with the least expenditure of resources—financial and personnel. In order to improve profitability, staff time should be allocated to activities that generate the highest revenues. The cost of airline ticketing, for example, ranges from $25 to $35 per transaction. With a 10 percent commission,

Advances in technology have not yet eliminated the need for paper in agency operations.

an agency would lose money on issuing tickets for fares less than $250 or $350, depending on the agency's particular overhead. The reissuing of tickets also results in added cost with no additional commissions. Consequently, it is necessary to analyze time and resource inputs versus revenues generated to achieve higher profits through improved staff productivity. Agency productivity can thus be analyzed in terms of transactions, agency product lines, and individual staff performance.

Transaction Productivity

An analysis of the costs related to different transactions such as ticketing, developing tour packages, and making sales calls, provides a basis for establishing standard costs for each transaction and evaluating its current profitability. Standard costs can also be used for projecting the profitability of undertaking new travel transactions and assigning staff accordingly.

Product Line Productivity

Product line analysis provides an overview of the relative profitability of travel products sold by an agency, including all services sold, such as airline tickets, rail tickets, car rentals, tour packages, and travel insurance. The staff can then be encouraged to sell the higher-yield products. Both transaction and product line analysis can be applied to analyze individual customer accounts to evaluate which accounts are profitable, marginal, or losing money, where agency costs exceed revenues from an account.

Staff Productivity

Finally, the productivity of each staff member must be measured to evaluate his or her performance. Staff involved in selling services can be evaluated in terms of their salary plus allocated overhead costs versus the revenues that they produce. Clerical and other support personnel may be assessed in terms of their activities and the average time required for each activity.

Technology and Productivity

Technology is one of the primary means through which agency productivity gains have been made. Employees output per hour can be dramatically improved and costs per ticket substantially reduced with the use of computer reservations systems (CRS). At the same time the quality of service can be improved. The use of automation for other office functions such as clerical and accounting can also enhance agency productivity. Nonetheless, travel is still a "people" business—people must ultimately operate the machines and, more important, interface with clients. Consequently, attention must be given to how the staff is organized and the process through which work is accomplished, including the technology in use.

Productivity Audit

A people-productivity audit of an agency might include consideration of the following questions, some of which were discussed in the section on organizational structure:

- How are job functions organized?
- Should counselors be generalists or specialists?
- Are jobs interchangeable?
- Is there idle time because employees are only trained for a particular job?
- What is the flow of work through the agency?
- What paperwork moves from person to person? Is it an organized process?
- Can work such as ticketing be batch-run at a particular time each day?
- Are employee hours keyed to the needs of clients or merely traditional operating hours?
- Will a mix of part-time and full-time employment be more productive?
- Are there office functions that can be eliminated or performed at a lower labor cost?[7]

In terms of measuring the actual productivity of an agency or its employees, several types of data need to be collected, including the following:

- Number of sales transactions and number of refund and reissue transactions
- Number of telephone calls and their duration and number of walk-in customers handled by each client
- Number of transactions done with preferred vendors and number done with car rental companies, hotels, and other suppliers
- Payroll costs including insurance, vacation, sick leave, and fringe benefits
- Total volume of commission earned by the agency and amount brought in by the employees

The analysis of productivity levels can assist the agency manager in deciding how to organize the work flow, where to spend promotional dollars, what products to emphasize, how to direct employee training and development, and other issues.

MANAGEMENT STYLES

Determinants of Management Style

The most effective management style for the travel agency will vary depending on the given circumstances and the people involved; it is now accepted by management scholars that there is no single, universally effective management style. Generally, the forces that affect the style are the manager's own personality, the nature of the tasks to be accomplished, the environment of the office, and the personalities and abilities of the staff. The manager's own personality is influenced by background, knowledge, and experience, which all affect his or her value system. The level of confidence in the staff as well as the importance attached to financial performance, growth of employees and the agency, and so on also influence the manager's inclination for a certain style. Environmental forces may affect management leadership style as well; these include such variables as time and budget constraints, competition, the agency's culture, and the professional maturity of the staff.

It is important for the manager to be aware of these different forces that affect management style and to work within them—the abilities of staff members, their general characteristics, and their followership styles. The successful manager will become familiar with each of his or her subordinates' personalities and abilities and treat them individually. When nonroutine agency work is to be assigned, for example, the insightful manager can then attempt to match the tasks with the most appropriate individuals who have the necessary attributes for completing them successfully.

Decision Making

Regardless of the agency's size, travel agency managers are faced with a myriad of decisions regarding anything from establishing new employee policies to deciding on whether to accept a new account that is marginally profitable. Decision making is an important management function that is strongly affected by management style. The range of management behaviors with respect to decision-making activities runs the gamut from authoritarian decision making where all decisions are made by the manager to participative decision making where group members determine the best alternative. In all but the smallest travel agency, it is possible that the most viable management style is one that alternates between decisions made solely by the agency manager on matters that do not have significant impact on employees to decisions fully shared with employees when their work routines, standards, or reward system will be affected.

MBWA

In addition to maintaining a good, communicative relationship with employees, the travel agency manager should also keep in close touch with the agency's customers. Even in a small office, a manager may be overly occupied with paperwork and other business matters to the extent that he or she loses touch with clients and employees. The practice called "Management by Walking Around" (MBWA) asserts that managers must have a good feel for what is happening in the home office with clients as well as what is happening with the competition. Instead of removing him- or herself from the operation in order to manage, a good manager will interact with both customers and staff.

THE PROFESSIONAL AGENCY

In today's deregulated business environment and consumer-oriented climate, it is extremely important for the travel agency to present a professional image before the general public. Professionalism entails technical competence in terms of use of computers and understanding booking procedures, knowing where to go for specific information, ability to construct fares, knowledge of geography, and familiarity with major destinations. It involves having a good understanding of industry trends and standards, changing conditions affecting the travel industry, and the competition as well.

Additionally, professionalism embraces a set of ethics, values, and practices that are peculiar to the profession itself. To ensure a high degree of professionalism among employees, management must first be committed to its achievement. Staff should be made aware of the agency's overall mission and their individual responsibilities to clients, and authority should be delegated in a manner commensurate with responsibility. There is nothing more frustrating for clients than to deal with employees who have no power to act on their behalf. When there are problems within the agency, staff should be made aware that their opinions, ideas, and suggestions are valued.

Participative management. By utilizing participative management and group decision-making techniques, the manager can help to develop more professional employees and at the same time run a more efficient operation. Participative management is particularly applicable when employees are in the position to provide useful and relevant information to the manager and when acceptance of a decision by employees is critical to its effective implementation. If employees feel they "own" the decision, they will be much more likely to support it.

Job enrichment.   Job enrichment, that is, giving employees more control over their work and a greater variety of tasks to perform, can also aid in the development of professionalism. It is a good idea to occasionally send counselors to attend association meetings and conferences so they can feel that they are a part of the management team. Management should encourage staff to attend training programs, for example, those leading to the designation of Certified Travel Counselors (CTCs), and assist with tuition if possible. By following these types of practices, managers can improve professionalism and encourage employees to feel more responsible and accountable for the overall success of the agency. Agents must view themselves as professionals and behave in an ethical and businesslike manner—the outward manifestation of professionalism is important.

Office appearance.   Diplomas, certificates, and other indications of professional competence should be displayed in the office rather than a clutter of brochures and posters. In the travel business, a cluttered desk is not the sign of a genius, as clients will undoubtedly question an agent's ability to organize a trip, a tour, or a cruise if the agent cannot organize the top of his or her desk. It is management's responsibility to ensure that the office reflects a professional image at all times.

The personal grooming of staff members is important as well, and for this reason many agencies have a dress code or provide uniforms or a company monogrammed jacket for their staff. Smartly designed uniforms not only enhance the professional image of the agency but are also a symbolic means of promoting group identity.

Phone calls.   Answering phone calls is another area that should be kept at a professional level. The phone call, which occupies about 15 percent of the agency staff time, often establishes a client's first impression of the agency and because many potential sales can be easily won or lost over the telephone, proper telephone etiquette should be followed at all times.

Preprinted forms.   Another way for an agency to enhance a professional image is to utilize preprinted forms and form letters. This saves time and minimizes the possibility of legal liability and negligence on the part of inexperienced staff.

Salesmanship.   Agents and counselors should be well trained in salesmanship and be able to provide clients with expert knowledge and a basis of comparison for whatever type of travel they are interested in purchasing. For example, the professional agent selling a pleasure package tour is able to compare the available tours according to price, duration, depth of sightseeing, admissions coverage, meal policy, items included, whether independent or escorted, amount of leisure time, and so on. The truly professional agent is also knowledgeable about the quality of the products he or she promotes. Keeping current via trade magazines and taking the time to learn about destinations and other travel products, the agent can tailor the tour to the particular client and thus provide the client with a service he or she is not able to obtain from a department store selling travel as a side venture or from a machine in the airport terminal.

For the agent specializing in meeting planning, well-planned, well-thought-out, pertinent questions addressed to the client demonstrate that he or she is an experienced professional making every effort possible to assist clients in achieving their goals. And for this professional expertise, there is a trend toward the belief that travel agents should work by appointment, charge for their time, and solicit narrowly targeted markets.

Impact of Technology

Ironically, it is the computer that will force travel agents to become true travel experts providing professional counseling services rather than acting as automated order takers. In the not-too-distant future, clients will be able to access directly through computers all sorts of information from airline seat availabilities to hotel vacancies and to purchase these products independently. As Home Information Centers, based on the concept of "electronic communities," spring up in heavily populated areas around the country, it is possible that "disintermediation" will occur. Disintermediation means that ticketing services provided by mediaries may be obviated—the customer can buy direct. It will be up to the travel agency, therefore, to perform marketing research, make comparisons between travel products, and develop data on their clients in order to provide expert advise and find the best-suited arrangements for future travel. More will be said about the impact of technology in Chapter 12.

SUMMARY

While the overall functions performed by a travel agency are fairly simplistic and straightforward, the agency manager must ensure that the organizational structure of the agency is designed to maximize efficient and effective operations. A policies and procedures manual is an important aid in operating a well-run office and minimizes employee-related problems as well. Regardless of the size or structure of the agency, organizational conflicts are inevitable and dealing with employees is one of management's most important tasks. It is up to the agency manager to handle conflicts in a way that will work toward the betterment of the agency. The manager should strive to develop a motivating organizational climate that encourages employees to develop professionalism and demonstrate professional behavior in their work with the agency's clients and suppliers.

DISCUSSION QUESTIONS

1. Identify and describe the various organizational structures utilized by travel agents. What are the advantages and disadvantages of each?
2. What options exist for the travel agency that is seeking growth?
3. Why is a policies and procedures manual so important? What are some of the topics that should be covered in such a manual?
4. Identify some of the options travel agency managers can utilize to motivate employees.
5. What can the travel agency manager do to ensure professionalism within the agency?

ENDNOTES

[1]"Survey: Average Volume Is under $2 million with 40% Air Sales," *Travel Weekly*, February 26, 1987, p. 124.

[2]Nadine Godwin, "Survey Reveals Average Sales Productivity of $520,000 per Agent," *Travel Weekly*, December 24, 1984, p. 12.

[3]Edward Placidi, "Twenty-Two-Year-Old Computer Whiz Starts 24-Hour Travel Agency," *Travel Age West*, May 7, 1984, p. 3.

[4]Mort Kauffman, "Getting Down to Basics: Who Should Be Doing What in Your Agency," *Travel Trade*, December 17, 1984, pp. 32–33.

[5]*Travel Weekly's Louis Harris Survey*, June, 1986, p. 24.

[6]V. H. Vroom, *Work and Motivation* (New York: John Wiley & Sons, Inc., 1964).

[7]American Society of Travel Agents. *Deregulation: Opportunities for Profit*, New York, NY: Thompson Communications Companies, Inc., 1980, p. 14.

SUPPLEMENTAL READINGS

LEHMANN, ARMIN D., *Travel Agency Policies and Procedures Manual.* Albany, NY: Delmar Publishers, Inc., 1988.

appendix a

EMPLOYEE POLICY MANUAL

FOR

PAX TRAVEL AGENCY

CONTENTS

Employment status	Termination
Business travel expenses	Salaries and wages
Pay periods	Employee benefits
Payroll deductions	Training
Hours of work	Other policies and practices
Attendance	Outside sales agents
Lunch	

Source: Association of Retail Travel Agents

NONDISCRIMINATION

The policies and practices of PAX Travel Agency shall be applied without regard to national origin, sex, age, marital status, race, or creed.

EMPLOYMENT STATUS

1. *Probationary Period.* Each new employee will be considered to be on probation for a period of three months. Periodic reviews will be conducted during this period.
2. *Part-time.* Employees whose regularly scheduled work week is less than 35 hours are considered part-time employees.
3. *Temporary.* Employees hired to handle seasonal or temporary work loads will have temporary status and will be paid on an hourly basis.

BUSINESS TRAVEL AND EXPENSES

All travel must be discussed with the management before any expense is incurred.

Receipts are required for travel, lodging, and other single items that exceed $25.00. Expenses under $25.00 should be itemized.

The Corporation encourages employees to develop business contacts and associate with clients and principals. Advance approval from the management should be obtained before entertainment expenses are incurred.

PAY PERIODS

Employees' compensation is stated as a monthly salary, hourly rate, or commission. Pay periods start on the first and sixteenth of the month.

Pay checks are distributed on the fifteenth and last day of the month by 5:00 P.M. In the event that either day falls on a Saturday, Sunday, or holiday, pay checks will be distributed on the last working day prior to the payday.

Commission checks are issued by the tenth day of the month following the month earned. Commission is earned only on sales that have been paid in full to the corporation net of any refunds. Commission will be forfeited on all sales not paid by the client within 14 days of the invoice date.

It is the Corporation's policy not to make salary advances except in extreme emergencies, and these requests must be approved by the President.

PAYROLL DEDUCTIONS

Each employee's paycheck voucher shows earnings and amounts deducted. All deductions are computed on a pay-period basis.

A. State Income Tax. The state income tax deduction is based on the tax withholding form completed at the time of employment. If there is any need to change the amount withheld, the management should be informed and a new form completed at least five working days before the next payday.

B. Federal Income Tax. This is based on the federal income tax withholding form completed at the time of employment. If there is any need to change the amount withheld, the management should be informed and a new form completed at least five working days before the next payday.

C. Social Security. Federal law requires the deduction of social security taxes. It also makes an equal contribution to your social security fund.

D. State Disability Insurance.

HOURS OF WORK

The normal work week consists of five 8-hour days, Monday through Friday. However, the office will be open from 8:30 A.M.–5:30 P.M. Monday through Friday except for the public holidays listed hereunder.

The office may be open on Saturdays during the season at the management's discretion.

1. *Overtime.*
    A. Overtime is defined as time actually worked beyond 40 hours in a week. Overtime must be authorized by the management prior to its being earned.
    B. Eligibility. Overtime pay at a rate of one and one-half times the hourly rate is paid to qualified employees who are required to work beyond 40 hours in any week (Monday through Sunday). If an employee takes leave and works overtime during the same week, straight time is paid for the first 40 hours actually worked, and the overtime rate is paid beyond 40 hours.

2. *Compensatory Time.* At the discretion of the management, compensatory time may be granted for time worked beyond 40 hours a week. Compensatory time must be approved prior to its being worked.

3. *Holiday Pay.* All employees, except temporaries, receive a day's pay for each holiday that falls within their regularly scheduled work week. If required to work on a holiday, those eligible employees will be paid for the hours worked at straight time and in addition the holiday pay, or granted additional time off in lieu thereof.

ATTENDANCE

Each employee is expected to report to work on time so they will be prepared to begin work at the appointed time.

LUNCH

A designated amount of time is permitted for lunch and each employee is encouraged to take it. The Management is responsible for assigning lunch hours and employees are asked to maintain their schedules as closely as possible—but *customers must be taken care of before going to lunch.*

Lunch must be eaten in the outside sales office or away from the premises and not at the employee's desk.

Lunch hours may not be split, and should be taken after 10:00 A.M. and must be completed before 3:00 P.M.

Other employees' desks or work areas may not be visited during the lunch period.

TERMINATION

1. *Notice in Cases of Resignation.*
   A. Written notice is required by the Corporation from employees who resign. This applies to all employees.
   B. Period of Continuous Employment   Notice
      Up to six months   one week
      More than six months   two weeks
   C. The amount of notice time may be less by mutual agreement between the employee and the management. If notice time given is less than that required and there is no mutual agreement, the amount of accrued vacation to be paid will be reduced by the amount required.
2. *Notice in Cases of Separation.* Notice shall be given by the corporation to the employee. The following schedule applies to all employees.
   A. Period of Continuous Employment   Notice
      Up to three months   None
      Three months to one year   one week
      Over one year   two weeks
   B. Normally an employee shall be required to work during the notice period. However, when it is desirable to terminate employment as quickly as possible, salary in lieu of the required notice period may be authorized by the President. Such salary is in addition to payment for vacation time.

C. The notice period or pay in lieu of notice may be voided by the President in those cases involving a criminal offense or other actions that could bring discredit to the corporation.

D. Prior to the issuance of a separation notice, every effort will be made to help employees to improve their service so that they may be retained. This will include adequate reviews and discussions with employees of their total work activity.

E. Any employee who is separated or who resigns and is subsequently re-employed will retain tenure from previous employment dates provided absence from the Corporation does not exceed six months.

SALARIES AND WAGES

1. *Confidentiality.* Salaries and wages are always determined on an individual basis and will be a confidential arrangement between employer and employee. Discussing salary with anyone other than the President or Vice-Presidents is cause for dismissal.

2. *Promotion.* To encourage employees to perform to their maximum potential and to reward them for outstanding service, it will be corporate policy to promote from within the organization.

3. *Review.* Salary and wage increases shall be neither predetermined nor routinely granted but are based on merit, performance, and longevity.

4. *Award to Employees.* From time to time, the Corporation will institute incentive plans to encourage employees' interest and productivity.

EMPLOYEE BENEFITS

1. *Medical Insurance.* Medical Insurance is provided by the Corporation at no cost to eligible employees, provided that there is no increase in premium. Enrollment must take place when eligible at the end of the probationary period of employment or during "open" enrollment periods. Coverage is also available for spouse and dependents and the cost of this additional coverage will be deducted from each employee's paycheck. A complete insurance packet will be made available to those participating in the plan.

2. *Vacation Leave.* This will be offered to all regular employees (both full time and part time) with the following schedule:

Period of Continuous Employment	Vacation
After six months of employment	five days
Annually thereafter	ten days

Vacation leave must be requested in advance and is subject to the approval of the management.

No more than five days may be taken consecutively without prior approval.

Vacation leave will not be accrued when an employee is on leave without pay.

Employees are encouraged to take their vacation during slow periods of the year.

Should an approved holiday fall during the employee's vacation, their vacation shall be extended by one day.

When the employee has completed six or more months of continuous service and is separated or resigns from the Corporation, the following policy applies: The employee will automatically receive a lump-sum payment for the full amount of credited vacation leave. The employee will forfeit this credited annual leave until any indebtedness to the Corporation of money or property is settled. Credited vacation leave will be forfeited if the employee is discharged for misconduct or behavior that brings discredit to the corporation.

3. *Sick Leave.* Full-time employees accrue two hours of sick leave per pay period. Temporary employees do not accrue sick leave. No sick leave will be granted during the first three months of employment. Absence due to sickness during the first three months of employment will be charged to leave without pay.

Up to twelve days of sick leave may be accrued.

Absence greater than the accrued sick leave available will be charged to vacation leave or leave without pay.

The management must be notified of the illness as soon as possible after the office opens.

Sick leave is not accrued when an employee is on leave without pay.

All accrued sick leave is forfeited when an employee leaves the corporation.

Sick leave may be used for absence due to any of the following reasons pertaining to an employee:
   A. Illness that prevents an employee from reporting to work
   B. Adequate time to recuperate from such illness
   C. Adequate time for medical/dental exams and treatment

4. *Special Leave.* When an employee must be absent from work due to the death of a relative, time off with pay will be granted as follows:
   A. Absence on account of death of a member of an employee's immediate family will be authorized for a period of up to three days. Immediate family includes husband, wife, son, daughter, mother, father, brother, and sister.
   B. Absence on account of death of other members of an employee's family will be authorized for one day.

Any additional time off, including leave for family illness, must be approved by management, and will be charged to vacation pay or leave without pay.

5. *Administration Leave.* The President may authorize administration leave because of inclement weather, breakdown of building support systems, or other special circumstances that effect the entire staff of the office.

6. *Jury Leave.* An employee who is summoned to serve on a jury is granted jury leave for the time such service is required. The employee must provide the management with an authorized document indicating the length of time for such jury duty and the dollar amount of compensation received. The employee may elect to be compensated in either of the two following ways:
   A. Jury leave at full pay may be taken for the entire time served if the compensation received while serving as a jury member is endorsed to the Corporation.
   B. Annual leave or leave without pay may be taken for time on jury duty and the compensation received for service as a juror may be kept.

   During the period that an employee is not actually involved in the jury process, that employee is expected to report to work.

7. *Holidays.* The Corporation will be closed for business on the following holidays, but if the holiday falls on a Saturday, the office will be closed the preceding Friday. If the holiday falls on a Sunday, the office will be closed on the following Monday.

   > New Years Day
   > Washington's Birthday
   > Memorial Day
   > Independence Day
   > Labor Day
   > Thanksgiving Day
   > Christmas Day

   Employees who wish to attend religious services on days not designated as holidays may do so on vacation leave. On these occasions, requests will be treated liberally.

8. *Confidentiality.* The Corporation deals with peoples' personal motivations and desires, much the same as other professions in their client relationships. It is essential that discretion be exercised in discussing our clients. You have serious responsibility to keep any information about a client strictly between you and your client.
   A. Telephone inquiries of clients and account activity must be carefully screened for proper identification before any information is divulged.
   B. All information about clients, including but not limited to names, addresses, and telephone numbers, belong to the agency and are not to be removed from the office.
   C. In discussing a client with other employees, adhere strictly to matters concerning the client's travel. It is no one's business who, what, when, where, or why the client is using the Corporation's services.

TRAINING

1. *General.*
   A. Local on-the-job training will be a consistent and continuous process.

B. Attendance at courses offered by airlines, cruise lines, and other suppliers is at the management's discretion.
C. When it is deemed in the best interest of the Corporation, the cost of
attending various courses, seminars, meetings, and training sessions
will be paid by the Corporation.
D. Attendance at social functions offered by suppliers are not compul-
sory events and can only be attended with the approval of the management. All invitations will be responded to by the management.
2. *Fam Trips.* Familiarization (Fam) trips are both an opportunity for learning
and a benefit to employees in the travel industry. Accordingly, the Corporation encourages employees to take Fam trips when it will improve the
employees' ability to serve our clients.

The following guidelines and rules of eligibility apply:

A. Management will determine which Fam trips are available and of-
fered to staff members.
B. Full-time employees will be given preference.
C. Employee must have been employed by the Corporation for not less
than twelve months if a 75AD pass is to be utilized.
D. Will be assigned based on employee specialization.
E. Agency sponsored trips will be paid by the Corporation. The employee must file a written report within two weeks of returning.
F. Since participation in Fam trips is totally optional, the employee shall
only be paid for normally scheduled hours.
G. Fam trips not endorsed by the Corporation may be taken but the
employee will charge the time away from the office to vacation
leave or leave without pay. Time away from the office for Fam trips
must be approved by the management.

OTHER POLICIES AND PRACTICES

1. *Amendments.* Conditions may require changes in corporate policies from
time to time and employees are responsible for keeping abreast of these
changes.
2. *Visitors.* Friends and family may choose to visit employees at work and
visits of not more than ten minutes are acceptable.

Visitors must leave if there are customers.

3. *Telephone Calls.* All incoming calls must be answered promptly, and if it
is necessary to place a call on hold this should be for the shortest possible
time.

When the caller wishes to speak to someone who is unavailable, either
render all possible assistance or ensure that the person called responds
at the agreed time. If an employee is occupied with a client inform the
caller and return the call as soon as possible, or at the time agreed with
the caller.

Personal calls are permitted, but should be kept to a minimum.

No business call is to be kept on hold for a personal call.

No outgoing personal calls are to be made when such a call will leave less than two lines open.

Personal calls billed to the Corporation will be billed to the employee.

4. *Personal Charges.* No employee is allowed to charge any personal travel to the Corporation.

5. *Agency Passes.* Airline and 75AD passes and their use are regulated by the management of the Corporation.

   Business trips are given first priority for use of airline passes.

   75AD passes are made available to eligible employees for Fam trips, international vacation trips, and for business trips.

6. *Trade Publications.* Trade publications are available to all employees, and should be read during lunch or at home.

   Always return publications to the assigned place.

   An employee wishing home delivery of a publication must subscribe.

7. *Supplies.* All agency supplies are to be ordered through the management. Emergency purchasing should be avoided if possible because it does not permit the Corporation to take advantage of bulk purchasing opportunities. Emergency supplies should be paid for out of petty cash and receipts are always required.

8. *Housekeeping.* Each employee is responsible for the appearance of their work area.

   Smoking will not be permitted in the front or outside sales offices to meet the requirements of the City Code. The ADS room will be designated our smoking area. Ash trays should be emptied and washed frequently.

   Drinking coffee or soft drinks is not permitted while waiting on a customer.

   It is the responsibility of all employees to assist in maintaining the appearance and cleanliness of the offices.

9. *Dress Code.* Employees should exercise common sense and be aware that personal cleanliness and neatness are essential to pleasant working conditions.

   Employees may not wear jeans of any color, or clothing of a revealing nature.

   All clothing worn should be in keeping with the professional image of the corporation.

10. *Mail.* Personal mail should not be sent to the office.

11. *Outside Employment.* Any employee engaging in outside activities for compensation should discuss this with the management in order to prevent the possibility of a misunderstanding or conflict of interest. As a matter of protection for both employee and Corporation, the employee or management may request a statement of approval be placed in the employee's personnel file.

12. *Charity Drives.* All solicitations of funds are to be directed to the management. Panhandlers are to be asked to leave the office.

13. *Fire and Safety.* All doors and aisles are to be kept clear of obstructions.

    Any fire should be reported to the management immediately. If a manager is unavailable, call the fire department and leave the building, closing the doors after you. The extinguisher outside the restrooms may be used to try and extinguish the fire.

14. *Equipment Repair.* All complaints or service requests are to be made to the management.

15. *Petty Cash.* Only a manager may issue change, cash checks, and issue funds except in case of extreme urgency.

16. *Alcoholic Beverages.* No one may keep or serve alcoholic beverages in any office without permission from the President. Drunkenness or drug use may be cause for dismissal with forfeiture of severance pay.

17. *Animals.* Animals are prohibited in PAX Travel Service's offices.

18. *Client Lists.* The client and mailing lists are the exclusive property of PAX Travel Service. No employee is to discuss current, past, or prospective future clients with anyone outside PAX Travel Service. This rule applies during and after employment.

OUTSIDE SALES AGENTS

1. *Office Availability.* Outside sales agents requiring to use the reservation computers or other office facilities will be allocated times at which they may use them by the management.

   The office will only be visited during normal business hours.

2. *In-House Assistance.* Each outside sales person will be allocated to one of the in-house staff who will render them assistance whenever needed.

3. *Organizing Groups.* All outside sales agents must submit full details of any proposals for groups which they wish to promote to the management for approval before they may be promoted under the auspices of PAX Travel Agency.

4. *Housekeeping.* Outside sales agents will be responsible for the tidiness of the offices used by them.

5. *General.* The rules with regard to dress, alcoholic beverages, food in the office, and all other matters will apply to outside sales agents the same as in-house staff, when the agents are in PAX Travel Agency's offices.

6. *Telephone Answering.* The telephone should be answered as quickly as possible, and outside sales agents are requested to assist whenever they are in the offices.

7. *Expenses.* When the Corporation incurs expenses (e.g., brochures, advertising, miscellaneous office expenses) arising from the work of outside sales agents, they will be billed for their share.

   Any debits charged back by the Corporation's suppliers will be charged to the agent who incurred them.

8. *Ticketing.* When quoting fares emphasize to the client that the fare quoted is only valid *if the ticket is issued at that time.*

9. *Checks.* All checks from clients must be made payable to PAX Travel Agency.

appendix b

TABLE OF CONTENTS

SECTION 6—EXCHANGE TRANSACTIONS

SECTION 7—PASSENGER TRANSPORTATION TAX

SECTION 8—CREDIT CARD SALES

SECTION 9—AIR TRAVEL CARD

SECTION 11—REFUNDS

SECTION 30—ARC BOND AND IRREVOCABLE LETTER OF CREDIT REQUIREMENTS AND INFORMATION

SECTION 60—APPLICATIONS

SECTION 70—AUDIT AND FRAUD PREVENTION PROGRAM

SECTION 80—AGENT REPORTING AGREEMENT

SECTION 90—TRAINING PROGRAM

SECTION 100—OFFICE OF TRAVEL AGENT COMMISSIONER

Airlines Reporting Corporation, *Industry Agents' Handbook,* Washington, DC: 1984.

chapter 7

Personnel Administration

LEARNING OBJECTIVES

- To know the importance of the job analysis, job description, and job specification to help match the right person for the right job
- To become familiar with the best places to look for new travel agency recruits
- To understand how training and development, evaluation and appraisal, compensation, and other incentives, such as fam trips, help motivate travel agency personnel

KEY TERMS

- Agency Training Schools
- Behavior Modification
- Bonus
- Cafeteria-Style Benefits
- Certified Travel Counselor (CTC)
- Equal Opportunity
- Federal Fair Labor Standards Acts

- Institute of Certified Travel Agents (ICTA)
- Job Analysis
- Job Description
- Job Specification
- Job Training, Formal and Informal
- Incentives

- Management by Objectives
  (MBO)

- Profit sharing
- Travel Schools

INTRODUCTION

The nature of the travel agency business is based wholly on service. As an agency's success depends almost entirely on the competence of management and the knowledge, professionalism, and expertise of the staff, there is no substitute for high-quality personnel in this business. The quality of agency staff will, to a large degree, determine not only the survival but the growth potential of individual agencies. Recruitment, selection, training, motivation, and retention of employees rank among the more critical functions of travel agency management.

Good travel people are becoming harder to find for many reasons. First, there is a recognized long-term shortage of labor for all entry-level jobs in the nation. Second, the industry continues to expand even in the face of intense competition, adding to the demand for good employees from a shrinking pool of available people. At the same time, many of the best employees are leaving the field for greater compensation and promotion in other fields. Travel agencies are also facing competition for trained agents from their suppliers, that is, airlines increasing their direct sales staff and nontraditional companies (for example, banks and department stores) entering into the agency business. Businesses that want employees well trained in automation and client contact service pose the biggest threat.

The general consensus within the field is that future agents will need to know more about the products they sell and less about the mechanics of processing sales. Much of the technical work previously done by agents is now handled by automated systems. The ultimate form of automation is immediately demonstrated on heavily traveled point-to-point flights in major hubs where customers may purchase tickets from automated ticketing machines (ATMs), eliminating the need for agent services. While computer and ticketing skills are important for the agency, the future may require a heavier emphasis on front-line counseling skills, sales and marketing expertise, product knowledge, and other cognitive skills to serve the needs of an increasingly sophisticated clientele and to attract new travel market segments. Training programs for travel agents will eventually have to address these requirements. Some larger agencies have initiated their own extensive training programs, finding that existing programs do not sufficiently train recruits to meet their specific needs.

RECRUITMENT ACTIVITIES

In order to avoid the costly expenses associated with high turnover and mistakes made by incompetent workers, every effort should be made to ensure the proper selection of employees, starting with making a thorough analysis of the job, writing a job description, and knowing the qualifications for the job. The *job analysis* entails the gathering of information on the details of the work, including the use or application of materials, equipment, particularly automated machinery, processes, procedures, and time structure. Appendix A at the end of this chapter provides an example of a job analysis questionnaire. The information from the job analysis is then used to prepare a *job description*, which specifies the job title, skills, and qualifications required. The job description may also include the amount of supervision given, areas of responsibility or self-direction, duties such as selling or counseling, possibilities for promotion in the position, and additional future responsibilities. An example of a job description for an entry-level travel agent is shown in Exhibit 7.1. Large travel agencies may want to go one step further by writing a *job specification* using the information provided by the job description. (See Exhibit 7.2.) The job specification states the skills and qualifications required to carry out primary responsibilities and functions of the job listed in the job description; it is used for advertising openings and other recruitment purposes. At this point, the agency is ready to recruit new staff.

RECRUITMENT SOURCES

The Travel Industry

The first place to look for travel agency recruits is within the travel industry itself. The industry comprises numerous interlinking businesses with an extensive pipeline through trade associations. For instance, offices of the American Society of Travel Agents (ASTA) and the Association of Retail Travel Agents (ARTA) often serve as intermediaries for experienced job-seeking travel counselors and prospective employers. An employer may also alert supplier representatives or other agencies about a job opening and receive referral applicants this way.

Employment Agencies

Another recruitment method is to use private employment agencies. In major urban centers, some agencies specialize in travel personnel, but in areas where these specialty agencies are not available, any employment agencies used should be checked first for their reputation and reliability. The travel agency should know the private employment agency's contract terms. If the employer is to pay the fee, a guarantee for refund should be provided in case the candidate leaves the agency within a specified period of time, usually during the trial employment period. Public employment agencies run by the state can also be a source for well-qualified applicants. When using employment agencies, it is important for the employer to provide a well-

EXHIBIT 7.1

PAX TRAVEL AGENCY
JOB DESCRIPTION FOR TRAVEL AGENT II

Under the general direction of the CEO of PAX Travel Agency, a level II travel agent will have the following primary duties and responsibilities:

PRIMARY DUTIES AND RESPONSIBILITIES

1. *Bookings and Ticketing.* Establish and modify PNRs on computer; determine the best options, including most efficient routing and least expensive fare following carrier rules; write and issue automated tickets; make hotel, car rental, and other bookings as required by clients; obtain confirmations; follow up with service calls. A productivity rate of seven to eight tickets or sales of $3000 per shift. (45% of time)
2. *Travel Counseling.* Confer with clients in person or by telephone; arrange travel itineraries for business trips or vacations, including land, air, and cruise particulars, using appropriate reference materials. (20% of time).
3. *General Office Work.* Prepare and file invoices and itineraries; compute costs and option dates; prepare forms. (15% of time)
4. *Supervision.* Supervise T.A. trainers in Apollo system. (5% of time)

OTHER DUTIES AND RESPONSIBILITIES

1. *Sales Calls.* During off-peak travel season, assist the CEO in calling on corporate, community, and social groups to generate new clients and to promote travel business. (10% of time)
2. *Familiarization Travel.* Take at least one fam trip each year to assist PAX Travel Agency to evaluate new suppliers and establish new commissionable accounts. (5% of time)

General Qualifications. Skills as described in Job Specification for an entry-level agent plus five years of field experience. Knowledge of Apollo system. CTC certification desirable but not mandatory.

Personal Characteristics. Friendly, neat, and well-groomed; strong ability to communicate with selling persuasiveness; ability to work at times under pressure.

EXHIBIT 7.2

PAX TRAVEL AGENCY
JOB SPECIFICATION FOR AN ENTRY-LEVEL AGENT

The entry-level travel agent must have the following basic skills and qualifications:

- Automation/CR5. Be able to create and modify basic PNR, determine the least expensive fare, access and understand fares and fare rules, issue an automated ticket, book hotels and cars, and access computer-stored information.

- Reference Materials. Be proficient in the use of the *North American OAG*, the *Worldwide OAG*, the *North American, European,* and *Pacific Travel Planners*, the *Official Hotel & Resort Guide*, the *Hotel and Travel Index*, and *Star Guide*. Also be able to read and interpret the *Consolidated Tour Manual*, the *Official Steamship Guide*, the *Worldwide Tour Guide*, the *Industry Agents' Handbook*, *Jax Fax*, and any tour or cruise brochure.

- Ticketing. Be able to write any basic accountable or nonaccountable document and know where to find the proper procedures for completing more complicated transactions.

- Geography. Be able to locate the world's major cities, countries, and tourist regions, as well as the states, major cities, and attractions of the United States. Also be able to read maps and atlases and decode the twenty-four-hour clock. Prospects should also know the agency's most frequently used tour operators and the areas that they serve.

- Fare Selection and Calculation. Be able to select airfares appropriate for clients' needs and interpret airline rate desk fare quotes, including such terminology as MPS, breakpoints, IMPs, IATA areas, EMAs, backhauls, circle trip minimums, HIFs, FCUs, and AMFs. Also be able to construct an air itinerary using such restrictions as advance purchase, minimum and maximum stay, open jaw, allowable stopovers, and cancellation.

- Sales Techniques. Be able to qualify clients' needs, turn features into benefits, change negative aspects into positive ones, overcome objections to booking, listen effectively, use proper telephone procedures, and close a sale.

- Travel Agency and Industry Operations. Know the basic structure of the travel industry, including such liabilities and responsibilities as the sales report deadline, correct ticket stock maintenance procedures, agency guarantee policy, charter cancellation and change policy, and customer complaint procedures. Also know the major hotel chains, car rental companies, and selected cruise lines.

Source: Ralph Lennon and Paula Moseley, "Hiring New Staff: What to Expect from Entry-Level Prospects," *The Travel Agent Magazine*, August 3, 1987, p. 47.

written job specification and/or a job description, which helps the employment agency screen potential candidates and match the best candidate for
the position before a referral is made.

Newspaper and Magazine Ads

Newspaper and magazine ads are other potentially productive sources for
recruiting employees, since almost everyone in the industry reads travel
trade gazettes and magazines, and well-qualified applicants also respond to
local newspaper ads. Since ad space is expensive, the ads should be well
written, describing the specific qualifications required. In reviewing the two
examples of classified ads found in Exhibit 7.3, the importance of identifying the specific requirements and benefits of the jobs becomes evident.

Travel Schools and Other Programs

Until fairly recently, on-the-job training was the rule of the travel industry.
The new employee learned by watching and questioning experienced travel
counselors and by performing backup tasks such as reservations and ticketing. Trainees would become familiar with all aspects of the agency's operations by osmosis and in some cases would wait up to two years before
dealing directly with a client. Travel agents served a kind of apprenticeship
without formal contractual obligations and were trained at the agency's expense. Today, a number of training options exist for those interested in a

EXHIBIT 7.3

The first ad provides basic information regarding the job; however, classified
ad 2 is much more specific and will attract a greater percentage of worthy
applicants.

CLASSIFIED AD 1

TRAVEL AGENT. Experienced. Must be able to take charge. Computer skills
necessary. Salary in mid-teens. Good benefits. Convenient downtown location.

CLASSIFIED AD 2

TRAVEL AGENT. Downtown agency convenient to Blue Line subway requires person with at least three years in booking air, hotels, and cruises,
who can also supervise less experienced employees in Sabre computer
training. Salary $XXXXXX. Liberal vacation and profit-sharing benefits.

---

travel agent career as well as for travel agency managers seeking recruits; however, the curriculum and objectives of the different programs need to be carefully examined.

Travel schools.   Travel schools are of two types: proprietorial institutions organized to train for a profit and schools that are associated with travel agencies and operated as secondary profit centers. These schools are a good source for recruits although there is generally little consistency among them regarding course of study, class hours, or program length. According to a recent ASTA survey, there are currently more than 700 travel schools with approximately 65 percent of all travel school graduates seeking employment with travel agencies.[1] While placement directors at these schools are anxious to introduce potential candidates, the applicants still require a fair amount of training that can only come from experience and exposure to the industry.

Travel schools generally offer an intensive course designed to teach students fundamental technical skills. A typical program might include six to nine weeks of instruction with daily classes lasting for five or six hours. For most schools only one course is offered, which is intended to be comprehensive. Subjects usually covered include domestic air, international air, tours, hotels, cruises, railroads, car rentals, hotels, office procedures, popular destinations, automated reservation systems, and selling skills.

Candidates from travel schools can handle the basic functions of an agency and are more attractive than applicants with no travel industry background at all, but they still must undergo supplemental training, particularly in counseling and selling skills. Since students from travel programs are generally well trained in a technical sense and eager to find an employer who will provide them with practical experience, many have the potential to become good travel counselors.

Agency training schools.   Agency training schools, whose sole purpose is to train future agents, provide another recruitment source. The quality of this training varies greatly, and employers should closely scrutinize each school's program. Training schools with accreditation from ASTA or the National Association of Trade and Technical Schools have met certain minimal standards. When recruiting from an agency or any other training program, several factors should be evaluated: the general reputation of the school, licensing from the state's education department, faculty credentials, a curriculum that addresses the needs of the agency, the amount of hands-on experience provided, and the school's general policies in regard to student recruitment, grading, and tuition. Like the other schools mentioned, placement officers at these specialty schools are eager to provide travel agencies with potential employees.

Correspondence courses. Travel agent correspondence courses concentrate on the acquisition of technical skills that can be expressed in written form: reservations, ticketing, procedures, use of reference manuals, geographical knowledge, and computer formats. The American Society of Travel Agents (ASTA), for instance, sponsors a correspondence course that is geared toward new employees and consists of basic indoctrination training covering all phases of the travel business from the employee's standpoint.

The typical correspondence course is divided into lessons or modules that cover different areas of travel. Regardless of the quality of the teaching material, there are some subjects, for example, sales techniques and counseling, that are extremely difficult to teach effectively using correspondence methods, and these skills will need to be developed at the agency.

Community colleges. Various community colleges throughout the country now offer two-year travel agent training programs. Graduates from these programs generally have the same travel agency-specific skills as students from travel schools. Additionally, they will have taken basic education courses in math, English, communications, history, psychology, geography, and the humanities. Because the needs of local agencies vary and out-of-state students may not be seeking employment locally, two- and four-year colleges generally do not offer courses geared to the specific needs of the local community. The two-year programs usually include some practical training through internships; therefore, job applicants from these programs would require somewhat less induction training.

Four-year colleges. The retail travel agency industry has been increasing its recruiting activities at four-year colleges and universities due to the growing sophistication of the travel agency industry and the trend toward offering professional subjects at the college level. The quality of travel-related programs available at four-year colleges varies greatly in terms of faculty credentials, student admissions criteria, curriculum design, course structure, and materials used. While most agency managers feel that a college education is not necessary for pursuing a successful travel agency career, others are reconsidering and recognizing the need for future employees to have a broader education beyond their immediate specialized training.

Because two- and four-year college graduates do not receive as much technical training as graduates of specialized travel schools, they are often not prepared to become productive agents immediately and will require more time than travel school graduates to absorb the latest fare and destination information. On the other hand, they have received a generalized education with a more solid grounding in subjects that contribute to their growth in counseling and management positions. To attract these college graduates, some agencies have raised starting salaries to improve their competitive stance in recruitment.

In-house training programs.   Some agencies still prefer to offer in-house training programs that provide training as an unpaid work experience for the trainee. The exchange of training for unpaid work should first be cleared with both state and federal regulatory agencies to make sure specific practices comply with the law. Despite the benefits, most agencies find that this concept is not as financially sound as it may first appear. Training entails a great deal of time and effort on the agency's part, not to mention the cost of errors made by the new trainee, and often these relationships end with misunderstanding and frustration on both sides. Trainees may feel exploited, especially if they have assumed an assured job at the end of the training program when this was not the case. On the other hand, the agency may feel it has wasted time and effort on a trainee who does not accept the agency's job offer.

Regardless of whether new employees go through an in-house training program or receive their initial training through one of the other programs discussed, the travel agency will still be required to provide a certain amount of additional training. Both formal and informal training programs can be effective in the development of a knowledgeable and professional staff and are discussed further in this chapter.

THE SELECTION PROCESS

The Job Application

A well-designed job application form does several things: it saves time, it is an aid in the hiring process, and it also provides important information for future reference. The use of a standard form assures the agency manager that the information is always in the same place and spares the interviewer from having to continuously hunt for the needed specifics.

The job application, like every other part of the selection process, is subject to federal and state regulations. Any questions that do not relate to performance on the job should be excluded. The lawful sections of an application are as follows:

1. *Personal Data:* name, address, telephone number, date available for employment, type of employment desired (part or full time)
2. *Education:* education, scholastic honors, memberships in professional groups
3. *Work Experience:* chronological description of jobs held and the specific duties and responsibilities involved
4. *Travel Experience*

Screening and Reference Checks

Job applications should be carefully screened and former employers contacted before calling potential candidates for final interviews. Many agencies screen applicants by telephone before calling them in for the initial personal interview. This not only saves a great deal of time but can also provide useful insight on an applicant's phone etiquette, voice technique, conversation and selling skills, and his or her ability to handle what many consider to be a stressful situation.

Desired Skills and Competencies

Important factors to consider in the selection process include the applicant's qualifications with respect to technical knowledge, office skills, and experience; former responsibilities handled and track record; personal appearance and telephone manner; potential health or transportation problems; types of references received from former employers; and an assessment of how well the person will fit into the agency.

For those being hired as travel counselors, personality and sales ability are important criteria. Generally, the more successful travel counselors or agents seem motivated to please others and enjoy using the art of persuasion. Other important character traits may include empathy, flexibility, ability to get along with others, responsiveness, self-confidence, and leadership. Computation and communication skills, knowledge of geography, and the ability to grasp and retain information are also necessary. In order to successfully sell profitable nonroutine travel, an agent must have the ability to do the following:

- Win the client's trust
- Get the client excited about a potential future trip
- Convey to him or her the satisfaction and benefits to be derived from the trip
- Discover his or her needs, wants, fears, and concerns about travel
- Close the deal

Clearly, the above requires competency in humanistic skills as well as product knowledge.

Personal Interviews

The final personal interview with job candidates provides an opportunity for the applicant and employer to know each other and for the employer to ask any remaining questions. The interview should take place in a private location, with the employer well prepared with questions and a detailed description of the job. Objectivity should be maintained throughout the interview.

In addition to asking questions regarding job skills, the interviewer should try to discern the applicant's sales personality, energy level, initiative, sensitivity to others, honesty (with questions concerning ethical practices or proprieties), and ability to work under pressure. Open-ended questions are most appropriate as they force the candidate to do most of the talking. The employer should explain, in detail, what the job entails, including level of responsibility, pay, and chances for promotion. Applicants should be asked to explain why they want the job and what they expect from the employer.

Final Selection

In making the final selection, all information on the better-qualified candidates should be collected and compared, with a measurement scale in mind. For instance, a point rating system or ranking system can be used to grade each applicant's various skills or characteristics. However, no evaluation sys-

Ward Grenelle Foster, near the brochure rack, oversees this 1928 Ask Mr. Foster employee training class in New York City.

tem is perfect, and the final choice often depends as much on the instinct and judgment of management as it does on factual information. The selected candidate must have the *potential* to produce in terms of quality and quantity and should be emotionally stable and able to fit in with the agency's culture and work environment. Making the right selection means satisfying anticipated needs and expectations on the part of both employer and employee.

"Equal opportunity" is also a consideration when hiring. Under the Civil Rights Act of 1964, no person can be denied a job, or fair treatment in that job, on the basis of ancestry, color, religion, gender, or national origin. The Age Discrimination in Employment Act of 1967 and the Rehabilitation Act of 1973 include the aged and the handicapped in this select group. These federal laws generally require that employers not discriminate with regard to classified advertising, hiring or firing, or paying unequal wages for equal work. Some states have even stricter laws with regard to discriminatory practices in recruiting and hiring. For instance, language skills may not be used as a means of discrimination unless it is a bonafide need in the job. It is in management's best interest to carefully review all employee selection procedures and eliminate or alter any that are not justified in determining a person's qualifications for employment. The argument that gender, for instance, may be a hindering factor in negotiating with travel wholesalers or suppliers is not defensible in the eyes of the law.

TRAINING AND DEVELOPMENT

Orientation

Every new employee should be given a proper orientation to the agency. The first thirty days of employment are always the most crucial and, therefore, a critical time for induction training. Orientation helps new employees integrate and identify with the firm's values and work ethic. A good orientation will (1) introduce the company's history and traditions, (2) share the owner's or proprietor's philosophy of business and vision of the future for the agency, and (3) provide information with regard to agency policies, ethics, and standards of practice. Regarding point three, the orientation may be used to review work procedures, to provide information on selling techniques and travel products, and to acquaint new workers with available resources and people who can help them become more effective and efficient. Naturally, work benefits and rules may also be discussed if these have not been fully covered during the hiring process. Orientations done in a warm and friendly manner start the working relationship off on the right foot and encourage the new worker to become a participating and contributive member of the agency team.

Staff Development

If the goal of every agency is to have its staff operate in a highly professional and efficient manner, then the staff must be well trained. Travel counselors should be proficient in the following three areas:

1. *Techniques:* use of reference materials, CRT, fare calculations, reservation procedures, ticketing, and documentation
2. *Sales:* product knowledge, confidence, and sales skills
3. *Office Procedures:* filing, use of forms, accounting procedures, general policies and practices

Even high-quality and experienced staff members cannot perform well unless they have been trained in how the agency wants the job done. Professionalism also involves becoming more experienced in the overall travel business and keeping abreast of all new developments in the industry.

Training as it relates to efficiency and productivity is particularly important. Most agents do well to generate one ticket per hour and more typically produce between four and six tickets a day. At this rate, commissions barely cover the cost of production and overhead, so small gains in efficiency can be quite significant when working with such small productivity ratios. Therefore, training should be continuous throughout the employee's tenure with the agency.

A needs analysis, both for new employees and as part of the ongoing training program, should precede any training program. The primary objective of a needs analysis is to ascertain the necessary skills and knowledge that are lacking in the agency's work force or with a particular employee. The needs analysis can save time, wasted effort, and money by identifying these shortcomings and targeting ways to deal with them. Although certain training needs to be individualized, some training needs, such as information sharing, are universal, and here, group methods can be more efficiently employed.

Informal Training

OJT.   On-the-job training is one effective way of training new employees or upgrading skills of existing staff members. The success of this method depends on the trainer's knowledge, the trainer's ability to impart that knowledge, and the level of respect the trainee has for the trainer. To conduct good on-the-job training, both trainer and trainee must know specifically what behaviors or skills need to be developed—obviously different for someone switching jobs within the industry than for someone entirely new to it. An overall training goal should be established for on-the-job training and then the specific steps the person must learn to achieve this goal outlined. Any skill should be demonstrated first, with an explanation of what the trainer is doing as well as why.

An important principle for all training is that one skill be mastered before another one is undertaken. For the travel agency, unlike for school exams, an accuracy rate of 80 percent is not sufficient; 100 percent *accuracy* must be stressed at all times. For example, an error in routing or sending a client abroad without proper documentation, even when everything else has been done correctly, is still a serious mistake with unfortunate consequences for the client once a trip is in motion.

Managers should know their employees' strengths and weaknesses and provide ongoing or supplemental training as necessary. One of the most effective ways to conduct training programs is to have the less experienced staff members work with the more experienced agents, who represent a valuable resource for the agency and whose knowledge should be shared within the organization. Handbooks such as the agency's policies and procedures manual or those provided by the ARC and IATAN can also be extremely helpful in explaining procedures to the new employee.

Meetings.   Regular office meetings can be another means of training. These meetings should be structured and separated into different topics so that staff members have a chance to sharpen their skills, exchange ideas, discuss current developments within the agency or industry, and learn more about the job. Topics can include not only product knowledge but also other necessary skills, such as letter writing, salesmanship, geography, and office procedures. Supplier representatives or wholesalers can be invited to make presentations, conduct seminars, or simply provide the agency with videos to improve the staff's destination expertise. Staff discussion during meetings should be encouraged since a one-way lecture is generally less effective for assimilation of knowledge.

Meeting time can also be used for one of the travel counselors to discuss a recent fam trip. Some agencies assign agents one destination a month to report on in depth. Fam trips are in themselves an important source of training on both product knowledge and evaluative techniques.

Role playing can be another valuable tool at training meetings, providing the staff with an opportunity to discuss different sales techniques and common problems, especially in the handling of client complaints and dealing with difficult personalities.

Other informal ways of helping train agency staff include developing a plan for routing information around to all employees, subscribing to trade publications so employees can keep current on new industry developments, and posting important information on a bulletin board. Overall, management should make an effort to continuously monitor and upgrade agents' skills so the agency can offer a professional, high-quality, and competitive service.

Employee newsletter.   An employee newsletter is an excellent way to supplement training by keeping employees informed on new products and services available to clients, as well as sales tips, special promotions, new data input in the computer system, latest fam trip supplier evaluation, and other useful information. Especially for the multiple unit operator, an in-house newsletter helps employees keep in touch with each other and be aware of personnel changes—resignations, new faces, and promotions—as well as personal events—marriages, new additions to the family, and so on.

An employee newsletter need not be an expensive undertaking. It may be produced using desk-top computer equipment and software that are becoming increasingly user friendly and inexpensive. Figure 7.1 shows the lead page of an in-house employee newsletter of Garber Travel Service, Inc., published weekly on Mondays to provide employees with updates on supplier discounts and special promotions, new tour packages, supplier changes, people in profile, kudos for exceptional performances, fam trip reports, and so on. The key to launching an in-house newsletter is assigning someone with good writing skills to serve as newsletter editor for a few hours each week with input from management, sales staff, and others.

Formal Training

Formal travel training programs are available to assist the training needs of every level of travel agency employment. It behooves the manager to make a commitment to an employee's growth by encouraging formal training for professional knowledge and advancement.

Certification course.   The Institute of Certified Travel Agents (ICTA) offers an advance-level management certification program to agents with at least five years of industry experience and evidence of ethical business practice. To assure the integrity and academic soundness of the program, an Academic Council of leading educators representing top 4-year institutions serves as an advisory body to ICTA. Already more than 9000 travel industry members nationwide have gone through the two-year program. Through the ICTA program, travel agents are awarded the title of Certified Travel Counselor (CTC), the highest designation in the travel agency industry. The following four courses must be completed, in addition to an independent project: (1) Travel Industry Business Management, (2) Management of Sales Personnel, (3) Marketing for the Travel Industry, and (4) Tourism for the Travel Agent. For the independent project, one of three options is available: (1) research paper, (2) evaluation of an ICTA executive management seminar, or (3) completion of a risk-management program. Those seeking the CTC designation can either join a local study group for the course requirement or do a directed independent study.

Agents with a CTC designation can continue the ICTA learning process through groups called forums, which are like local alumni associations and

MONDAY MORNING news

The official employee newsletter of Garber Travel Service, Inc.

Margaret Finn Blank, Editor	August 22, 1988	Laura E. Quinn, Asst. Editor

Boston Herald

TICKET TO RIDE

Garber Travel is excited about the Boston Herald's new game, "Ticket To Ride." You may have seen the mysterious television advertisements announcing the new promotion, or read about it in the Herald.

"Ticket to Ride" offers readers a chance to win one of ten trips for two aboard the Venice Simplon Orient-Express, or one of several cruises to Bermuda, or one of many weekends in Montreal.

Garber Travel will be planning the travel for the lucky winners. As a matter of fact, Peg Willard, Manager of Foreign Sales in Brookline, is in the process of booking the first winner on the Orient-Express. The 85-year-old winner is looking forward to this luxurious adventure which will include two nights in Venice and two nights in London. Peg will be in charge of all arrangements for the Orient-Express winners.

The Bermuda cruises and Montreal weekends will be handled by Debbie Lee, Manager of our Commonwealth Avenue branch.

Garber is handling the "Ticket to Ride" promotion thanks to our association with the Boston Herald on a corporate travel level and thanks to Edith Elkin's daughter, who works for the Herald's New York advertising agency. Edith is our foreign exchange specialist in the Accounting Department.

Herald Staff photo by Steven LaBadessa

GARBER TRAVEL

FIGURE 7.1.
Source: Garber Travel Service, Inc., *Monday Morning News*, August 22, 1988, p. 1

meet several times a year. ICTA also sponsors a Travel Career Development Program to prepare agents for the CTC program. Courses for this program include The Travel Product, Selling Travel, Office Policies and Procedures, and How Travel Agencies Function. Other ICTA programs include a correspondence course that emphasizes international airfares and ticketing and a series of ten destination and sales training courses.

Trade association programs.   In addition to these established programs, many travel trade associations and suppliers of travel products provide training courses, seminars, and workshops on various topics. The Cruise Lines International Association, for example, offers quarterly training programs around the country. The Airlines Reporting Corporation (ARC) maintains a full-time training function that offers frequent and convenient opportunities for agency personnel to acquire basic skills in the preparation of carrier documents and knowledge of how these documents are properly submitted through ARC to the carriers. ASTA offers seminars that range in length from one to four days and cover such topics as developing and managing commercial accounts, selling skills for travel agents, improving managerial effectiveness, developing a profitable outside sales team, increasing agency productivity, and the lucrative world of incentive travel. Training is also available through allied associations such as the National Tour Association's Certified Tour Professional Program.

Short-term courses, in particular, can be useful when employees are deficient in specific areas of knowledge or skills or when industry changes require employees to obtain an information update. An example of the latter is the rapid changes that have recently occurred in the legal environment of the travel agency business. Technical information of this type is best obtained through a seminar conducted by a legal expert.

Importance of formal training.   As the travel industry continues to expand, evolve, and become more complex, every agency staff member should take advantage of some formal training. Although this means time and money on the part of the employer, it also results in better managed agencies and more professional, knowledgeable staff members. Given the increased competition of travel agencies and the drastic changes that have occurred since the mid-1970s, including the loss of exclusivity, formal travel training is no longer a luxury but part of the solution to marketplace survival. In the absence of any standard measure of quality for the industry, these training programs represent an important step in the development of professionalism within the travel agency business.

EVALUATION AND APPRAISAL

Feedback on performance is essential for and generally desired by all employees. While continuous informal feedback is important on a day-to-day basis, formal evaluations that focus on past performance and future development and expectations should be done once or twice a year. Managers generally have better performance results and increased loyalty when they take the time to recognize staff for a job well done and pinpoint ways in which employees can improve performance. The annual evaluations are important for determining an employee's salary increase, and they also provide such information as the employee's potential for promotions, ability to assume more responsibilities, and setting of development goals.

Determining Criteria

A standard set of objective criteria should be used for assessing the past performance of each employee. For the travel agency, performance is often quantitatively measured in terms of such factors as dollars generated in sales or the number of new accounts developed. For larger agencies, supervisors and branch managers are often evaluated on the basis of group figures, even when managers may not have complete control over these figures.

Since volume alone does not fully reflect an individual's performance, other general standards should be set, such as those that measure *how* the employee does the work. These are more subjective criteria and hard to quantify. Such things as attitude, ability to work with others, appearance, willingness to learn new aspects, organization, judgment, punctuality, and contribution of new ideas all fall under this category. Table 7.1 provides a partial listing of both qualitative and quantitative performance factors.

A well-written job description can help to develop performance standards. It is, of course, important for employees to know what standards they are being measured against. Employees should agree that the standards are fair and help participate in the setting of individual standards. Both the employee and manager should clearly understand what the employee is accountable for and specifically what the employee's job entails.

TABLE 7.1 PERFORMANCE CRITERIA

Quantitative	Qualitative
Dollar sales volume	Product knowledge
Tickets-sold count	Customer complaints or compliments
Cruise- and packages-sold count	Attitude
New accounts	Loyalty
Profit ratio	Ability to work with others
Number of new contacts	Judgment
"Hit" ratio (sales to presentations)	Personal characteristics
Service calls	Flexibility
	Initiative
	Maturity

For the manager, personal feelings should be kept out of the evaluation. Care should be taken to avoid the "halo effect," where one fault or outstanding quality of a favored or less favored employee may influence the entire appraisal. When the written evaluation is completed, the manager should discuss it with the employee, thus putting the evaluation to constructive use.

To prepare for the appraisal interview, the manager should review the employee's performance since the last appraisal and note changes on a standard agency evaluation form. Exhibit 7.4 is an example of a performance review form specifically designed for travel agencies.

One evaluation technique involves the employee and appraiser filling out the same form and then making a comparison. The appraisal interview should concern three primary questions: How is the employee doing? What is expected? How can there be improvement or further development?

Management by Objectives

This last question is future oriented and has to do with goal setting and employee development. Management by Objectives or MBO is a popular management technique that addresses goal setting and performance accountability by mutual agreement between superior and subordinates. MBO specifies that for objective criteria, such as volume of sales or the generation of new accounts, goals should be measurable and mutually agreed upon, tailored to the individual and the job, realistic, and yet challenging. For instance, a goal to "increase sales" is not specific enough; instead, it should be written as "increase sales by 20 percent." This gives the employee something to aim for, thus providing a source of motivation.

If goals are set that are too difficult or unrealistic, they will not be accepted and may even result in negative motivation. The goals need to be written so that agency employees are competing with themselves and not other staff members. Performance rewards should be personalized, although equitable, and predetermined, based on how well objectives or goals are met. Although establishing goals for subjective criteria is difficult, the appraisal interviewer needs to address these behaviors as well. Positive qualities, such as the ability to get along with other staff members, should be complimented and rewarded as a means of reinforcement, and negative behavior should be discussed with specific goals set for improvement.

Performance and Pay

Employee pay increases should be tied to formal evaluations, thus linking reward with performance. According to the organizational behavior modification theory, if an employee is performing well and this results in a pay increment that the employee values, the behavior of performing well will be positively reinforced. If an increment is given regardless of performance, the reward system will have no effect on improving performance in the future and may in turn discourage good performers who see others receiving equal reward for unequal contributions. In essence, the ultimate purpose of the evaluation is not its use as an academic exercise but as a management tool to motivate and develop better employees.

EXHIBIT 7.4

PERFORMANCE REVIEW FORM

Name _____ Self Review ( ) yes ( ) no

General Office ( ) Travel Counselor ( ) Commercial Agent ( )

Outside Sales ( ) Group Sales ( ) Manager ( )

Date of Employment _____ Date of current classification _____

Reviewed by _____ Date Prepared _____

Give a general job description for this person: _____

_____

_____

_____

_____

Note brief comments on performance in each area:

Technical performance _____

_____

_____

_____

Personal and professional _____

_____

_____

_____

Administrative _____

_____

_____

_____

Following is the level of performance of this person, related to the performance expected of most persons in this job classification, considering the job description and any other factors you consider pertinent:

(Suggested performance rating chart with broad examples:)

	Not Applicable	Performance Level			
		4	3	2	1
Technical performance					
1. Computer usage.					
2. Knowledge of procedures/forms.					
3. Knowledge of airfares.					
4. Written communications.					
5. Oral communications.					
Client relations					
6. Enthusiasm under pressure.					
7. Positive attitude.					
8.					
9.					
10.					
Personal and professional					
11. Maintains work area.					
12. Flexibility.					
13. Integrity.					
14. Plans and controls work.					
15.					
16.					
17.					
18.					
Administrative					
19. Delegates.					
20. Assumes responsibility.					
21.					
22.					
23.					
24.					

OPTIONS FOR USAGE:

A. Use form as shown expanding items to suit your agency mix and needs. Numerous and detailed items will be needed.

B. Use one basic form with designated heading, e.g., Travel Counselor, and then list performance items that would usually only apply to that job description. Shorter controlled list.

A staff "brainstorming" session will help to work up and clarify your original performance review form.

A. Last performance objectives. _____

_____

B. Status of that objective. _____

_____

_____

C. Future objective, course of action, time for completion. _____

_____

_____

D. Comments: _____

_____

_____

_____

Discussed and agreed:
(To be signed by both participants)

Name: _____
                                                          title   date

Name: _____
                                                          title   date

Source: Dorothy A. Purdie, "Performance Planning and Appraisal," Institute of Certified Travel Agents (unpublished article, 1981).

COMPENSATION

Salary Programs

Practices regarding compensation vary greatly in the travel agency business. They include paying (1) a minimum salary with extensive travel benefits, (2) the "going" rate or just above that, (3) straight salaries only, (4) a base salary plus a monthly commission, or (5) a base salary plus a monthly commission and a bonus. One ASTA survey reports that 67.5 percent of travel agency employees are paid a salary, 21.9 percent are paid on a commission basis, and 10.6 percent get part salary and part commission.[2] Whatever the method of compensation, it is apparent that too many agencies tend to hire the person who is willing to accept the lowest compensation, which generally results in high turnover and less experienced staff and is in the final analysis a costly policy. As a rule, it is better to hire the best people available and pay them as much as the business can afford, resulting in stronger sales and loyalty to the company. Underpaying often causes employees to seek employment with a competitor or to open their own agency.

A general guideline for compensation is that total payroll should not exceed 50 percent of the agency's total revenue for the year. While travel agent salaries historically have been considered relatively low, a survey done by the Travel Education Center of Cambridge found that in 1985 salary increments averaged approximately 9 percent for the travel agent versus the 6.5 percent national average for all service occupations. This is clearly a step in the right direction.[3]

Overtime

Overtime is very common in the travel agency business, so certain guidelines should be followed. Both federal and state laws control overtime pay and compensatory time off in addition to minimum wage. According to the Federal Fair Labor Standards Act, the hourly rate must be equal to or exceed minimum wage, and any employee is entitled to overtime pay equal to one-and-one-half times the employee's regular pay for any work over forty hours per week. This is calculated on a consecutive, seven-day, twenty-four-hour-a-day period. For instance, just because an employee worked more than eight hours one day, he would not be eligible for overtime pay unless his weekly total exceeded forty hours.

When an employee is *required* to attend a meeting, cocktail party, or fam trip, these hours do qualify as work time. However, if these events are made *optional*, it is not considered work time under the law. If employees are on regular work time during a fam trip, they should sign a contract specifying that they will not work more than their regular hours without prior approval from an authorized supervisor. Certain administrative and executive employees are exempt from this law; however, an attorney or appropriate governmental agency should be consulted before classifying any employee as exempt.

Overtime can be a very costly expense for the employer and should be kept at a minimum or avoided altogether. Another way to handle overtime is to give compensatory time off, but again, certain requirements must be met. The employee must be given one and one-half hours off for each hour of overtime worked, the compensatory time must be used during the same pay period in which the overtime was accrued, and the employee must voluntarily agree to these arrangements.

Familiarization Trips

Familiarization or fam tours are the primary means for educating travel agents about destination tourist facilities. They provide another form of incentive, though there is considerable debate over whether fam trips should be considered rewards or training and education opportunities. While many employees view these trips as incentives, others see them as strenuous exercises requiring hard work. Most managers agree, however, that from the perspective of the employer, they should be judged by their educational value and not by their pleasure attributes. If agents feel that the trip is "earned," they may see it more as a reward to enjoy than as an opportunity to gain knowledge of a new travel destination, and consequently, their time may be spent vacationing rather than evaluating.

Fam trips should be for everyone in the agency as a part of their training and development. It is usually best for the organization when trips are spread around equitably—the manager should never accumulate them for personal use. Some agencies hold periodic drawings for trips for the administrative staff so they, too, can enjoy travel benefits. Each agent should take at least one fam trip a year, as it improves product knowledge at little cost to the agency except for the cost of employee time. The destinations selected for fam trips should be those that are most popular among clients.

To assist agents in their appraisal of each place visited, it is often helpful to devise an evaluation form or checklist. Appendixes B and C at the end of the chapter provide examples of evaluation checklists for a hotel and a cruise. For example, when inspecting a hotel, the information advertised in the hotel guides or brochures should be compared against the realities of the hotel itself. A hotel may be evaluated in terms of its cleanliness, maintenance, attractiveness, service, type of clientele, size of rooms, amenities, restaurants, recreational facilities (very important in resort hotels), safety of the surrounding neighborhood, location, and accessibility. Meeting rooms, banqueting facilities, and business center services that may be important to corporate clients should be closely inspected. As the variables of a hotel property include both tangible and intangible elements, fair evaluation can be challenging, informative, and good training all at the same time.

Agents who are attending the fam trip should always be aware that they are representatives of the agency and that they have a responsibility to conduct themselves in a professional manner that will strengthen business relationships between the various suppliers and the agency. To avoid possible labor law problems, it is also wise to have the employee sign an agreement prior to the trip that he or she will not be performing more than the regular hours of work while away from home. Some agencies have the agent take a paid leave of absence with expenses fully covered, to avoid potential overtime problems.

Other Incentives

Wages and fringe benefits. The agency's policies and procedures manual should set forth all policies with respect to wages and fringe benefits. Even for the smallest of agencies, all details should be clearly spelled out to avoid potential disputes with employees. The employment contract, if utilized, provides another vehicle for outlining details regarding pay and fringe benefits.

Fringe benefits provide the travel agency employer with a vast array of options with which to produce a creative and motivational package for employees. What works best is usually an individual matter between employee and employer, and every program should be tailored to suit the agency's situation. Some agencies now offer "cafeteria-style" fringe benefit programs, in which staff members pick among optional benefits and create their own individual package up to a certain dollar value.

The most common fringe benefits are health insurance, life insurance, sick leave (on an accrual basis), disability coverage, holidays, and vacation. Other employee benefits for the travel agency can include personal time, low-interest loans, paying trade association dues, treating employees to memberships in golf, tennis, or health clubs, and allowing agents to travel with their spouses at discounted rates.

Commission plans and bonuses.   For the travel agency, another common form of incentive is the commission or bonus plan. While the commission is an amount of money paid on a regular and frequent basis, the bonus is usually paid annually or semiannually. For the employee who is aggressive and highly competitive, a low salary with a high commission plan may prove more attractive than a high salary with low or no commission. In many agencies, a minimal sales quota must be achieved before a commission is paid, whereas other agencies may operate only on a straight commission basis. For motivational purposes, commissions should be distributed as frequently as possible.

Many agencies give bonuses to employees in recognition of or to provide incentive for outstanding performance. When agencies use bonus plans, there is usually a predetermined percentage of net profit allocated to the bonus pool. The amount of bonus each employee receives can be determined by years of service or as a percentage of commission earnings or salaries. Alternatively, the employer may choose to distribute the bonus pool equally among all employees or on a discretionary basis. If a bonus plan is considered at all, the principle is to use bonuses as a part of the reward system that helps improve operational efficiency.

Profit sharing.   Profit-sharing plans also encourage workers to increase company profits. Some of the retirement profit-sharing plans have been very successful in building up savings for employees, as well as aiding in the development of loyalty as the employee's savings account grows. The IRS allows employers to contribute 15 percent of the total annual compensation (up to a maximum of $36,000) for each employee to the profit-sharing account and to write this off as an expense, which is not taxed until it is withdrawn. The advantage of the profit-sharing plan over the pension plan, whether it is distributed annually or put into a retirement fund, is that the contribution from the employer is contingent upon a profit. Profit sharing rewards employees in good years and penalizes them when sales are below par. As in the case of the bonus plan, there are a number of different ways to set up the profit-sharing plan.

Nonmonetary incentives.   Despite the importance of monetary rewards, it is crucial for the travel agency manager to be aware of and take advantage of nonmonetary incentives as well. The list of reinforcement options provided in Chapter 6 shows that the range of possible incentives is extensive. For the agency that is not able to provide high salaries or extensive fringe benefits, rewards such as challenging, stimulating work, a pleasant working environment, job security, recognition, industry benefits, and an opportunity to grow personally and professionally should be used as important motivational tools.

SUMMARY

Given the intangible nature of the product sold, the travel agency builds its reputation on the performance of its personnel. If the agency lacks a knowledgeable, motivated, loyal, and professional staff, any advantages it has in terms of marketing plans, technological advancements, or financial backing will be quickly dissipated. Personnel-related costs are also an agency's major expense. The management of personnel, therefore, is probably the most vital function of the agency manager. The tasks of recruiting, selecting, training, appraising, and compensating employees must be undertaken with careful consideration and with full knowledge of state and federal laws guiding such practices. As the travel agency business becomes increasingly complex and agencies face competition from less traditional sources, a well-run, efficient organization with a professional and satisfied staff will be a critical element in any agency's survival.

DISCUSSION QUESTIONS

1. What are some of the reasons for the shortage of trained agency personnel?
2. What is the difference between a job analysis, a job description, and a job specification? Why are they important?
3. Discuss some of the ways to recruit travel agency personnel. What are the advantages and disadvantages of each?
4. What are some of the qualifications for a travel counselor?
5. What are some of the advantages of a well-trained staff?
6. Discuss the importance of the performance appraisal.
7. Should familiarization trips be viewed by management as an incentive or training?

ENDNOTES

[1]Bob Brooke. "How Good Are Travel Schools?" *ASTA Travel News,* June 15, 1986, p. 57.

[2]1984 ASTA Census, cited in "News Events of 1985," *Travel Market Yearbook,* December 31, 1985, p. 27.

[3]Nick Verrastro. "Agent Wage Hikes for '84 Will Average 8.5 Percent, Survey Shows," *The Travel Agent,* February 16, 1984, p. 3.

SUPPLEMENTAL READINGS

DERVAES, CLAUDINE, *The Travel Agent Training Workbook,* Sections I–VI. Tampa, FL: Solitaire Publishing, 1982.

STEVENS, LAURENCE, *The Travel Agency Personnel Manual.* Wheaton, IL: Merton House Publishing Company, 1979.

THOMPSON, DOUGLAS, AND ALEXANDER ANOLIK, *A Personnel and Operations Manual for Travel Agencies.* San Francisco: Dendrobium Books, 1986.

appendix a
Job Analysis Questionnaire*

Step by step: the information to obtain when doing a job analysis

Identifying information

Organization/unit
Title
Date

Brief summary of job.   This statement will include the primary duties of the job. It may be prepared in advance from class specifications, job descriptions, or other sources. However, it should be checked for accuracy using the task statements resulting from the analysis.

Job tasks.   What does the worker do? How does he or she do it? Why? What output is produced? What tools, procedures, aids are involved? How much time does it take to do the task? How often does the worker perform the task in a day, week, month, or year?

Skills, knowledge, and abilities required.   What does it take to perform each task in terms of the following?

1. Knowledge required
    a. What subject matter areas are covered by the task?
    b. What facts or principles must the worker have an acquaintance with or understand in these subject matter areas?
    c. Describe the level, degree, and breadth of knowledge required in these areas or subjects.
2. Skills required
    a. What activities must the worker perform with ease and precision?
    b. What are the manual skills required to operate machines, vehicles, equipment, or to use tools?
3. Abilities required
    a. What are the nature and level of language ability, written or oral, required of the worker on the job? Are there complex oral or written ideas involved in performing the task, or simple instructional materials?
    b. What mathematical ability must the worker have? Will he or she use simple arithmetic; complex algebra?
    c. What reasoning or problem-solving ability must the worker have?

*Adapted from U.S. Civil Service Commission

d. What instructions must the worker follow? Are they simple, detailed, involved, abstract?

e. What interpersonal abilities are required? What supervisory or managing abilities are required?

f. What physical abilities, such as strength, coordination, visual acuity, must the worker have?

Physical activities.   Describe the frequency and degree to which the incumbent is engaged in such activities as pulling, pushing, throwing, carrying, kneeling, sitting, running, crawling, reaching, climbing.

Environmental conditions.   Describe the frequency and degree to which the incumbent will encounter working under such conditions as these: cramped quarters, moving objects, vibration, inadequate ventilation.

Typical work incidents

1. Situations involving the interpretation of feelings, ideas, or facts in terms of personal viewpoint

2. Influencing people in their opinions, attitudes, or judgments about ideas or things

3. Working with people beyond giving and receiving instructions

4. Performing repetitive work, or continuously performing the same work

5. Performing under stress when confronted with emergency, critical, unusual, or dangerous situations or in situations in which work speed and sustained attention are make-and-break aspects of the job

6. Performing a variety of duties, often changing from one task to another, of a different nature without loss of efficiency or composure

7. Working under hazardous conditions that may result in violence, loss of bodily members, burns, bruises, cuts, impairment of senses, collapse, fractures, electric shock

Worker interest areas.   From the following list identify the preferences for work activities suggested by each task.

1. Dealing with things and objects

2. Concerning the communication of data

3. Involving business contact with people

4. Involving work of a scientific and technical nature

5. Involving work of a routine, concrete, organized nature

6. Involving work of an abstract and creative nature

7. Involving work for the presumed good of people
8. Relating to process, machine, and technique
9. Resulting in prestige or the esteem of others
10. Resulting in tangible, productive satisfaction

appendix b

**PAX TRAVEL AGENCY
ON-SITE HOTEL EVALUATION SHEET***

Hotel Name: _____
City: _____ Date: _____
Contact: _____

_____

Exterior

Location: _____
Parking facilities: _____
Airport shuttle bus or limousine/escort service: _____
Taxis available: _____
Hotel cars: _____
Car rentals: _____
Number of stories, availability of: _____
Proximity to shops, restaurants: _____
Appearance of hotel: _____

Lobby:

Size: _____
Seating available: _____
Cleanliness: _____
Shops: _____
Front desk: _____
Bellmen available: _____
Concierge: _____
Elevators: _____

Check In/Check Out:

Efficiency: _____
Quality of service: _____
Personnel knowledge of hotel services, points of interest in area: _____

_____
Knowledge of various languages: _____

Recreational Facilities and State of Maintenance:

Beach: _____
Swimming pool: _____
Towels and cabanas: _____
Cocktails: _____
Food service poolside: _____

Golf courses: _____

Pro shop: _____

Rentals available: _____

Green fees: _____ Starting times: _____

Tennis courts: _____

Pro shop: _____

Lighted: _____ Rentals: _____

Fees: _____ Lessons: _____

Health/fitness center: _____

Disco/nightclub: _____

Live entertainment: _____

Dancing: _____

Other: _____

Guest Activities:

Planned: _____

Continuous: _____

Children's activities: _____

Activities for elderly: _____

Special tours/cruises: _____

Food:

Room service: _____

Coffee shop: _____

  Appearance of food: _____

  Service: _____

  Price: _____

  Scope of menu: _____

  Hours open: _____

Restaurant: _____

  Appearance of food: _____

  Service: _____

  Price: _____

  Scope of menu: _____

  Hours open: _____

Group Facilities:

General assembly capacity: _____ Break-out rooms: _____

Total number of meeting rooms and capacities for each room: _____

_____

Audio-visual equipment: _____

_____

Display space: _____

_____

Catering facilities: _____

_____

Room Inspections:

	Minimum	Standard	Superior

Location in hotel: _____

Size of room: _____

Drawer space: _____

Closet space: _____

Furniture: _____

Decor: _____

Lighting: _____

Television: _____

Cable TV; HBO: _____

Radio: _____

Coffee makers: _____

Other amenities: _____

Bed size: _____

View: _____

Cleanliness: _____

Noise level: _____

A/C: _____

Heating: _____

Bathroom: _____

   Shower only: _____

   Shower & tub: _____

   Lighting: _____

   Towels/washcloths: _____

Other amenities: _____

Maid service: _____

Frequency: _____

Timing: _____

Turndown service: _____

Other comments: _____

Phone Service:

Courtesy: _____

Wake-up calls: _____

Conference calls: _____

Special Services:

Laundry: _____

Mending, alteration: _____

Services for handicapped: _____

Other: _____

Executive Center:

Separate floors: _____

Typing: _____

Telex: _____

Secretary: _____

Translation services: _____

Clientele:

Age group: _____

Air or car arrivals: _____

FIT or package: _____

Business or vacation: _____

Party mix (families, singles, couples): _____

Foreign visitors: _____

Dress: _____

General behavior characteristics: _____

Socio-economic status: _____

Price range: _____

Source: Adapted from Lynn Sorensen, "Checking Out What Your Clients Check Into," *The Travel Agent,* January 22, 1981, p. 41.

appendix c

PAX TRAVEL AGENCY
CHECKLIST FOR SHIPBOARD INSPECTION

Company: _____

Ship: _____

Sailing Date: _____

Number of Days: _____

Port of Embarkment: _____

Itinerary: _____

Public areas	Excellent (1)	Good (2)	Average (3)	Below average (4)	Unsatis- factory (5)	Comments
1. First Impression						
Exterior						
Entrance						
Cabin						
Dining room						
2. Food						
Presentation						
Quality						
Variety						
Special orders						
Meal hours						
Deck buffet						
Gala buffet						
3. Service						
Cabin						
Dining room						
Lounges						
Deck						
Other						
4. Facilities						
Deck						
Sports						
Spa						
Deck chairs						
Disco						
Casino						
5. Other						
Beauty shop						
Shops						
Masseur						
Other						
6. Entertainment						
Music						

Shows					
Professional staff					
Activities					
Pax participation					
7. Shore Excursions					
Professionalism					
Efficiency					
8. On-Board Charges					
Tipping policy					
Beauty shop					
Bar					
Shore excursions					
Cash or charge					
policy					
Photos					
9. Last Impression					
Exterior					
Interior					
Cabins					
Minimum					
Average					
Service					
Pax satisfaction					
Money's worth					

Cabins	Stateroom #___ Category ____	Stateroom #___ Category ____	Stateroom #___ Category ____	Stateroom #___ Category ____
Size				
Decor				
Lighting				
Beds				
Linen (quality)				
Bathroom size:				
conveniences				
tub/shower				

Other Observations and Comments:

Single Policy:

Handicapped Facilities:

General Comments:

chapter 8

Travel Agency Accounting

LEARNING OBJECTIVES

- To define how accounting systems contribute to the successful management of a travel agency
- To identify the different needs of various decision makers for accurate accounting information
- To introduce the rudiments of an accounting system, including definitions of basic accounts and a typical chart of accounts for a travel agency
- To know how to construct balance sheets and income statements and what they mean to a travel agency

KEY TERMS

- Assets
- ASTA Travel Agency Accounting System
- Balance Sheet
- Bonding
- Booking and Commission Report
- Capital Accounts
- Cash Disbursements Journal
- Cost of Sales
- Creditors
- Credits
- Debits
- Employee Productivity Report
- Equity
- General Ledger
- Generally Accepted Accounting Procedures (GAAP)

- Income
- Income Statement
- Liabilities
- Payroll Journal
- P & L Statement
- Revenues

- Sales/Cash Receipts Journal
- Statement of Changes in Financial Position
- Supplier Productivity Report
- Working Capital

INTRODUCTION

Accounting truly is the language of business. Accounting systems are designed to record, summarize, and report financial information concerning the operations of an organization. Accounting system outputs are financial statements. In addition, the system provides the financial foundation for management reports used in planning and controlling the travel agency.

Accounting terminology and procedures vary among countries, often dramatically so. Regulatory and taxation reporting differences alone may cause income, expense, asset, liability, and equity transactions to be realized differently in various countries. The framework presented here follows the generally accepted accounting principles (GAAP) that prevail in the United States. However, we have discussed only retail travel agency operations in this chapter to simplify presentation of basic accounting concepts. Wholesale operations apply the same basic principles, although specific accounts change to reflect unique features of wholesalers.

USERS AND USES OF ACCOUNTING INFORMATION

As noted, accounting systems must provide information to a host of decision makers, and each user group may place its emphasis on a different aspect of the entire set of financial data presented by the accounting system. Even so, the usefulness of financial information is based on a few basic principles.[1]

Accounting System Requirements

Foremost, the system must provide accurate information. The accuracy standard rests on several basic concepts. Accounting is concerned only with facts that can be expressed in monetary terms, and these financial facts must be objective and verifiable. Most often, then, accounting measures costs and prices paid at the time they are realized, which means that these may correspond to real value over time.

Useful accounting systems also must present financial information in an understandable fashion, which, in some cases, may necessitate preparation of several sets of financial statements. More important, users must be able to rely not only on the integrity of financial statements but on the assurance that they have been developed in accordance with GAAP.

Finally, accounting systems must provide financial information on a timely basis. All accounting data is designed to facilitate decision making. If the system cannot provide accurate and understandable information to users before or at the time a decision is to be made, it is not particularly useful and may cause decisions to be made without information. Therein lies the value of an accounting system to users of financial statements and reports.

User Perspectives

Users of financial information most often are classified according to the specific decisions they are facing. Some users are interested in the long-run profitability of the travel agency, others in day-to-day operations. Some users are concerned with an agency's profitability or operations only to the extent it determines if they, the users, will be paid. These interests generally are reflective of the concerns expressed by owners, creditors, suppliers, managers, and governmental agencies.[2]

Owners

Owners, whether sole proprietors, partners, or equity holders in a corporation, are concerned with managing their investments. They are assumed to be concerned with the long-run success of the agency or return of invested capital. Although numerous reports may be important, the income or profit and loss (P & L) statement tends to be the primary source of information, summarizing the sales and expenses of the agency and thus its profitability for a particular period.

Aggregate measures of revenue and expense, while necessary, may not be adequate by themselves for informed decision making. For example, an owner very likely will be interested in the composition of the revenue stream to the agency. Overreliance on a single corporate account may mean that profits, while currently good, may be risky in the future. The absence of any commission revenue from cruise lines, for instance, may signal that a profitable agency could be even more profitable if cruises could be added to the agency's sales mix. P & L statements are useful for both financial (external) and managerial (internal) accounting purposes.

Creditors

Creditors are a second group of financial statement users. They represent persons and institutions who have loaned funds to the travel agency. Their primary concern then becomes one of whether the agency can repay the debt owed as of a current date. This concern may encompass short-run debt-paying ability, long-term debt-paying ability, or both.

Historically, it has been assumed that the balance sheet provided the most useful financial information to creditors. Because the balance sheet presents a financial snapshot or picture of agency operations at a point in time, it was thought to provide the best indication of loan security. The relationship between assets owned by, funds loaned to, and funds invested in the agency goes a long way toward determining the agency's ability to pay bills as they come due.

Going a long way toward determining debt-paying ability is not, however, the same as determining debt-paying ability. Increasingly, creditors realize that the ability of an agency to cover loan repayment is a function of the agency's ability to generate a profit, information that is found in the P & L statement, not the balance sheet.

Suppliers

Technically, vendors or suppliers are creditors of the agency. Arguably, they are the single largest creditor group of any retail travel agency. Primary suppliers, such as airlines, hotels, cruise lines, and tour operators, for whom the agent is collecting revenue, have obvious concerns with the agency's debt-paying ability. Supplier regulatory organizations such as ARC and IATAN (discussed in Chapter 2) impose financial standards, designed to ensure an agent's creditworthiness among other things, on all agents before they can receive a conference appointment.

IATA-appointed agents must submit to ongoing bank verifications and external audits of financial statements. The IATA agent also must meet minimum standards for current asset, working capital, and equity positions, and agencies frequently must likewise be bonded as a condition of appointment. For example, the ARC requires a minimum of $20,000 and a maximum of $70,000 to be posted. To secure these bonds, agencies typically must maintain specified levels of working capital, net worth, and owner-invested capital.

Managers

Managers use financial information as input to operating decisions, decisions geared to achieve profitability objectives established by owners. Of course, the predominant pattern in retail travel agencies is for the owner to be the manager. However, with the trend toward dealerships, franchises, and even incorporating and issuing stock to raise capital, ownership increasingly will be separated from management and the need for financial information will become even more exacting.

To improve profits, management can increase revenues, decrease expenses, or ideally achieve a combination of the two. An improved revenue picture can come through increased volume, sales of higher-commission products and services, changes in the sales mix, and other means. Expenses can be reduced by cutting bad accounts, such as those requiring an excessive amount of time or rewrites without a corresponding increase in revenue. In all cases, management needs accurate, understandable, and timely financial information.

Booking and commission report.   It is clear that managers at least need the information contained in basic financial statements—the balance sheet and P & L statement. It is equally obvious that agency managers require additional information, not contained in financial statements, if they are to make informed decisions.[3] A Booking and Commission Report, showing product lines sold in terms of dollar volume and percentage of overall revenue mix, can prove invaluable (see Exhibit 8.1). Proposed on a monthly, year-to-date, and year-to-year basis, this report highlights trends that will help in planning and control, particularly marketing decisions.

Employee productivity report.   An Employee Productivity Report is essential to effective management (see Exhibit 8.2). Studies suggest that employee compensation, wages, and benefits represent over 50 percent of the typical agency's total operating cost, more than four times greater than the second largest expense category, location. The need to improve productivity, whether agents are paid on a commission or a salary basis, is obvious.

Proposed on a monthly, year-to-date, and year-to-year basis, the Employee Productivity Report looks at employee bookings and commissions by product line for the accounting period. This is analogous to other retailers who require each salesperson on the floor to attain a minimal quota of sales each day, week, or month. A particular employee may not be generating enough sales for the agency in total. Alternatively, an agent's total bookings could be adequate, but undue emphasis is being given to low-commission

EXHIBIT 8.1

PAX TRAVEL AGENCY
BOOKING AND COMMISSION REPORT

Product	Bookings $	%	Commissions $	%
Air	330,000	33	29,700	31.66
Tours	240,000	24	19,200	20.47
Commercial	210,000	21	18,900	20.15
Hotels	160,000	16	22,400	23.88
Car rentals	60,000	6	3,600	3.84
TOTAL	$1,000,000	100	$93,800	100.00

EXHIBIT 8.2

PAX TRAVEL AGENCY
EMPLOYEE PRODUCTIVITY REPORT
SALESPERSON: T. RAVEL

Product	Bookings $		Commissions $	
	Period	YTD	Period	YTD
Air	41,250.00	82,500.00	3,712.50	7,425.00
Tours	30,000.00	60,000.00	7,500.00	15,000.00
Commercial	26,250.00	52,500.00	6,562.50	13,125.00
Hotels	20,000.00	40,000.00	2,800.00	5,600.00
Car rentals	7,500.00	15,000.00	1,875.00	3,750.00
	$125,000.00	$250,000.00	$22,450.00	$44,900.00

products. A productivity report could clue the manager to redirect the employee's time to more profitable lines in the revenue mix.

Supplier productivity report. The accounting system also contains information to generate supplier productivity reports. Volume generally means clout, which in turn translates into profits, most often through overrides. In addition to cumulative discounts and overrides, the agent may find the opportunity to increase profits on a per-order basis. Per-order, or group, and per-annum incentives offered by suppliers are now the norm rather than the exception. The agency must develop its own Supplier Productivity Report, rather than relying on the suppliers themselves to tell the agent what and how much it is selling (see Exhibit 8.3).

EXHIBIT 8.3

PAX TRAVEL AGENCY
SUPPLIER PRODUCTIVITY REPORT

Date	Supplier	Client	Gross $	Commission $
9/8/88	Avis	Smith	$500.00	50.00
9/10/88	National	Jones	300.00	50.00
9/15/88	Presidential Tours	Brown	800.00	72.00
9/27/88	AMEXCO	Kennedy	1,000.00	120.00
TOTAL			$2,600.00	$292.00

Government

The final user group is made up of governmental agencies, of which tax authorities, federal and state, are the most important. Income and payroll taxes are of particular importance, but local taxes, depending on location, also may be significant. Finally, the continuing interest of the U.S. Department of Transportation (DOT) in the travel industry may yet affect accounting practices, because certainly, the DOT often calls upon the industry to supply financial information for regulatory proceedings.

The interests of the primary users of financial information—owners, creditors, suppliers, managers, and government—are not mutually exclusive. Managers must understand and anticipate how owners will interpret financial information. Similarly, both owners and managers must understand how creditors will view the agency based on its financial statements, while simultaneously meeting the financial standards required by conferences. Understanding the various uses to which financial information can be put is the crux of financial management (which is the subject of Chapter 9).

THE BASIC ACCOUNTING SYSTEM

Accounting systems can only account for transactions that can be expressed in monetary terms, be objectively measured, and be verifiable. Fortunately for the travel agent, most transactions invoke a paper trail (known as an audit trail), including checks, invoices, deposit slips, vouchers, credit card indemnity forms, and other pieces of paper. This facilitates maintenance of sound bookkeeping systems—the foundation of sound accounting systems. Bookkeepers record the transactions that, when summarized, are used to build the financial statements and reports used by decision makers.

Primary Journals

A basic bookkeeping system in a travel agency records all transactions in three primary journals. The Sales/Cash Receipts Journal is used to record all sales made and cash received. Cash outflows are recorded in the Cash Disbursements Journal, akin to an ordinary checkbook. Finally, all payroll-related transactions are recorded in a Payroll Journal. Totals from each journal are compiled monthly and posted to the General Ledger. The information required to generate the financial statements and reports mentioned can then be taken from the General Ledger.

ASTA System

The American Society of Travel Agents (ASTA) recommends a slightly more elaborate bookkeeping system. ASTA's system incorporates many of the concepts in the simplified system discussed above, but it has the advantage of being specifically designed to generate ARC reports and facilitate adoption of the numerous back-office computer systems now available.

The Invoice/Receipt (I/R) is a key source document in the ASTA system. All transactions affecting revenues generated and/or due from a client are recorded on an invoice/receipt, with copies maintained in a log. An I/R would be written for any client-related transaction involving a charge for a ticket, voucher, or service payment to the agency with cash, check, or credit card; and the agency issuing a refund.

Nonclient revenues received are recorded in the Miscellaneous Receipts Log (MRL), which is the only source document for recording revenue-generating transactions for nonclient sources. A typical agency would use the MRL for tracking retroactive commissions, overrides, supplier refunds, operating expense reimbursements, and similar transactions.

Individual I/Rs and the MRL are combined in the Summary of Invoices and Receipts (SIR), which is useful in controlling accounts receivable, meeting ARC reporting requirements, and compiling financial statements. In most respects, it is a specialized version of a Sales/Cash Receipts Journal.

The Cash Disbursements Journal, and in some cases the Payroll Journal as well, is replaced by the voucher check. Voucher checks are used to record all disbursements of agency funds, classify disbursements, recognize revenue when net payment is made, accrue certain liabilities, charge accounts receivable when payment is made for a client, and record account adjustments. Unless a separate Payroll Journal is maintained, the voucher check system records all payroll transactions. All information from voucher checks are then summarized in a Payment Recap.

Basic Funds Flow Accounts

Regardless of whether an agency has adopted the ASTA-recommended accounting system or is using a more generalized one, all transactions must be recorded consistently. Consistency begins with recognizing that the system basically is accounting for funds the agency earns, spends, owes, and retains. Accounting systems classify these fund flows into five basic types of accounts.

1. Assets.   Assets formally have been defined as the probable future economic benefits obtained or controlled by the agency as the result of past transactions. Essentially, assets can be expected to eventually increase the cash inflows to the agency. In some cases, the assets are highly liquid, that is, expected to generate inflows in the near future, such as cash and accounts receivable. Alternatively, certain assets such as office equipment may contribute to profits over the long run.

A special word about accounts receivables and credit is warranted. Travel agencies in the past often were not too meticulous in their credit policies with regard to large commercial accounts, permitting them to owe payment for thirty days or longer. When the agency must itself pay the carrier once a week, the agency is in effect financing due charges over the time difference. Permitting large accounts receivables to build up can jeopardize the cash flow position of an agency, so a ten days credit policy, that is, payment due within ten days of invoicing, should be followed. Travel agencies, after all, are not banks.

2. Liabilities.   Liabilities are the converse of assets; they represent claims against agency assets. More precisely, liabilities are future sacrifices of economic benefits arising from agency obligations to transfer assets or provide services to others as a result of past transactions. As with assets, liabilities are classified by order of liquidation. Current liabilities, such as ARC payable, generally are due within one year or accounting period while long-term liabilities, such as mortgage payable, fall due greater than one year.

3. Capital.   Capital accounts are somewhat more difficult to define. Usually capital accounts represent the original amount of paid-in capital by owners, additional paid-in capital, and funds earned in the agency. Alternatively, the value of capital accounts can be defined as a residual, where owners' equity is equal to the difference between the value of what is *owned* by the agency (assets) and the value of what is *owed* by the agency (liabilities). Capital accounts represent the *net worth* of the agency to owners.

Asset, liability, and capital or equity accounts are summarized in an agency's balance sheet, together giving a picture of where the agency is now. At the same time, they tell decision makers about the future. As balance sheets summarize the value of funds owed to and owed by a travel agency, they also say much about future profit potential.

4. Income.   Income accounts are of particular importance and represent revenue from sales, such as airline commissions or tour income and interest. Cash flows to the firm (inflow) for services rendered.

5. Expenses.   Accounts of expenses, also of special importance, show the costs of doing business. The agency must pay or realize a cash outflow in order to pay for services provided or rendered to it (inflow).

The concept of inflows and outflows is used in accounting to maintain a balance in reporting: Every inflow must be accompanied by a corresponding outflow. Accounting systems are based on the concept of double-entry bookkeeping; there is no such thing as a unilateral transaction. The two halves of the accounting couplet are referred to as debits and credits; debits record increased asset and expense balances while credits record increases in liabilities, or decreases in net worth or income. When ARC is paid, cash balances are reduced but so are accounts payable. A cash sale may mean an increased asset, but it also entails an increased liability, an amount payable to the ARC.

Each of these five accounts—assets, liabilities, capital, income, and expenses—however, must be elaborated upon in actual practice. The fully developed accounting system, regardless of industry, is referred to as a chart of accounts. Although many charts of account could be used by the travel agent, perhaps the best system is the Chart of Accounts developed by ASTA.

ASTA Chart of Accounts

The ASTA Travel Agency Accounting System was developed by Touche Ross and Company.[4] All of the accounts are numbered, 100 through 699, and each of the three digits in each account number conveys information to the user. The first digit identifies the type of account: asset, liability, and so on. The second digit identifies the specific division of the category, for example, accounts receivable from airline sales. Broadly defined, the ASTA accounting system is as follows:

Type of account	Statement	Account numbers
Assets	Balance sheet	
Current		100–199
Long term		200–299
Liabilities	Balance sheet	
Current		300–389
Long term		390–399
Capital	Balance sheet	400–499
Revenues	Income statement	500–599
Expenses	Income statement	600–699

The exact specification of the ASTA Chart of Accounts follows below. Becoming familiar with these accounts helps in gaining a better understanding of how a travel agency differs from other businesses. Any three-digit account not fully specified is considered to be "open" and subject to definition at a future date and to meet specific agency requirements.

BALANCE SHEET ACCOUNTS

100–299	Assets

100–199	*Current assets*
110	Cash in bank
111	Checking account
112	Savings account
120	Petty cash
121	Petty cash—bank A
130	Accounts receivable
131	A/R—Domestic air
132	A/R—International air
133	A/R—Hotel
134	A/R—Package tours
135	A/R—Steamship
136	A/R—Refunds
137	A/R—Miscellaneous/general
138	A/R—Car rental
139	A/R—FIT
140	A/R—Own tour/group
141	A/R—Foreign rail
142	A/R—Bus
143	A/R—Charter
150	Investments
151	Marketable securities
170	Notes receivable
171	Notes receivable—firm A
190	Other current assets

200–299	*Long-term assets*
210	Automobiles
220	Accumulated depreciation—automobiles
230	Office equipment
240	Accumulated depreciation—office equipment
250	Furniture and equipment
260	Accumulated depreciation—furniture and equipment
270	Leasehold improvements
280	Other long-term assets

300–399	Liabilities

300–389	*Current liabilities*
310	Accounts payable
311	A/P—ARC
312	A/P—Carrier A
313	A/P—Carrier B
314	A/P—Carrier C
315	A/P—Amtrak
316	A/P—Insurance
317	A/P—Car hire vouchers
318	A/P—Steamship tickets
319	A/P—Bus tickets

BALANCE SHEET ACCOUNTS (Continued)

	Liabilities
350	Accrued liabilities
351	Federal income tax withheld
352	State income tax withheld
353	Local tax withheld
354	FICA tax withheld
355	Other payroll tax withheld
370	Notes payable
371	Notes payable—bank X
390–399	*Long-term liabilities*
391	Mortgage payable

	Capital
400–499	Capital
410	Common stock
420	Invested capital
421	Proprietor or partner A
422	Partner B
450	Retained earnings
451	Profit/loss for period
452	Dividends
470	Withdrawals
471	Proprietor or Partner A withdrawal
472	Partner B withdrawal

	Income statement accounts
500–599	*Income*
510	Operating income
530	Commission income
531	C/I—Domestic air
532	C/I—International air
533	C/I—Hotel
534	C/I—Package tour
535	C/I—Steamship
536	C/I—Service charge
537	C/I—Miscellaneous/general
538	C/I—Car rental
539	C/I—FIT
540	C/I—Own tour/group
541	C/I—Foreign rail
542	C/I—Bus
543	C/I—Charter
544	C/I—Insurance
545	C/I—Amtrak
550	Investment income
570	Special project income
590	Extraordinary income

BALANCE SHEET ACCOUNTS (Continued)

	Income Statement Accounts
600–699	*Expenses*
610	Personnel costs
611	Sales salaries
612	Office salaries
613	Executive compensation
620	Other payroll costs
621	Tax—FICA
622	Tax—Federal unemployment
623	Tax—State
624	Tax—Local
625	Other employee benefits
630	Selling expenses
631	Automobile
632	Commissions—outside sales
633	Travel—general
634	Travel—tour expense
635	Entertainment
641	Advertising and promotion
650	Administrative expenses
651	Office expenses
652	Office supplies and printing
653	Office repairs and maintenance
654	Postage and express
655	Communications
656	Dues and subscriptions
657	Teleticketing charges
660	Other administrative expenses
661	Legal fees
662	Educational expenses
663	Bad debt and collection expenses
664	Contributions
665	Licenses and fees
666	Accounting fees
667	Business insurance expense
668	Interest expense
669	Taxes—general
670	Occupancy expenses
671	Rent
672	Utilities
690	Accrued expenses—year-end adjustments
691	Depreciation expense
692	Leasehold improvements

FINANCIAL STATEMENTS

Financial statements are the formal outputs of any accounting system. Users must rely on the integrity of the system of accounts and accurate recording of all transactions in the financial statements as a basis for making rational decisions concerning the future of the travel agency. Depending on the decisions to be made, users may turn to either the balance sheet or income statement for information.

The Balance Sheet

The balance sheet presents the financial position of the travel agency at a point in time and therefore is often more correctly known as a statement of financial position. It details the resources of the firm (assets) and how they are financed, either by those lending funds to the agency (liabilities) or by those investing capital in the enterprise (equity). The balance sheet, therefore, is merely an extension of the fundamental equation of all accounting: Assets must always equal the sum of liabilities plus owners' equity.

A sample balance sheet is presented in Exhibit 8.4. It is built upon the definitions of assets, current and long-term; liabilities, current and long-term; and equities as defined in the chart of accounts. The definitions change between the bookkeeping and more formal accounting phases.

The balance sheet conveys much useful information to the reader, and for this reason, various tools for analyzing financial statements are discussed in Chapter 9. However, some aspects of Exhibit 8.4 can be highlighted as an indication of this statement's usefulness.

An agency's *working capital* is defined as the difference between current assets and current liabilities. The PAX Travel Agency has $45,000 in working capital, indicating that in general it has the ability to pay bills as they come due in the short run. The working capital position of the PAX agency is important in at least two other regards: (1) IATA minimum working capital requirements are met and (2) bonding agent requirements will be met.

The balance sheet can monitor the status of the PAX Travel Agency in several regards beyond whether it is meeting conference and bonding requirements. The general performance of progress of agency operations can be determined through periodic comparisons of balance sheets at different points in time. These comparisons also become useful in controlling cash, receivable, and payable account positions.

The P & L Statement

While the balance sheet offers a point-in-time snapshot view of an agency's assets, liabilities, and equities, the profit and loss (P & L) statement, also known as the income statement, provides information on an agency's profitability over a given time period, for example, a month, quarter, or year. (See Exhibit 8.5.) The varied use of the terms *income* and *profits* in published reports often causes confusion, so it is helpful to clarify each of the items in a P & L statement.

EXHIBIT 8.4

PAX TRAVEL AGENCY
BALANCE SHEET
DECEMBER 31, 19XX

Assets

Current assets		
Cash	$23,000	
Accounts receivables	40,000	
Marketable securities	20,000	
Prepaid expenses and deposit	2,000	
Total current assets		$85,000
Long-term assets		
Automobile	$7,500	
Furniture and fixtures	4,500	
Equipment	6,500	
Other assets	2,500	
Total long-term assets		21,000
Total assets		$106,000

Liabilities

Current liabilities		
Accounts payable	35,000	
Accrued expenses payable	3,000	
Accrued taxes payable	2,000	
Total Current Liabilities		$40,000
Long-term liabilities—notes payable		5,000
Total liabilities		$45,000

Equities

Paid-in capital	$60,000	
Retained earnings	1,000	
Total equities		61,000
Total liabilities and equities		$106,000

EXHIBIT 8.5

PAX TRAVEL AGENCY
INCOME STATEMENT
FOR YEAR ENDED DECEMBER 31, 19XX

Revenues		$1,507,000
Payments to carriers/suppliers		– 1,371,400
Commission income		$ 135,600
Operating expenses:		
Salaries	$50,000	
Administrative and office	33,900	
Selling	12,400	
Total operating expenses		– 96,300
Net income before tax		39,300
Income tax expense		– 8,300
Net income after tax		$ 31,000

Revenues is usually the first item listed on an income statement. The amount of revenues is a measure of total agency sales, and provides an indicator of the volume of business transacted during the time period under consideration. The revenues reported in the income statement would exclude any refunds or cancellations. Revenues generated from sales should not be confused with commissions and other income to an agency, that is, the monies that an agency receives for its services.

The second major item shown in Exhibit 8.5 is payments to carriers and suppliers, also referred to as *cost of sales*—equivalent to the *cost of goods sold* category used in statements for other retail businesses. The payments reflect the amount remitted to carriers and suppliers for airline tickets, tours, and hotel rooms that were sold to agency clients.

Revenues may indicate volume, but commission income is a more accurate measure of an agency's performance. Commission income is the monies which an agency receives from carriers and suppliers for its services. It is equal to revenues minus payments to carriers and suppliers. Commission income would also include any overrides and incentives earned during the time period covered. The term *gross profit* is often used instead of commission income to describe the monies received by an agency for its services. Gross profit is a better description of agency income, especially when an agency earns income from other sources as well as commissions.

The next major item following income is *operating expenses*, which include the cost of personnel, supplies, office space, brochures, advertising, telex, and other resources used in the course of doing business. An agency is producing net income or profits if commission income exceeds total operating expenses. Losses occur when operating expenses exceed income.

Net income is the amount that people generally think of as profits for an agency. However, the amount of monies actually available may be substantially reduced due to federal, state, and local taxes on business profits. The net income remaining after taxes can be used to pay dividends to owners or to increase owners' equity as retained earnings, which is shown on the balance sheet as an increase in the owners' net worth.

From a management perspective, the income statement provides important data for financial planning and monitoring agency performance against planned profit goals. Information from both the balance sheet and income statement is used to assess the financial well being of an agency, a subject which is discussed in Chapter 9.

Statement of Changes in Financial Position

The final basic financial statement is known as the Statement of Changes in Financial Position, which details the sources and uses or application of funds moving into and out of the agency. In essence, the statement further explains how working capital accounts, as defined above, change over the course of an accounting period.

SUMMARY

Accounting is a systematic way of recording, summarizing, and reporting financial information concerning the internal operations of the travel agency. It is the basis for all important documents concerning the financial health or position of the organization, providing information for five basic groups of users: the agency owner(s), creditors or lenders, travel suppliers, agency management, and the government. Each group of users will require or emphasize different aspects of the financial reports.

In the basic accounting system, good bookkeeping—the routine recording of all business transactions—is essential and requires in its simplest format the use of three primary journals: Sales/Cash Receipts, Disbursements, and Payroll. The ASTA system, on the other hand, provides a more elaborate classification of accounts and has been designed to assist the generation of ARC reports and facilitate adoption of agency back-office computer systems. Regardless of the system adopted by an agency, all transactions must be recorded consistently and must account for funds that the agency earns, spends, owes, and retains. The inflow and outflow of funds may be recorded into five basic types of accounts, including assets, liabilities, capital, income, and expense.

Finally, the data generated by the accounting system will provide information for the Balance Sheet—a point-in-time picture of the financial health of the agency—and the Profit and Loss Statement—a report on the agency's profitability over a given period of time—as well as for other financial reports desired by management. In the next chapter, we will discuss financial controls that rely on sound accounting as the basis for making strategic and short-term financial decisions to safeguard the economic viability of the agency.

DISCUSSION QUESTIONS

1. Who are the primary users of financial statements? How do their interests differ?
2. What are the criteria against which accounting systems are measured?
3. What types of reports are needed by travel agency managers in addition to financial statements?
4. What are the primary source documents in the ASTA accounting system?
5. What are the five primary categories of accounts in any chart of accounts?

ENDNOTES

[1]C. T. Fay, R. C. Rhoads, and R. L. Rosenblatt, *Managerial Accounting for the Hospitality Service Industries*, 2nd ed. (Dubuque, IA: Wm. C. Brown Publishers, 1976), p. 29.

[2]D. L. Madden, *Management Accounting for the Travel Agency Executive* (Wellesley, MA: Institute of Certified Travel Agents, 1978), pp. 11–13.

[3]P. G. Davidoff and D. S. Davidoff, *Financial Management for Travel Agencies* (Albany, NY: Delmar Publishers, Inc., 1988), pp. 71–84.

[4]Touche Ross & Co., *ASTA Travel Agency Accounting and Information System* (Washington, DC: American Society of Travel Agents, 1979), pp. 2.1–2.14.

SUPPLEMENTAL READINGS

BATHAM, M. J., *Guide to Travel Agency Accounting*. Wheaton, IL: Merton House Publishing Company, 1979.

MONCARZ, E. S., and N. J. PORTOCARRERO, *Financial Accounting for Hospitality Management*. Westport, CT: AVI Publishing Co., Inc., 1986.

chapter 9

Financial Analysis and Controls

LEARNING OBJECTIVES

- To understand financial ratio analysis for travel agencies
- To understand break-even analysis and be able to calculate the break-even point for an agency
- To understand cash flow analysis and develop the cash flow statement for an agency
- To recognize how long-term and short-term financial planning work together to help a travel agency manage its resources
- To know pro forma income statements and how to assess the return on investment in an agency

KEY TERMS

- Accounting Rate of Return
- Activity Ratios
- Break-Even
- Cash Flow
- Cash Flow Statement
- Collection Period

- Committed Fixed Costs
- Contribution Margin
- Current Ratio
- Debt-Equity Ratio
- Discounted Cash Flow Methods

- Fixed Assets Turnover
- Fixed Costs
- Leverage Ratios
- Liquidity Ratios
- Payback Period
- Profitability Ratios
- Profit Margin

- Pro Forma Income Statement
- Return on Assets
- Return on Equity
- Semifixed
- Times Interest Earned
- Total Assets Turnover
- Variable Costs

INTRODUCTION

Money and skilled personnel are the two fundamental resources of a travel agency. The latter, however, is often better understood than the former, especially in the small travel organization without a professional fiscal officer on its staff. For an agency to succeed, management must have at least basic knowledge of financial management, recognizing that profit margins tend to be narrow in the sales of most travel products.

Travel agencies can encounter problems with their finances due to the high volume of high-cost–low-yield transactions involved in servicing clients, meeting weekly cash flow needs, and achieving planned profit goals. Financial mismanagement can lead quickly to disaster since travel agencies generally have limited assets to secure extended borrowing from banks or other financial institutions. Proper financial management, moreover, provides the basis for informed decision making and can identify opportunities to improve an agency's profitability.

This chapter will complete our previous discussion on agency accounting and familiarize readers with key concepts concerning financial management for travel agencies. The chapter covers financial ratio analysis as a basis for analyzing the financial health of an agency and then considers investment decision making and financial planning and control. The emphasis is focused on the application of key concepts and principles, using a small agency example to simplify understanding.

FINANCIAL RATIOS

The underlying premise in analyzing financial ratios is that they are key indicators of a company's financial health. Ratios can be analyzed at one point in time and also over several time periods to identify any trends. To the extent that data are available, it is also useful to compare one's own situation with industry averages. Four types of ratios are usually calculated to analyze specific aspects of an agency's performance: liquidity ratios, activity ratios, leverage ratios, and profitability ratios.

Liquidity Ratios

An agency must be able to pay its bills on time in order to remain in business. Liquidity ratios provide measures of an agency's ability to meet its immediate obligations and to survive any unexpected short-run financial needs. The two most commonly used liquidity ratios are the current ratio and quick ratio.

The current ratio compares current assets to current liabilities. Current assets as shown for the PAX Travel Agency in Exhibit 9.1 include cash, accounts receivable, marketable securities, and prepaid expenses. Current liabilities include accounts payable, accrued expenses, and accrued taxes. The current ratio is calculated by dividing current assets by current liabilities as in this example:

$$\text{Current Ratio} = \frac{\text{Current Assets}}{\text{Current Liabilities}}$$

$$= \frac{\$85,000}{\$40,000} = 2.1$$

A high current ratio is an indication that an agency can meet its current obligations. Low values, especially those less than one, may foretell the possibility of short-run financial difficulties. In manufacturing companies where inventory is considered a current asset, the quick ratio, which considers only liquid assets such as cash, receivables, and marketable amenities, is also determined to account for the fact that unsold inventory is not as rapidly convertible to cash. Travel agencies typically do not have a physical inventory of products; therefore, the current ratio will suffice.

Activity Ratios

Activity ratios provide measures of how well an agency manages its assets. These ratios are also called turnover ratios because they reveal how rapidly assets are converted, that is, turned over into revenues. High turnover ratios are generally associated with good asset management. The two turnover ratios calculated below are the fixed assets turnover and total assets turnover. A third measure of asset management is the collection period, which indicates the efficiency of an agency's collection policy.

Using the data from Exhibits 9.1 and 9.2, the fixed assets turnover of the PAX Travel Agency example is calculated by

$$\text{Fixed Assets Turnover} = \frac{\text{Revenues}}{\text{Fixed Assets}}$$

$$= \frac{\$1,507,000}{\$21,000} = 71.7$$

EXHIBIT 9.1

PAX TRAVEL AGENCY
BALANCE SHEET
DECEMBER 31, 19XX

Assets

Current assets

Current liabilities

Accounts payable	$35,000	
Accrued expenses payable	3,000	
Accrued taxes payable	2,000	

Total current liabilities — $40,000

Long-term assets:

Automobile	$7,500	
Furniture and fixtures	4,500	
Equipment	6,500	
Other assets	2,500	

Total long-term assets — 21,000

Total assets — $106,000

Liabilities

Cash	$23,000	
Accounts receivable	40,000	
Marketable securities	20,000	
Prepaid expenses and deposit	2,000	

Total current assets — $85,000

Long-term liabilities—notes payable — 5,000

Total liabilities — $45,000

Equities

Paid-in capital	$60,000	
Retained earnings	1,000	

Total equities — 61,000

Total liabilities and equities — $106,000

Similarly, the total assets turnover is

$$\text{Total Assets Turnover} = \frac{\text{Revenues}}{\text{Total Assets}} = 14.2$$

Turnover ratios for agencies tend to be relatively high because only minimal physical assets are necessary. Comparable ratios for manufacturing companies may range as low as 1.3 to 2.0 due to their requirements for large plants and equipment. The theory is that high assets turnover indicates high productivity output from assets, thus, the higher the ratio, the better the utilization in assets.

The collection period is calculated as follows:

$$\text{Collection Period} = \frac{(\text{Receivables}) (365)}{\text{Revenues}}$$

$$= \frac{(\$40,000) (365)}{\$1,507,000} = 9.7 \text{ days}$$

The PAX Travel Agency's collection period of 9.7 days would indicate an effective collection policy for an agency since the bulk of agency sales, that is, airline tickets, must be remitted each week. The extension of credit may result in additional sales, but then the cost of providing credit to clients and potential cash flow problems must be accounted for.

Leverage Ratios

Leverage ratios measure the extent to which an agency has financed its investment by borrowing. Debt financing usually increases the risk of investment in an agency so that a high leverage ratio is associated with more risk. A low ratio, on the other hand, may mean poor leverage. There are times when it is more advantageous to use borrowed capital than one's own funds, for instance, when the return from operations is much higher than the cost of debt and one's own funds can be put to other profitable use. The leverage ratio presented below is the debt-equity ratio, and the debt-servicing ratio discussed is times interest earned.

The debt-equity ratio compares the total debt of an agency to owners' equities. Referring again to our example of PAX Travel Agency, Exhibit 9.1, the debt-equity ratio would be:

$$\text{Debt-Equity Ratio} = \frac{\text{Debt}}{\text{Equity}}$$

$$= \frac{\$45,000}{\$61,000} = 0.74$$

A ratio exceeding one would mean that an agency financed its investments with more debt than equity. In the above example, a ratio of 0.74 indicates that more equity than debt was used to invest in the agency.

EXHIBIT 9.2

PAX TRAVEL AGENCY
INCOME STATEMENT
FOR YEAR ENDED DECEMBER 31, 19XX

Revenues		$1,507,000
Payments to carriers/suppliers		– 1,371,400
Commission income		$ 135,600
Operating expenses:		
Salaries	$50,000	
Administrative and office	33,900	
Selling	12,400	
Total operating expenses		– 96,300
Net income before tax		39,300
Income tax expense		– 8,300
Net income after tax		$ 31,000

Times interest earned provides a measure of an agency's ability to service its debts. Assuming that PAX Travel Agency had $500 in interest expense, then times interest earned would be computed as follows:

$$\text{Times Interest Earned} = \frac{\text{Net Operating Income}}{\text{Interest Expense}}$$

$$= \frac{\$39,000}{\$500} = 78.6$$

A high times interest earned ratio indicates that an agency can easily pay its interest obligations. Creditors obviously would prefer a high ratio for times interest earned but a low ratio for debt-equity.

Profitability Ratios

Profitability ratios describe an agency's past profitability. The correlation between past and future profitability is subject to speculation, so a single year's profitability should not be taken to forecast future performance. In business there are no guarantees, but long-term profitability can be a fair indication of sound management and a healthy agency. The three most common profitability ratios are profit margin, return on assets, and return on equity.

Profit margin shows the percent of every sales dollar that an agency was able to convert into net income—the bottom line. In the case of PAX

Travel Agency, the profit margin was

$$\text{Profit Margin} = \frac{\text{Net Income after Tax}}{\text{Sales}}$$

$$= \frac{\$31,000}{\$1,507,000} = 2.1 \text{ percent}$$

Return on assets measures how profitably an agency used its assets. From Exhibits 9.1 and 9.2,

$$\text{Return on Assets} = \frac{\text{Net Income after Tax}}{\text{Total Assets}}$$

$$= \frac{\$31,000}{\$106,000} = 29.2 \text{ percent}$$

Return on equity indicates the rate of return earned on the book value of owner's equity. That is,

$$\text{Return on Equity} = \frac{\text{Net Income}}{\text{Equity}}$$

$$= \frac{\$31,000}{\$61,000} = 50.8 \text{ percent}$$

Both the return on assets and return on equity are relatively high in the example given, but this assumes only a minimum investment in the agency operations and has not taken into account possible losses and/or lower income for other years, as discussed later under financial planning.

FINANCIAL TARGETS AND CONTROLS

In order to achieve financial success, agency management must be able to determine the minimum volume of sales necessary to cover costs. Break-even analysis can be used to establish financial targets as guide posts to achieve the desired level of profits. On the controls side, an agency needs minimum liquidity (that is, cash on hand) to stay in business. An agency with successful sales can still falter if it does not have the cash to support its volume of sales. Cash flow analysis is used to deal with temporary cash shortages during the normal course of an agency's business. Both of these techniques are covered below.

Break-Even Analysis

The concept underlying break-even analysis is that an agency should generate sufficient income to cover total operating expenses. As simple as the concept may seem, its application requires a solid understanding of the sources of agency revenues, the nature of agency costs, and the capacity of agency resources. The ultimate goal would be to not only cover operating costs but also generate profits for owners to earn an adequate return on their investment.

Before describing the techniques of break-even analysis, the complexities involved in applying it realistically should be discussed. For travel agencies, revenues from a different mix of clientele will have different performance implications and thus different cost incurrence. Commercial clients who are apt to change itineraries, sometimes up to the last minute, need up-to-date information, making access to computerized reservations almost a minimum requirement if they are to be properly served. Rewriting of tickets or carrying large commercial accounts beyond ten days also adds to the cost of doing business. Dealing with seasoned vacation travelers who want expert counseling would require knowledgeable and experienced staff who may command higher salaries. Selling international travel requires higher expertise than selling only domestic travel. Clients' needs, therefore, will determine to some extent the type of skilled resources an agency must have to be successful. In turn, the quantity and quality of resources will affect the level of operating costs.

Classification of agency costs. The operating costs of an agency can be categorized according to their relationship to changes in volume, measured by sales and number of clients served. In analyzing the nature of agency costs, it is important to specify the planning or budgeting period under consideration and the extent of discretion that management has to change the type and/or level of cost incurred. The planning period could be a month, a quarter, or a year. The shorter the planning period, the larger the proportion of costs that will be constant or "fixed" over a given range of sales. If management has little or no discretion to change the type or level of cost over the planning period, then most of the costs should be treated as more or less fixed. Labor cost, for instance, is often treated as a variable cost. If an agency is operating at the minimum staffing level, however, management does not have much discretion in reducing labor costs; in this case, labor costs are essentially fixed.

The actual behavior of costs over the planning period and management's discretion to change them are determining factors in realistically categorizing the nature of specific agency costs. Agencies in general do not have high capital expenditures. Their level of fixed costs is substantially lower than that of other travel businesses such as airlines, hotels, and ground transportation companies. The cost structure of an agency also can be modified within a short time period, since few of the expenditures involve extensive planning or construction time.

Fixed costs of an agency. Nevertheless, for management purposes, many of the expenditures tend to be fixed for a given range of output or level of services. Fixed costs are those that remain constant regardless of the level of sales expected (or achieved) during the planning period. Two types of fixed costs can be distinguished: committed and discretionary or budgeted.

Committed fixed costs are expenses that management cannot change over the planning period, and they concern maintaining the organization to conduct agency business. Examples of committed fixed costs would be rent, insurance, and equipment. Salaries for a minimum staffing level also can be considered to be committed fixed costs up to a certain volume of sales, beyond which additional staff would be necessary. Discretionary or budgeted fixed costs include items such as advertising, sales promotions, employee training, and market research, which have been budgeted at a fixed level over the planning period. These discretionary costs are fixed in the sense that they have been allocated in advance and do not change with sales. They are discretionary only to the extent that management is able to change the budgeted amounts in response to critical or unforeseen circumstances. In practice, many firms may budget on an annual basis but allow for quarterly and/or monthly revisions in allocated costs.

Variable costs of an agency.   Variable costs are the opposite of fixed costs, as they change in proportion to sales and clients served during the time period covered. The costs of delivering or mailing tickets to clients, making reservations, and collecting payments from clients are examples of an agency's variable costs. Within a given period, very few true variable costs exist in agency operations. Many expenses instead have both fixed and variable elements and are considered semivariable. Items like telephone, fax, and telex charges, for instance, have fixed monthly charges plus per-unit charges for long-distance calls and each telex sent. If the fixed and variable components can be separated, they should be allocated to the respective categories before analyzing the cost structure of an agency.

The figures presented in Exhibit 9.2 are based upon a small agency of three persons located in an urban area. Salaries, rent, and other expenses will differ by location, but the nature of the costs, that is, fixed, variable, semivariable, would be similar. In the example presented, approximately 85 percent of the total operating expenses are considered to be fixed (committed or discretionary) costs that are necessary to maintain a basic organization over the planning period. The remaining 15 percent represent variable costs. In order to reduce the level of fixed costs, elements of the basic organization, such as the number of staff, equipment, and so on, would have to be modified. The high proportion of fixed costs in this example does not allow much leeway with regard to achieving a break-even volume of sales, which is covered next.

Break-even sales volume.   The break-even volume of sales can be expressed in terms of dollar sales volume and/or the volume of sales transactions. The break-even dollar sales volume provides a useful guideline in establishing targets for sales revenues. Sometimes overlooked, the break-even volume of sales transactions is critical for evaluating the adequacy of an agency's physical resources to handle the target volume of sales. It also provides the basis for measuring the productivity of agency resources, such as the number of sales transactions per staff and the average required number of weekly sales.

In calculating the break-even volume of sales, a manager has to depend upon the budgeted or estimated costs for the time period under consideration. Past experience and historical records may assist in developing cost estimates; however, these estimates are typically subject to revisions as an agency encounters unanticipated changes or events during the operating cycle. As costs are revised, the break-even volume of sales also must be revised accordingly to reflect changes in budget estimates.

The break-even volume of sales transactions can be determined in several ways. One method uses a contribution approach, another uses a percentage margin approach, but all of the methods can be simplified to the basic break-even model as in the following outline.

TI: Total income, which in this case would be equal to commission income (to simplify the calculations, minor sources of noncommission income are excluded)

ACI: Average commission income per sale

TC: Total operating costs (excluding payments to carriers and suppliers)

FC: Total fixed costs

VC: Total variable costs

AVC: Average variable cost per sale

TC: $FC + VC$

Vb: Break-even volume of sales transactions

p: Planned profits

The break-even point would be where total income (TI) equals total costs (TC). The break-even volume can be derived as follows:

$$Vb = \frac{FC}{ACI - AVC}$$

The average contribution margin (ACM) would be equal to ACI — AVC, which alternatively could be expressed in percentage terms. Knowledge of average variable costs per sale is desirable for management to make rational decisions regarding commissions, pricing, and the volume of sales. Within the budgeted range of operations, average variable cost per sale (excluding payments to carriers and suppliers) can be roughly approximated by dividing total variable costs by the forecasted or expected total number of sales transactions for the time period.

To illustrate, using the figures from the PAX Travel Agency Exhibit 9.2, let us say that variable costs are equal to 15 percent of total operating expenses, which is $96,300, and the average commission earned is approximately 9 percent of total sales; that is, $135,600 divided by $1,507,000 is equal to 9 percent. Assuming that the average dollar amount per sale is $500, the average commission income per sale would be $45, with the average variable cost per sale being $4.79. The break-even volume of sales transactions would be

$$Vb = \frac{FC}{ACI - AVC}$$

$$= \frac{(\$96,300)(.85)}{\$45 - \$4.79} = \frac{\$81,855}{\$40.21}$$

$$= 2037 \text{ Sales Transactions}$$

Assuming that the planning period is one year, the break-even volume indicates that the PAX Agency must average approximately 39 sales averaging $500 per travel invoice each week, generating $19,500 in target sales revenues and $1755 in commission income. The influence of seasonality can be incorporated into the sales targets by assessing historical patterns in sales. In addition, the sales targets in both dollar amounts and number of sales transactions can be used as guidelines in evaluating the productivity of agency resources. With two salespersons, the number of weekly sales per staff would have to average, for example, about twenty-one sales per salesperson or $10,000 in sales revenues. The analysis also can be extended to compare the amount of income generated per dollar of resource cost for each cost item under consideration.

Planned profit goals. Break-even analysis can easily incorporate planned profits in determining the desired volume of sales. Planned profits can be treated similarly to fixed costs in the sense that they are a requirement of doing business, reflecting a return on investment necessary to justify and maintain owners' or investors' capital in its present use. The volume of sales required to achieve planned profit goals (Vp) is

$$Vp = \frac{FC + p}{ACI - AVC}$$

Let us assume for illustration purposes that a before-tax profit (p) of $45,000 is desired. To account for the planned profits, the previous figures would be adjusted as follows:

$$Vp = \frac{FC + p}{ACI - AVC}$$

$$= \frac{\$81,855 + \$45,000}{\$45 - \$4.79}$$

$$= 3155 \text{ Sales Transactions}$$

With a planning period of one year, the planned profit volume indicates that the agency now must average about 61 sales per week, generating $30,500 in target sales revenues, in order to achieve the planned profits of $45,000. The revised target sales figures similarly can be extended as guidelines for assessing the productivity of agency staff and other resources.

Break-even analysis provides a useful technique for analyzing sales volume and managing agency resources profitably over a given planning period. The financial status of an agency, discussed in the next two sections on cash flow analysis and financial planning, also must be closely monitored.

Cash Flow Analysis

Unlike many other businesses that may purchase on monthly credit, travel agencies must operate on a cash basis for payment of airline tickets which comprise a substantial, if not the largest, proportion of their sales. While the actual cash might not be drawn against an agency's bank account until a week later due to the time lag in the clearing process, the cycle of payment is established on a weekly basis. Given the importance of air ticket sales, an agency's cash flow cycle is usually structured to account for air ticket payments.

Cash flow analysis is critical to agency operations, especially for those with limited assets to secure additional borrowing on short notice. The weekly cycle is such that the financial situation of an agency is very sensitive to changes in the daily inflow of cash. An agency must meet its airline ticket payments or risk losing its appointment from the respective airline conferences.

Managing an agency's cash flow begins with the projections of both inflows and outflows of cash. Past performance provides a starting point for developing the projections. Additional information on the payment schedule for budgeted costs, collection cycle on accounts receivables, and trends in recent sales is also needed to improve the accuracy of the projections. In the present deregulated environment, unexpected changes are common, and management judgment is an important factor in developing projections.

Before detailing the technique of cash flow analysis, it should be emphasized that its purpose is to provide advance knowledge of an agency's expected cash situation so that management can plan appropriate courses of action. Periods of cash surpluses, for instance, can be opportunities for short-term investments to enhance agency profitability. Anticipated cash deficits must be handled by carrying over surplus cash from other time periods or arranging for short-term borrowing.

Exhibit 9.3 provides an example of projected cash outflows for an agency. The projections are usually summarized in a monthly statement covering each week separately. They can be combined with projections of cash inflow to generate a cash flow statement, which is shown in Exhibit 9.4.

EXHIBIT 9.3

PAX TRAVEL AGENCY
PROJECTED CASH OUTFLOW FOR AUGUST 19XX

Projected outflows	Week 1	Week 2	Week 3	Week 4
Airline ticket payments	$20,000	$20,000	$12,000	$17,000
Payments to other suppliers	5,000	3,000	5,000	2,000
Payroll (15th and 30th)		1,500		1,500
Operating expenses				
Rent	400			
Telephone and telex			200	
Advertising	200			
Other			300	
Periodic expenses				
Travel				500
Insurance	400			
Printing and mailing		800		
Total	$26,000	$25,300	$17,500	$21,000

EXHIBIT 9.4

PAX TRAVEL AGENCY
CASH FLOW STATEMENT FOR AUGUST 19XX

	Week 1	Week 2	Week 3	Week 4
Projected cash inflows				
Cash/credit card sales	$17,500	$16,100	$11,900	$13,300
Collections on accounts	10,500	9,000	8,500	6,000
Total inflows	$28,000	$25,100	$20,400	$19,300
Projected cash outflows				
Airline ticket payments	$20,000	$20,000	$12,000	$17,000
Payments to other suppliers	5,000	3,000	5,000	2,000
Rent and payroll	400	1,500	—	1,500
Subtotal:	$25,400	$24,500	$17,000	$20,500
Other expenses	600	800	500	500
Total outflows	$26,000	$25,300	$17,500	$21,000
Cash surplus <deficit>	$ 2,000	<$200>	$ 2,900	<$1,700>

The cash flow statement should be reviewed weekly to verify the agency's situation and update projections as necessary.

With computerization, an agency can easily ascertain its cash situation, which enables management to control it more effectively. It should also be noted that an agency must review its credit policies for its clients carefully to ensure that clients' accounts warrant extension of credit. In most instances, credit should not be extended. Most clients find it convenient to charge travel on their Travel and Entertainment (T & E) credit cards such as American Express and Diners Club, or bank cards such as Visa and Master Charge, which allow them thirty days or more for payment. But the agency can quickly convert credit card sales into cash without penalty since airline carriers pay the credit card discount. An agency's cash situation is such that extending its own thirty day's credit to clients would be costly.

In analyzing cash inflows and outflows, summaries can be prepared for various time periods—a week, a month, a quarter, or a year according to management information needs. The longer time periods allow management to analyze trends in cash receipts and disbursements and anticipate the cash situation several months in advance to implement plans for appropriate action. The following section discusses forward financial planning extending beyond one year.

Long-Term Financial Planning

In order to assess the amount of resources needed for an agency's growth, management must plan beyond its current year by developing projections of agency operations over future years. Annual projections for the upcoming year are augmented by longer-term projections covering two to five years into the future. The longer-term projections attempt to identify the growth pattern of agency operations, additional resources needed to support growth, agency profitability, and return on investment. The latter is of particular importance to owners' and/or investors' capital budgeting decisions regarding alternative uses of funds.

Developing financial projections for future years is at times mistaken as a "numbers game" involving only the manipulation of financial data to correspond with profit objectives. If developed properly, the financial projections in fact reflect a complex set of assumptions regarding future demand for agency services, changes in operating expenses, resource capacities, and the competitive environment. Changes in the travel industry are highly dynamic—so much so that the accuracy of projections is likely to decrease with the length of the projection time period. Experienced judgment is necessary to develop realistic projections of future operations, and the projections must be updated in light of new trends.

Long-term financial planning is essentially for the purpose of developing strategies in anticipation of projected agency growth and establishing financial goals against which agency performance may be assessed. Moreover, the projected amount of resources and estimated profitability provide information for investors to assess the risk of operating the agency vis-à-vis adequate return on their investment.

Pro forma income statement.   A variety of projected or pro forma statements are developed for long-term financial planning. The discussion here focuses on the pro forma income statement since it summarizes projected agency performance with respect to sales, expenses, and profits. A condensed five-year pro forma income statement for a new agency is presented in Exhibit 9.5.

As is evident from the projected pattern of growth for PAX Travel Agency in Exhibit 9.5, the agency is expected to lose money during the first year when it is just beginning to develop its client base. This situation is similar to the introduction stage of the product life cycle and also has relevance to the learning curve since sales are affected by staff skills and experience. The agency will recover almost all of the first year losses by the end of the second year and is expected to be profitable from the third year onward. The expected profits are based on sales doubling in the second year and continuing to increase to more than threefold in volume over year one by year four. Costs, on the other hand, are expected to increase by only one and one-half times over the five-year period.

With a first-year loss of $22,700, the agency probably has to be capitalized at a minimum between $50,000 and $60,000 to meet conference requirements, bonding, and cash flow needs. Otherwise, it will not survive the first year, and subsequent years of projected profitability will never materialize. New agencies are frequently overly optimistic about initial sales and fail due to undercapitalization, which prevents them from surviving a full year of losses.

Return on investment.   In regard to financial goals, the return on investment in the agency can be calculated and compared to a minimum target rate of return acceptable to investors and/or the cost of capital. The accounting rate of return is equal to the average net income after tax (NIAT) divided by the initial investment in the agency. Assuming an initial investment of $60,000, the average rate of return based on the net income after-tax projections for the five-year pro forma in Exhibit 9.5 is as follows:

$$\text{Accounting Rate of Return} = \frac{(\sum_{i=1}^{n} NIAT_t)/n}{\text{Initial Investment}}$$

$$\text{ARR} = \frac{\overset{\text{Yr.1}}{(-\$22,700} + \overset{\text{Yr. 2}}{0} + \overset{\text{Yr. 3}}{\$21,200} + \overset{\text{Yr. 4}}{\$31,000} + \overset{\text{Yr. 5}}{\$26,000})/5}{\$60,000}$$

$$= 18.7 \text{ percent}$$

EXHIBIT 9.5

PAX TRAVEL AGENCY
FIVE-YEAR PRO FORMA INCOME STATEMENT

	Year 1	Year 2	Year 3	Year 4	Year 5
Revenues (sales)	$490,000	$1,090,000	$1,308,000	$1,507,000	$1,658,000
Commission income	$ 44,100	$ 98,100	117,700	$ 135,600	$ 149,200
Less: operating expenses	–66,800	–75,800	–90,600	–96,300	–102,500
Net income <loss>	< –22,700 >	22,300	27,100	39,300	46,700
Loss carried forward	– – –	–22,300	–400	– – –	– – –
Net income before tax	– – –	0	26,700	39,300	46,700
Less: federal corp. tax	– – –	– – –	–4,100	–6,300	–7,700
	– – –	– – –	22,600	33,000	39,000
Less: state corp. tax	– – –	– – –	–1,400	–2,000	–2,300
Net income after tax	– – –	– – –	$ 21,200	$ 31,000	$ 26,700

The accounting rate of return, however, ignores the timing of the cash flows. Discounted cash flow methods such as the internal rate of return and net present value can be used to account for the time value of money, resulting in a lower rate of return than that calculated above. Furthermore, potential investors may view the initial loss of $22,700 and zero returns until the third year as high risk in view of the competitive environment and the industry failure of new agencies. Consequently, the pattern of growth may have negative attributes that may outweigh the expected rate of return, and investors should assess these factors in light of their respective situations.

Another method that can be used to evaluate the investment in an agency is the payback period, equal to the length of time required for earnings from an agency to return the initial investment. The initial investment of $60,000 in the previous example would not be returned or paid back until profits from a sixth year of operations are earned; that is, the net income after tax accrued over the five years would be only equal to $56,200 after accounting for the first-year loss of $22,700. A payback period of six years may be too long a time horizon for some investors since risk is usually perceived as increasing with time.

The payback period also can be used as a rule-of-thumb method for estimating the maximum rate of return for an investment. Assuming that operations will continue for at least twice the length of the payback period, the reciprocal of the payback period will provide an estimate of the maximum rate of return that can be expected from an investment. The payback for the example would be soon after the fifth year, so the maximum rate of return would be somewhere between 16.7 percent ($\frac{1}{6}$) and 20 percent ($\frac{1}{5}$). It should be cautioned that the actual rate of return achieved can be lower than the maximum rate estimated from the payback that defines the upper limit.

SUMMARY

From a management perspective, the reasonableness of the projections must be evaluated in regard to market potential, resource capacities, and structure of the agency. Here, experienced management, operational knowledge, and judgment about the marketplace are critical to ensure that the financial projections are attainable. Each year's financial targets with regard to sales, expenses, and profits must be further detailed in quarterly, monthly, and weekly projections for the current year of operations. Long-term financial planning is an ongoing process that provides the basis for short-term planning as it fits within the overall pattern of growth for future years. Rather than an end in itself, financial planning is actually the beginning point for the management of all agency resources.

DISCUSSION QUESTIONS

1. How are financial ratios used to assess the financial health of an agency?
2. How are agency costs classified?
3. How can break-even analysis be used to establish sales targets for an agency?
4. What method can be used to incorporate planned profit goals?
5. Why is cash flow analysis critical to an agency?
6. What factors should be considered in selecting a method for evaluating an investment for a new travel agency and an existing agency?

SUPPLEMENTAL READINGS

DAVIDOFF, P. G. AND D. S. DAVIDOFF, *Financial Management for Travel Agencies.* Albany, NY: Delmar Publishers, Inc., 1988.

MADDEN, D. L., *Management Accounting for the Travel Agency Executive.* Wellesley, MA: Institute of Certified Travel Agents, 1978.

STEVENS, LAURENCE, *Budgeting for Profit and Managing by Goals.* Wheaton, IL: Merton House Publishing company, 1982.

chapter 10

Travel Agency Automation

LEARNING OBJECTIVES

- To be able to state how automation has changed and continues to change the travel industry
- To understand the process of automation and how computerization works
- To know the major computer reservations systems (CRS) and the different methods of communication
- To define what functions or applications comprehensive travel agency automation may encompass

KEY TERMS

- Airline Tariff Publishing Company (ATPCO)
- Apollo
- Automation
- Biased Display
- Cathode Ray Tubes (CRT)
- Central Processing Unit (CPU)
- City-Pair
- Computerization
- Data Base Management System
- Floppy Disk
- Hard Disk
- Hardware
- Host Carrier
- Passenger Name Record (PNR)
- Point System
- Queue System

- Sabre
- Software
- Spreadsheet

- Telemarketing
- Turnkey System

INTRODUCTION

"Automation" is a slippery term, and in one sense it is nothing new to most travel agents. Copying machines, teleticketing machines, and more recently telefax machines are but a few examples of how agencies have adopted technology to improve operations. What is new to many agents is the automation of most primary functions in the office. Reservations, ticketing, accounting, and most forms of management reporting now can be done with the aid of the computer.

Computerization in travel agencies comprises many issues. Agenices first need to consider the process of automation, what it entails, its goals, and its impacts. Next is the question of how to automate. After management decides to support automation, the agency must evaluate vendor offerings, undertake financial planning, install the system, and train the staff. These decisions and activities arise most frequently when an agent is automating front-office functions, such as reservations capabilities.

The airline industry is at the forefront of travel industry automation and vigorously markets computer reservations systems (CRS) to travel agents. More recently, agents have been able to automate their control and management activities. Although not as widely used as reservations systems, back-office systems are making significant inroads into travel agency management. As the technology continues to evolve, improving computer capabilities while simultaneously reducing the cost of computers, travel agencies will strengthen their position as one of the most highly automated industries in the country.

THE PROCESS OF AUTOMATION

Automation can be defined as controlling a process by electronic or other devices, reducing human intervention to a minimum. A computer is an electrical apparatus capable of carrying out repetitious operations at high speeds. Computerization is controlling, storing, and performing operations on information by and in a computer. Merging these definitions, computerization is the control of repetitious processes by a computer. Much of travel agency operation is repetitive and therefore ideally suited to automation.

But in terms of systems selection, computers are more than what the simple deifinitions imply. Users must choose between mainframes, minicomputers, and microcomputers, and each is significantly different. Even within a particular category, such as microcomputers, significant differ-

Sheraton unveils Reservation I in 1958, the first automatic electronic reservations system to serve the hospitality industry.

ences exist between machines of the same manufacturer and, of course, between machines of different manufacturers. Peripherals must also be considered. A keyboard, mouse, and optical scanners may all be used to put data into the computer. Data may be output on display screens, printers, and teleticketing machines. All of these data must be stored in the computer's internal memory and external storage devices. Even after spending thousands of dollars on hardware, the user must also buy software, which provides the operating instructions for the hardware. For example, the sole purpose of some software is to permit each peripheral to communicate with the computer and with other computers. Each hardware and software option represents a choice for the travel agency managers.

Operational requirements provide some guidance for computer choices. The number of repetitive transactions, their nature and complexity, and the information to be derived from them define computer needs. Travel agents deal with hundreds of travel facts for each client served, and these data are inputs to the computing process. The computer in turn assists management in giving meaning to the data by turning them into information. The data, or information, needs of travel agency management establish what is needed from the computer.

Agency operations likewise define constraints on automation, as computers must work within the financial and physical environment of the agency. If what an agency wants from a computer is not financially feasible, the agency may have to redefine its computer needs or perhaps abandon computerization altogether. Even if automation is financially viable, the equipment simply may not fit in the office, and again, the manager may be forced to explore alternative avenues of automation. Finally, it must be remembered that some staff will be computerphobic; personnel assignments will change, and computers may eliminate some positions. These and other factors are part of the process of making decisions about automation.

Computers

Computers are defined in terms of four functional parts, which are shown in Figure 10.1. The central processing unit (CPU) is, technically speaking, the computer. It contains the microprocessor, which gives the computer its arithmetic and logic capabilities, and also houses internal memory where the computer stores programs, instructing the computer what to do, and

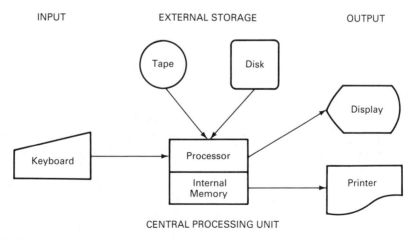

FIGURE 10.1   A simple computer system

information. The more information to be processed at one time and the more complex the processing, the larger the internal memory must be. Even simple functions require a lot of storage space; thus, memory is measured in multiples of 1024, represented by "K." A 64K computer has 65,536 internal memory positions, which would be the minimum available space necessary for business applications, although 640K is rapidly becoming the benchmark for basic systems.

Not all memory is readily available to the user. Read Only Memory (ROM), for example, cannot be changed by the user. Some programs are "burned" into ROM at the factory; for example, instructions on what the computer should do when it is first turned on are found in ROM. On the other hand, the user can write into and read from Random Access Memory (RAM), so if the manager were building an income statement on the computer, it would be in RAM.

There are limits to how far internal memory can practically be expanded. Beyond a certain point, it is more economical to store information externally rather than in internal memory. On some machines, information can be stored on cards and read into the computer's internal memory only when needed. This is a rather cumbersome form of external storage used for mainframe computers and is gradually being replaced. Early personal computers employed cassette tapes for external storage, but although relatively inexpensive, cassettes are generally too slow and awkward for business applications. Floppy and even hard disks are the norm for office use today. Floppy diskes, so-called because of their Mylar base, can be read very quickly by a disk reader, are easily stored, and can be transported. Hard disks provide even more external storage. It is not uncommon for a basic system to have a 10-megabyte hard disk capable of storing 10 million characters of information that can be accessed more quickly than on floppy disks. Its cost, however, makes it uneconomical for smaller offices.

Information is entered into internal memory and onto disks through a variety of input devices. A typewriter-like keyboard is the most common and inexpensive unit. Optical scanners are also being used more frequently. The technology long used in retail outlets, especially grocery markets, is being applied to other business tasks. Another device allows the user to read from any written page with a scanner that communicates the text to the computer. The most user-friendly input device is a voice-recognition unit, which, although somewhat limited, very expensive, and still in the infancy stage, will soon make it possible for people to talk to their computers in everyday language.

In most cases, the user wants to see what the computer has done. Cathode ray tubes (CRT) visually display to the user what has been written into, and output from, the computer. If a hard copy or paper copy of the output is required, printers for written text and plotters for graphics are available to meet most needs.

Software links all of the hardware together. Some software is application specific, such as financial analysis or word processing, while other software is the same regardless of the specific application, such as the operating system software. Programming done by users should be distinguished from prepackaged software that may be bought from a vendor and is available for most conceivable business tasks. Each option, just as with hardware choices, delineates the benefits to be derived from computerization.

Goals of Automation

The hardware and software components of a computer system can perform simple, repetitive tasks quickly and can reason to the extent that, for example, "2" is larger than "1" or "B" is after "A" in the alphabet. However, they cannot think; the travel agency manager must still define relevant input and output.

Automation may reduce or even eliminate many of the repetitious manual tasks that typify travel agency operations. Filing, sorting, counting, and other clerical functions are ideally suited to computerization. Once data is entered into memory, they may be accessed and analyzed anytime. The space saved from eliminating many paper records and the time saved from no longer maintaining and using these records may be redirected to more profitable activities, such as client services.

Computers also give the manager access to more information. New vendor services and fares are known before or as they occur, not afterward. Information formerly found piecemeal in the clutter of paper can now be used to better control operations and serve clients.

Current automation allows the agent to display worldwide airline schedules and fare information, make reservations, and price itineraries for customers. The same capabilities are available for the hotel, tour, car rental, rail, and cruise segments of the industry. The tickets, itineraries, and invoice documentation for each service booked can be mechanically produced. Even the most experienced agent cannot manually review product offerings, make the necessary phone calls, and manually write documents as fast as the computer. Automation saves valuable time and increases revenue potential. All told, it has been estimated that computers enhance agent productivity by up to 50 percent.

The basic documents of booking travel can serve as the basis of market research. Computers may be used to develop client profiles that track preferences on seating, hotel accommodations, car rentals, meals, and other travel variables, a capability that is increasingly important in marketing to both leisure and corporate clients.

Operational and internal control are also enhanced by automation. The manager can review weekly or monthly reports on total bookings by carrier and by segments, bookings by particular travel counselors, and hotel and car reservations. By monitoring clients and commissions, management is in a better position to make informed decisions on bad accounts and vendor incentives. Again, the effect is to improve profits and productivity.

Accounting and finance can also be improved. Not only can financial reports be produced more quickly but more accurately, improving internal control and client billing. Historic cash flow problems can be highlighted and unpaid commissions tracked down automatically on the computer. Furthermore, most computers allow managers to ask "what if" questions to determine the bottom-line effect of their decisions and enhance profit management.

Finally, a travel agency may decide to automate for the sake of competitiveness. With the vast majority of airline reservations now being made on computers, agents may find they must automate to maintain customer confidence, or they may just adopt computers due to the "me too" syndrome. The appearance of the documents presented to clients is also important. A mechanically produced itinerary and ticket or a graphics-enhanced report to a corporate client, detailing monthly travel expenditures, is likely to be perceived as more professional than one that is handwritten.

The benefits of automation do not come without cost. Space must be found in both the front and back office for computer equipment. Staff must be trained, costing the agency lost time and, possibly, additional money. Some personnel may become expendable with computerization, obviously presenting a human relations problem to management. Some employees may be inhibited by computers; others may not readily accept the altered maintenance records and redirected work schedules that are the inevitable result of computerization. In the end, the dollar outlay for equipment may thus actually be one of the least costly elements of automation. For these reasons, management must carefully consider how to automate.

How to Automate

The decision to automate and the automation process starts with top management. Given its expense and impact on operating costs and revenue, automation must be supported by the travel agency manager if it is to succeed. This process starts with identifying the goals of automation and where these goals are applicable in the agency's operations. Any activity that requires more accuracy, more frequent reporting, or more frequent communication than is currently possible is a candidate for automation. Similarly, any repetitious task requiring overtime or merely more time than seems reasonable should be considered for automation.

With the scope of activities defined, management is faced with a series of questions. They include: How many transactions must be performed? How many people perform these operations? What is the current cost of performing these functions? What is the revenue potential affected by the functions? Do these functions warrant the expense of automation? Are the necessary funds available to automate? Answers to these questions serve as the basis of an initial feasibility study. Management can consult trade publications, sales brochures, and other travel agents to provide preliminary answers to the questions raised and to determine which, if any, automation system meets the agent's needs.

Vendor selection. If automation appears feasible, the manager must decide on the type or types of vendor(s) to use. Some vendors offer the agent a turnkey system, providing hardware and preprogrammed software in a single package, which holds the advantage of being relatively convenient and simple for first-time users. The drawback is that the software has not been developed to meet the particular needs of each travel agency operation. To overcome this problem, some vendors offer a programmable system, providing the hardware and only very basic software. The agent is then able to develop operation-specific programs and gain flexibility at the cost of the additional personnel, training, and time associated with programming. If even more flexibility is desired, the hardware and software may be purchased separately to best suit the agent's needs. Another alternative is to buy computer time on another company's machine. This saves the capital cost of computers but may be more expensive in the long run, due to record maintenance costs and comparative lack of flexibility. Finally, the agency may use a combination of vendors to achieve its automation objectives.

When choosing a specific vendor, the travel agency should review and evaluate the vendor's financial statements, organizational chart, sales brochures, and users list. It is a headache to purchase a computer system one week and find the vendor has closed its doors the next. The vendor is a partner in automation, trouble shooting, debugging programs, offering advice, and performing required maintenance.

Other considerations. Next, the hardware and software must be considered. Besides being capable of performing what the manager hopes to acheive, it must be usable. The accompanying documentation must be thorough, clear, and user friendly. Unfortunately, some documentation is almost completely unintelligible to the computer user. Poor documentation is one of the major reasons why some machines are purchased and never used. For this reason, some vendors are including on-screen help messages with the computer and software; if a question arises, rather than turning to the user's manual, the user asks the computer for help in dealing with the problem. This is a particularly valuable form of documentation.

The after-sales service also needs to be evaluated. The amount and cost of training, the maintenance agreement, and the purchase or lease agreement vary from vendor to vendor. Each will affect the degree to which objectives are accomplished. Perhaps the best way to evaluate a company, its system, and its service support is to visit other travel agents where the system is used. They, more than documents, can say how successful the system is in use. Visits also help visualize how automation changes the physical layout and staff duties of an agency.

Finally, the manager must decide how to finance automation. Very few small agents are able to pay cash for a system, and even if sufficient funds are available, debt may be a more economical means of purchasing equipment. Alternatively, automation may be financed with a lease. The question of whether to purchase or lease depends upon the agency's working capital, the marginal tax rate, and the interest rate appropriate to the firm. In some instances, the after-tax cost of leasing may be less than the after-tax cost of buying, but in other circumstances, the reverse may be true.

The process of automation can and has taken many forms in travel agencies. Computers have been most successfully and widely employed in the sales functions as, spurred on by airlines, most travel information is available from and bookings made on computers. More recently, computers have been applied to other travel sectors and travel agency functions, including accounting and reporting. Each of these applications is discussed in the following sections.

AIRLINE RESERVATION SYSTEMS

Perhaps nothing is more critical to establishing a clientele and revenue base than continued access to accurate and timely information on air carrier schedules, fares, and seat availability. Prior to widespread automation, this information was obtained manually. The agent would determine client preferences with respect to all aspects of the flight and, using the *Official Airline Guide* (OAG), would identify which scheduled flights most closely matched the traveler's needs. With the OAG data in hand, the agent would refer to carrier tariffs to ascertain the applicable fares and restrictions. Finally, the agent would contact the carrier to confirm all information, make the reservation, and write the ticket for the traveler.

Due to the rapid growth of air travel in the 1960s, and the explosion of price and service offerings precipitated by airline deregulation in the 1970s, the dissemination of flight, fare, and seat availability via OAG, carrier tariffs, and the telephone became both cumbersome and inefficient. The computer technology that emerged during this period gave rise to the idea of making this information available to the travel sales distribution system via computer, as well as offering computerized reservations, ticket writing, and even accounting systems to appointed agents.

Today, airline computer reservations systems (CRS) are installed in some 95 percent of all agency locations, accounting for approximately 90 percent of airline revenues generated by travel agents. These systems evolved from a single effort to the point where five systems are marketed by airline vendors and one by a nonairline vendor. Each system has some common characteristics and some unique features, and all present opportunities and problems for the travel agency manager.[1]

Historical Perspective

The first attempt at developing a joint carrier, agent, and supplier CRS was the Donnelly Official Airline Reservation System (DOARS). Initiated in 1967, the DOARS soon failed when the parties could not agree on how to finance the development and installation of the system. The Automatic Travel Agency Reservations Systems (ATARS), begun in 1970, was the second effort at a common CRS. ATARS was slightly more successful than its predecessor, as it was submitted to the Civil Aeronautics Board (CAB) for review. Interestingly, the CAB was investigating the competitive implications of CRS when the parties to ATARS voided the joint agreement. Shortly thereafter, the Joint Industry Computerized Reservations System (JICRS) was proposed. This system was nearing completion in 1976 when first United, then American, and finally Trans World Airlines decided to individually place their Apollo, Sabre, and PARS CRS in travel agencies. The JICRS was continued by the American Society of Travel Agents (ASTA) and International Telegraph and Telephone, who renamed the system Mars Plus. This system was sold in 1981 to Tymshare which continues to market it; it is the only non-carrier-owned system currently available. Lastly, Eastern and Delta entered the CRS market with their Soda and Datas II systems in 1982.

Travel agents tended to resist the early systems. In particular, agents did not readily accept automation, especially CRS that were not jointly developed. To overcome this, Sabre, Apollo, and PARS initially contained information for most flights and almost all airlines, but even so, the economics of placing CRS in agency locations and continued travel agent apprehension restricted automation to high-volume agents. Only 4000 agencies had CRS by mid-year 1980.

Deregulation proved to be the spur necessary to gain wider acceptance of automation as airlines were forced to enhance their systems to keep pace with their rapidly changing industry. CRS were improved technologically and economically. Also, widely fluctuating airline fares, service, and tour package options helped travel agent management overcome its earlier hesitancy in accepting automation.

By 1988, 39,210 agency locations employed 168,460 airline reservations sets or CRTs.[2] Table 10.1 points out the importance of CRS and details several patterns. The vast majority of travel agents are automated, and most locations have more than one CRS set, with some using more than one vendor's system. Finally, the CRS market is dominated by Sabre and Apollo.

Ownership patterns are not as direct as when the systems were first developed and marketed. Single carrier distribution has tended to give way

TABLE 10.1   CRS USE IN THE UNITED STATES

System (vendor)	No. of (CRT)	Market share (pct. of CRT)	No. of locations	Market share (pct. of locations)
Sabre	62,000	36.80	14,000	35.71
Apollo	44,360	26.33	9,160	23.36
Pars	20,000	11.87	5,400	13.77
System I	28,100	16.68	7,150	18.24
Datas II	14,000	8.32	3,500	8.93
Total	168,460	100.00	39,210	100.00

Source: "Automation Report," *Travel Weekly,* August 22, 1988, p. 55.

to multiple carrier arrangements. System One, developed by Eastern, became part of the Texas Air Corporation conglomerate when the former was acquired by the latter. United has sold shares of its Apollo system to USAIR and a host of international air carriers. American considered selling one-half of its Sabre interest to Delta. TWA has likewise sold one-half interest in its system, in this case to Northwest.

Most of the U.S. systems have moved into the international arena, pairing with other international airlines to form even more far flung distribution systems. Delta is exploring cooperative ventures through Fantasia, a CRS developed by JAL, Quantas, and ANA. PARS carriers TWA and Northwest are participating in two international consortiums: (1) the Gemini CRS formed by Air Canada and Canada International, and (2) the Abacus system initiated by Singapore Airlines and Thai International. Recent agreements between Continental and SAS will bring System One into the Amadeus system developed by several European carriers. The competing Galileo CRS is participating with Apollo carriers. Only Sabre at the present time has remained relatively unaffiliated in the international marketplace.

General Operating Characteristics

CRS are essentially a sophisticated means of data collection, transmission, and analysis. Travel data are input into the system via a keyboard similar to that on a typewriter. The information is displayed on a cathode ray tube, or CRT. The keyboard/CRT set is linked to a small computer, the central processing unit or CPU, which is connected via a modem to telephone lines that communicate information to the airline computer.

Methods of communication.   Information can be communicated or transmitted to the carrier's CRS in several ways. Carriers marketing their own system provide for direct access to their computer, usually over dedicated electrical and telephone lines. If an agent wishes to make travel arrangements via the CRS on the CRS vendor, also known as the host carrier, communication between the agent and carrier is direct. If the agent wishes to book travel via the CRS on a carrier other than the CRS vendor, but the carrier is a co-host who has paid the host carrier for the privilege of being displayed in the system, then there is less direct, off-line communication. Aeronautical Radio, Inc., more commonly referred to as AIRINC, was incorporated in 1929 to meet the communications needs of the airline industry. Primarily owned by U.S. airlines, AIRINC provides services not only for the airline industry but for a variety of corporations and government agencies as well. For CRS, AIRINC provides switching services from the host carrier's computer to the co-host carrier's computer. To book a flight off line, the agent communicates directly with the host carrier's computer, which switches the message to a co-host carrier's computer via AIRINC. The response to the inquiry is communicated over AIRINC lines to the host computer, which then communicates with the agent's CPU and displays the information on the CRT.

Two other methods of communication are found in CRS. In some cases, the host and co-host carriers contract to provide direct communication between each other's computers. Rather than switching any intercarrier communications through AIRINC, the systems are linked directly, which may considerably enhance the accuracy and speed of data transmission.

The final method of communication with carrier computers is referred to as a multi-access reservation system. Multi-access systems permit agents to communicate directly with all carriers participating in the system. Reducing intercomputer communication further increases the speed and accuracy of data transmission. Of course, to access carriers who do not participate in the multi-access CRS, the agent returns to one of the three methods identified above: (1) direct to host; (2) offline, switched via AIRINC; and (3) off-line direct link to co-host.

Display and information formats.   The travel agent works with several types of travel information, or display formats, which are common to most CRS. Schedule, flight, and seat availability and fare displays are those typically available to agents. Schedules and availability are generally called up and displayed on the CRT, in response to an agent's queries on a city-pair (origin and destination) market arranged around requested time of departure or arrival. Along with flight and availability, the agent may request fare information in general, as well as fare and seat availability for a specific city-pair market and date. Additional variables, such as flight number, connecting cities, airline, the type of aircraft, and even meal service, may be used to delimit the information displayed on the CRT.

The schedule information format is based on the OAG, even in the age of automation. Carriers continue to submit their schedules, on computer tape and on "hard copy" or paper, to the OAG, which consolidates the information and makes it available to other carriers and travel agents, also on tape and/or hard copy. Those carriers purchasing tape load it or enter it into their in-house computer for use in their CRS. Alternatively, carriers submitting tape to the OAG may also give the tape directly to host carriers for display in the CRS.

The hard copy of the OAG contains both direct and connecting flights, on and off line. Typically, however, only direct flight information is used in CRS, whether from OAG tape or submitted directly to the host carriers. Host carriers program their system to construct connections through a specified list of connecting hubs. The program then constructs all possible connections through these points, taking into account connecting times and other information.

Fare formats are generated in a similar fashion. The Airline Tariff Publishing Company (ATPCO) is jointly owned and operated by airlines to consolidate, publish, and distribute fares and cargo rates, along with associated rules, to the travel industry. ATPCO tariffs are distributed to subscriber carriers on a daily basis, and carriers owning CRS load the ATPCO tariffs into their system. Again, some carriers may bypass the clearinghouse and submit hard copies or tape directly to host carriers.

The multiplicity of fares and rules makes fare construction very difficult for the ATPCO and CRS; therefore, some rules cannot be programmed into the computer and are given to host carriers on hard copy only. The carriers may then spend substantial time and effort programming these rules into the system, or the rules and tariffs may be eliminated from the CRS altogether.

Fare displays have been an area of controversy with CRS. The delay and deletion of fares due to the complexity of programming, according to host carriers, may mean that non-CRS-owning carriers are discriminated against. Some have also suggested that fare loadings are intentionally delayed to give host carriers time to review competitors' fares and to discourage their use by travel agents.

The final common information format is the seat availability format. Carriers can, of course, sell seats from their inventory, seats available on scheduled flights, through their own sales outlets—field ticket offices (FTO), city ticket offices (CTO), and centralized reservations offices—and through travel agents. Airlines also typically allow other carriers to sell tickets from their inventory of seats. Tickets sold in this manner are referred to as interline sales.

Interline sales are governed by agreements between participating carriers, allowing one carrier to sell seats on another. Each carrier maintains its own inventory of seats and controls whether a particular flight is open or closed for booking. For interline sales, the airline must communicate the availability status to its partners. As with schedule information, availability information is communicated or switched between carriers through AIRINC or directly for display on CRS.

Passenger name record and queue system.   If, using the flight, fare, and availability formats, the agent is able to make suitable travel arrangements, a passenger name record (PNR) is generated. The PNR, which remains in the carrier's location in a central site, basically represents a completed transaction and is a means of storing all information received from the computer. The PNR, usually consists of the following:

1. Passenger name
2. Passenger telephone number
3. Ticketing information
4. Form of payment (check, cash, charge)
5. Remarks
6. Booking agent received from

The PNR is assigned an identifying number by which it may be accessed. If the customer wishes to be ticketed at a later date, then the agent can readily refer to the PNR by its identifying number. Similarly, between the time the reservation is made and the trip is taken, the airline may make fare or schedule changes. The PNR automatically reflects these changes and brings them to the attention of the travel agent. Lastly, both travel agents and airline management can use the PNR as the basis for customer profiles, helping them more effectively market their services.

The queue system is another storage device common to airline reservation systems. The queue may be thought of as an electronic mailbox or card file in which carriers place messages for the agent and agents place messages for themselves. Messages updating PNR, reminders to the agent to issue tickets by a specific date, and similar information are the basis of the queue system.

A well-documented PNR and queue system are the keys to automated management. Queues should

- Increase effective communication
- Bring information automatically to the agent's attention
- Prioritize work
- Minimize unnecessary paper work
- Reduce errors

To effectively manage and realize these benefits, travel agent management may find it desirable to establish specific queues for

- Boarding passes
- Hard copy requests
- Quality control
- Prepaids
- Deposits
- Problem bookings
- Personal accounts

PNRs, queues, and the three primary information formats for flight, seat, and availability are found in all CRS, giving travel agent management the ability to reduce frustration and errors and to increase communication and productivity. Each system differs in some aspects, which is evident in reviewing the Sabre and Apollo systems.

American's Sabre System

Before entering the Sabre system, the agent needs two pieces of information from the client—where the client wants to travel and when the client wants to travel. When the agent types this information on the keyboard, it is simultaneously displayed on the CRT and communicated to American's in-house system. These are the key search parameters of the availability display, the one most frequently used by travel counselors. After the request is transmitted to American, the computer rapidly completes two processes before responding.

In the selection process, flights are reviewed and retrieved for possible display on the first screen shown to the agent. Up to twenty flights may be selected by the computer, according to its programming in response to each request. Selection is made from flights leaving two hours before to two hours after the requested departure time, with direct flights considered first, followed by connecting flights. This group of flights is further narrowed by displacement time, the differences between requested and actual departure time. The smaller the displacement time the more preferred the flight in the selected group. If two flights have the same displacement time but one departs before and one after the requested departure time, the latter trip will be chosen.

If two flights depart at the same time, they will be listed in ascending flight number order. Sabre will select the lowest flight number in the case of a requested time that precedes the departure time for the tied flights and the highest flight number when the departure time is later than the tied flights' departure time. After narrowing the list of flights, according to the rules above, Sabre then applies a sort process.

The sort process, of up to the twenty flights under consideration after the selection process, is based on service factors that American believes most closely approximate the traveler's service preferences. This is done by assigning points to each of several flight factors. The flight with the lowest total points is displayed first on the CRT, with the remaining flights shown in descending order.

Total elapsed filght time and displacement time are important elements in the point system. Since travelers generally prefer shorter flight times and departure times closer to their desired departure time, each minute of time is assigned points. Likewise, penalty points are assigned to inter-airline connections and direct flights with more than two stops.

Some penalty points are assigned on the basis of carrier status. American, as host, is assessed no penalty points, while co-hosts, those paying American to be displayed in Sabre, are assessed some penalty points. Sabre adds a substantial number of penalty points to the direct flights of carriers that do not pay American to participate in the system.

Sabre tallies the points assigned to each flight to arrive at a single value used to sort the display. The six lowest total point flights are displayed on the first primary screen. If the first screen does not show any flights acceptable to the passenger, the agent may call up successive screens until the original list of selected flights is exhausted. If no suitable flights are found in these displays, then Sabre selects another list according to the selection instructions outlined above.

Fare information is shown by two basic means. Any itinerary chosen by the travel agent will be priced automatically by Sabre. Alternatively, the agent may search city-pair markets by fare. This search would display flights by fare amount, carrier, fare class, and applicable restrictions, information that is then used to cross reference flights in the availability display.

Sabre supports several types of data processing equipment that are available from American through Agency Data Systems. Reservations and ticketing equipment interface with or can be connected to and communicate with accounting and other managerial software. Management reporting, invoice printing, and accounts receivable control systems help make Sabre one of the leaders in the CRS market.

United's Apollo System

United's Apollo system was remarkably similar to Sabre when both were introduced in 1976; since then, however, the two have become significantly different. Today's system, marketed through United's Covia subsidiary and running on IBM's new PS/2 computer system, bears little resemblance even to previous editions of Apollo.

Apollo has stayed nearly the same as the OAG. The system selects and stores flight choices in the following order:

1. Direct flights in departure time order
2. Connecting flights on a single airline
3. Connecting flights on carriers with interline agreements
4. Connecting flights on carriers without interline agreements
5. Flights involving two or more plane changes

Agent queries on availability initiate a selection of flights from these categories. Beginning two hours prior to the required departure time, Apollo chooses sixteen flights from the list of available direct flights, exhausting all possibilities before moving to the list of connecting flights, and so on. The OAG-like selection and display of flights may reflect both United's belief that travelers are primarily concerned with departure time and the wide acceptance of the OAG by travel agents.

The flights selected for consideration are then sorted to determine the order of display on the CRT. Apollo sorts in a manner similar to Sabre, giving most importance to elapsed travel time and displacement time. Each minute of flight and waiting time is penalized one point; the lower the points, the higher the placement in the CRT display. Any flights tied in points are sorted for display on a random order basis.

Apollo also assigns points based on carrier status. In some cases, a number of points are deducted from United point totals, and ties in point totals are broken in favor of United. This type of display is an example of a so-called "biased" display and is permissible under certain circumstances. In other situations, United cannot legally be favored, but Apollo is permitted to assign a larger number of points to flights flown by carriers who do not pay to participate in the system.

The total points for each flight are summed and serve as the basis of display order. The eight flights with the lowest total points are shown on the first CRT screen. If no options are acceptable to the passenger, then the remaining eight flights are displayed with the lowest point flights shown first. Should the second screen also be unacceptable, Apollo returns to the original presorted list of flights for the city-pair market and continues as described.

Apollo provides a fare guide to determine the applicable fare. Within a fare category, fares are listed from highest to lowest by a two-letter carrier code. The agent then returns to the availability format to complete the transaction.

Apollo Business System (ABS) is United's proprietary software and equipment designed to support its reservations capabilities. Itinerary and invoice printing are basic to the system. ABS also gives the agent back-office capabilities in terms of payables, receivables, and management reports.

International CRS

Fear of U.S. airline dominance over the profitable European and fast growing Asian travel markets have led to the relatively recent formation of international computer reservation systems and consortiums.

Amadeus and Galileo are the two leading European CRS and represent
the first attempt at multi-national automation consortiums. These two were
initially planned as one system but later bifurcated into two because of technical disagreements, primarily over the computer system to be used. Announced in 1987, Amadeus was described as a $300 million joint airline
reservation system co-sponsored by Air France, Iberia, Lufthansa, and SAS
which would be ready for operation in 1989. Galileo is a similar joint venture co-sponsored originally by British Airways, KLM, Swissair, and Austrian
Airlines and later joined by Alitalia, British Caledonian, Aer Lingus, TAP Air
Portugal, and a few others.

Abacus, an Asia/Pacific CRS, was developed in 1987 with the objective
of countering the powerful American-European alliances. Initially, Abacus
was intended to be one system, combining the forces of airlines in Australia,
Japan, and Southeast Asia. Disagreements among the airlines cleaved the partnership between Qantas/JAL and the Southeast Asian axis of Cathay Pacific,
Singapore Airlines, and Thai International. The Australian axis eventually split
with Australian Airlines and Ansett, the two domestic carriers, striking a partnership with Galileo, giving that European system its first Asia/Pacific
foothold. Several months later Qantas announced the formation of the Sabre-
based Fantasia with the "active sponsorship" of American Airlines, JAL, and
ANA.

World-wide CRS Participating Carriers

The American Systems

Apollo/Covia	United Airlines, US Air
System One	Eastern, Continental
Pars	Northwest, TWA, Air Canada, Canadian
Sabre	American
Datas II	Delta

The European Systems

Amadeus	Linked with Pars and Abacus. Participating airlines: Lufthansa, Iberia, Air France, Air Inter, SAS, JAT, Finnair, Braathens, Icelandair, Adria
Galileo	Linked with Apollo/Covia. Participating airlines: British Airways, Alitalia, Swissair, Olympic, KLM, Sabena, TAP, Aer Lingus, Austrian Airlines, Ansett, and Australian

The Asia/Pacific Systems

Abacus   Cathay Pacific, Singapore Airlines, Malaysia Airlines, China
               Airlines, Phillippine Airlines
Fantasia   Quantas with American Airlines, Japan Air Lines, and All
               Nippon Airways as "active sponsors"

COMPREHENSIVE TRAVEL AGENCY AUTOMATION

Automation implies more than the ability to access airline information more effectively and efficiently. The inclusion of cruise lines, railroads, tour operators, car rentals, and hotels on CRS means that the entire travel package is available via the computer. Back-office systems complement reservations capabilities, giving travel agent management more control over operations and financial planning, but this advantage is not without cost. Much of the technology available to travel agents is also available to consumers—for example, anyone with a personal computer may now scan schedule availability and fare displays on user-friendly versions of TWA's PARS and American's Sabre systems. Some have even suggested that CRS give airline vendors the ability to bypass travel agents, especially in dealing with corporate clients. Finally, management may find that the economic and personnel costs of automation are quite high. As technology improves, however, such costs will be reduced as automation comes closer to the goal of a paperless office.

Other Participants in CRS

Communication between travel agents and their nonair suppliers has also been affected by automation. The 800 number is gradually being replaced by direct computer linkups between agents and vendors and by vendor offerings in airline-owned CRS. Airlines have given impetus to this trend, incorporating more services into their systems to make them more attractive to travel agents. Many hotel chains and car rental firms report that more than half their trade bookings are now coming over CRS. Cruise lines, railroads, and tour operations have joined this trend, as shown in Table 10.2.

Most major car rental firms are displayed in CRS. Whereas agents are somewhat hesitant to book hotel rooms on the computer, making car reservations is widely accepted. It has been suggested that agents are more comfortable switching a client from one car to another or from one firm to another than they are altering hotel plans for the client in the event that something goes wrong.

The risk of lost messages and delays in confirmation is often linked to the communication system. Many agents blame AIRINC for these problems. Even though this may be more a perceived than a real problem, airlines and car rentals are taking steps to remedy the situation. American, United, TWA, and Eastern have announced plans to explore direct links between their systems and the car rental agencies. Hertz, Avis, and Budget are among the firms actively seeking direct access to airlines' CRS.

Rates have also been a problem for car rental display in the systems. Programming limitations have restricted the number of rates that may be displayed. For example, a given CRS may display only one fare per car type when several rates may be available under certain restrictions. Also, due to the time lag between when the rate schedule is submitted to the airline vendor and when it is available for display, car rental companies generally have not guaranteed their rates. Recent programming and communications enhancements, however, have largely overcome this problem and more guaranteed rates are expected in the near future. The trend toward automated rental bookings should continue as smaller agencies are replaced by larger agencies. Some travel industry experts predict that within a few years 90 percent of bookings will be made via CRS.

Hotels have actively pursued automation on their own. Holiday Inn was a pioneer in the field, introducing its Holidex system in 1965. Today Holidex III allows every front desk employee to transmit information to and receive information from other reservations centers concerning inventory at that and other properties, maintain connections with airlines, and maintain corporate profiles.

Communciations between hotels and airline reservations systems take several paths. Some hotel computers can communicate directly with CRTs placed in very large agencies, other systems communicate directly with the airline CRS, avoiding the need to switch via AIRINC. Mariott's in-house system utilizes both means of communication. An interesting variation is Woodside's Advanced Reservation Management System, a multi-access system available to its agents; Ramada Inns is one of several noncarrier participants in the system. Finally, the growth of hotel bookings via airline CRS has necessitated a third party clearinghouse to perform the same functions for hotels that the ATPCO and the OAG provide for airlines. DenCom consolidates the tapes describing the properties and rates of prescribing chains, translates them into formats and languages readable by carrier systems, and forwards the consolidated data to host carriers for display.

Airlines have taken many steps to promote the use of the systems to book hotel and car rentals. As an incentive to use their system, airlines typically give agents $1.00 for each booking, followed up with special seminars and training sessions designed to encourage greater use of the system. Large agencies, particularly those with large commercial volume, may find the benefits of booking hotels and cars via a CRS to be very profitable.

The cruise industry is also sharpening its marketing program with increased use of automation. While some lines have direct access to carrier systems—for example, Holland America is a direct participant in Apollo—most have automated through a third-party information service. Cruise-

TABLE 10.2 CRUISE, RAIL, AND TOUR PARTICIPANTS IN CRS

	Sabre	Apollo	Datas II	Soda	Pars
Participants	CruiseMatch	Holland America	Costa Cruises, Norwegian Caribbean Lines	CruiseMatch	CruiseMatch
Capabilities	Information fo 23 lines, availability for 11++, booking	Information, availability, and booking	Information only	Information for 23 lines, + availability for 11++, booking for 5+++	Information for 23 lines, + availability for 11++, booking for 5+++
Documents	Written confirmation	Written confirmation	None	Written confirmation	Written confirmation
Participants	Amtrak, BritRail, French National	Amtrak, BritRail, French National	BritRail	BritRail**	Amtrak, ***BritRail***, German Rail***
Capabilities	Amtrak: Information, booking, ticketing; BritRail: Information ticketing for passes; French National: Info and booking for FNR and Eurail	Amtrak: Information; BritRail Information, ticketing for passes and ordering for point to point; French National: Information and booking for FNR and Eurail	Information, ticketing for passes	Information, ticketing for passes	Amtrak: Information, booking, ticketing for passes and ordering for point to point; German Rail: Information and booking for GR and Eurail
Documents	Amtrak: Tickets; BritRail: Flight coupon issued, redeemable for pass; FNR: confirmation, pass mailed to agent	Amtrak: Confirmation; BritRail: Flight coupon issued, redeemable for pass, point to point ticket sent to agent; FNR: Confirmation pass mailed to agent	Flight coupon issued, redeemable for pass	Flight coupon issued, redeemable for pass	Amtrak: Tickets; Brit Rail: Flight coupon issued, redeemable for pass; GermanRail: Confirmation passes mailed to agent

Participants	To be announced	Aspen Ski Tours, Creative Leisure, Fantasy Holidays, Funway Holidays, Hadden Tours, Medallion Tours, MTI Vacation, Percival Tours, Pleasant Hawaiian Holidays, Runaway Tours, Jack Stovall, Tavek Tours, Trade Wind Tours, United Airlines Fly-Drive, United Vacations	Insight Tours, Certified Tours Fitzpatrick Tours***	None	Tauk Tours***, Cosmos/Tourama***, Globus-Gateway*** Allied Tours
Capabilities		Information, availability, booking	Information, availability, booking		Information, availability, booking
Documents		Confirmation	Confirmation		Confirmation

Available to Sabre users subscribing to Total Access Option; **Not available to MARSPLUS users; ***Not available to MARSPLUS and PARS II users. American Cruise Lines + + +, American Hawaii Cruises + + +, Bahama Cruise Line, Carnival Cruise Lines, Commadore Cruise Line, Costa Cruises, Cunard/NAC + + +, Delta Queen Steamboat Co. + +, Eastern Cruise Lines + +, Fantasy Cruises, Holland America Line, Home Line Cruises, Norwegian Caribbean Lines, Paquet French Cruises + +, Pearl Cruises of Scandinavia + +, Premier Cruise Lines + + +, Princess Cruises + + +, Royal Caribbean Cruise Line, Royal Viking Line, Sea Goddess Cruises, Sun Line Cruises + +, Western Cruise Lines + + +

Source: Travel Weekly, July 31, 1985, p. 76.

Match can provide information on twenty-three ship lines and sixty-five ships, availability on eleven of the lines, and booking on five of them.

Computer tape and hard copy are submitted to CruiseMatch, which inputs the data into its computer. The participating lines are also given direct access to the computer for input of selected data. The CruiseMatch computer is directly linked with System One, Pars, and Sabre and through these systems is available to the agent. Internal PNR and queue systems mean that CruiseMatch is compatible with and familiar to travel agents already using CRS.

Railroad participation in airline reservations systems is not surprising for European railroads but has come as a major breakthrough for AMTRAK. Inclusion in Sabre, Apollo, and Pars has opened thousands of new retail agents to the U.S. rail passenger network. AMTRAK's acceptance into the Area Settlement Plan should further spur rail bookings via computer.

The BritRail system is one of the most unique in the industry. An agent booking on BritRail writes the ticket on British Airways stock, which is given to the customer. The airline coupon is then redeemed for a rail pass at a railway ticket office or station.

The number and variety of tour offerings have tended to inhibit their inclusion in the CRS in the United States, although some operators in the United Kingdom, such as Thompson, have been very successful, generating some 80 percent of bookings on the computer. United has been the most ambitious operator in automating tour sales—the Instant Tours program in Apollo gives agents access to more than a dozen tour operators.

Outside of Apollo, communications and programming difficulties have been a problem. Some operators are now able to enter availability and updates directly into some systems, but further progress on direct communication will have to be made before tours are more accessible on an automated basis. One effort is Travel Search, which, like other third-party clearinghouses, consolidates the offerings of several operators and communicates this information to the airline system. To date, the firm has programmed some 9000 tours and cruises into its computer and is available for informational purposes to retail agents on an experimental basis.

Other Major Applications

Videotex.   As airline systems incorporate more nonair services, they are rapidly approaching the videotex system, which has gained wide acceptance in the United Kingdom and is coming to be accepted in the United States. British Telecom launched its viewdata system, Prestel, in 1979, and today it is used by more than 90 percent of agencies in the United Kingdom.[3]

Simply put, Prestel combines the capabilities of carrier-owned CRS, CompuServe's and others' electronic mail, telex, and electronic newspapers into a single user-friendly system. Prestel seemed ideally suited to the U.K. travel market for the following reasons:

- Provides an answer to the threat of direct sales to travelers
- Helps in the difficulty of disseminating information to a geographically dispersed travel agent network
- Relieves congestion of vendors' lines during peak booking periods
- Combats rising communications costs
- Coordinates the amount and volatility of travel information

The parallels to the United States travel sales distribution system are self-evident.

The basic components of Prestel are a color television that serves as a display, a keyboard to input questions and data, and an adapter that permits communication from the agent to the central computer to be carried over telephone lines. Catalogued on the in-house computer are thousands of pages of text describing destinations as well as the offerings of tour operators, railroads, ferries, hotels, and airlines. Prestel even includes up-to-date news stories on these services and can draw simple diagrams. By an easy switch, the agent has direct access to vendor computers and can make reservations using a standard format.

Many in the United States are advocating a videotex system for this country. Some have suggested that the current airline systems could be enhanced in information content and technology to duplicate the success of Prestel. Others have advocated Western Union's EasyLink, which already encompasses electronic mail, telex, and a data base system, as a short-term solution. Still others in the industry endorse development of an entirely new system.

Telemarketing.   Airline-owned CRS and videotex systems are primarily concerned with improving the marketing of vendor services—travel agent marketing benefits only indirectly by having access to more current and accurate information. The marketing of travel agent services has benefited more directly from automation with the introduction of telemarketing.[4] Telemarketing is based on a two-way device that allows businesses to make preprogrammed calls to clients, announcing new services or reminding them of an upcoming event and accepting messages from customers. The system is already widely used in the real estate, insurance, and finance industries.

The system introduced to travel agency management can store upwards of 2000 telephone numbers (including the 23-digit numbers of Europe and Asia) and 99 messages and can be programmed to automatically dial up to 25,000 calls per month. This represents the capacity to efficiently communicate with clients, advertise and promote the agency, and help establish agency identity. Because the machines can also be programmed to accept customer comments, telemarketing machines assist wtih market studies and reports. Some agents report that they have more than doubled sales volume within a year of installing telemarketing devices.

Back-office and interface functions. Telemarketing and reservations are often referred to as "front-office" automation, but the computer has also been applied to "back-office" functions—those not seen by clients. Accounting, finance, and customer profiling are but a few of the functions that have been automated. To date, however, back-office systems have not been as widely accepted as front-office systems and are found in only about forty percent of agency locations.[5] The top ten vendors of these systems and their market shares are shown in Table 10.3.

Four of the five top systems are sold by CRS vendors. In addition to Agency Management, American, Delta, United Airlines, and Eastern have been most successful in automating back offices. Several factors account for this trend. Foremost, CRS vendors have had to enhance their product to remain competitive, including the development of back-office systems. Vendor-developed systems hold the added advantage of being interfaced—able to communicate—with the reservations systems. Agents can transfer data directly from the CRS display to other records, including customer profiles, general ledgers, balance sheets, Airlines Reporting Corporation (ARC) reports, and employee records. The direct communication between the back-office computer and CRS computer helps to ensure the accuracy of information entered into the system and to save time in data input. Some vendors are developing the capability to handle back- and front-office functions on a single computer, a large step toward comprehensive agency automation.

TABLE 10.3   TOP TEN VENDORS OF BACK-OFFICE SYSTEMS

Vendor	Agency locations
Agency Data Systems	4700
Delta Airlines Plus	2272
Covia TSZ000	1500
Agency Management Services	822
System One TRI	595
Travel Computer Systems	500
Cobrasoft	425
ASTA Marketing Services	385
Travel Agency Systems	300
Travel Agency Management Systems	300

Source: Nadine Goodwin, "Survey Reveals 42 Percent of Agencies Automate Back-Office Functions," *Travel Weekly,* September 8, 1988, pp. 1–4.

Smaller agencies, and even somewhat larger agencies that do not handle a large amount of commercial business, may find that an in-house, back-office system is not economical. Productivity gains attributable to time savings are the primary reasons for automating reports. If reporting is a small portion of total time and cost, then automation in house may not be justified. The agent still has options for automating, however.

Many accounting firms or other service bureaus will contract to provided computer-generated reports for the travel agent. Travel agents can accumulate the customary accounting records and, rather than tally them by hand, deliver them to the accounting firm, which will then enter the data into its computer and generate the desired reports. The agent will typically pay a one-time fee for the initial programming of report forms and a monthly service charge for the actual reports provided thereafter. These costs are offset by eliminating the need to invest in automated equipment and software and the possibility of reducing some clerical costs. Of course, this option is less convenient than an in-house accounting system and introduces additional room for error.

Timesharing is another alternative open to agency managers. With this arrangement the agent pays for time used on another business computer. The cost to the agent includes the expense of a CRT that communicates with the computer of the timesharing partners and a charge for time used. Although somewhat more expensive than the services of an accounting firm, timesharing generally provides more rapid turnaround—receipt of reports after the data is communicated.

Data base management system and spreadsheet.   A final option for automating back-office functions is for agencies to develop their own computer programs using off-the-shelf software available for the computer. A data base management system (DBMS) allows the user to enter, organize, analyze, and retrieve data. The airline reservations systems are essentially very sophisticated DBMS. Programs may be written to format the CRT screen to resemble the hard copy document with which the agent is familiar—instead of entering data on paper, it is entered on the CRT. The data may then be retrieved by name, date, city-pair, or any other combination.

The DBMS frequently may be interfaced with spreadsheet packages to meet the agent's accounting needs. Spreadsheets are analogous to an accountant's worksheet, summarizing the business in cost and revenue relationships. Once these relationships are defined, or modeled, the agent may generate reports on current volume and may see the bottom-line effect of changes in volume. Some spreadsheets give the user the ability to optimize models, identifying where the agent can improve operations within the defined relationships of cost to revenue.

Spreadsheets and DBMS may be linked to other software for generating custom-designed reports. Word processing software provides for quick and easy editing of most documents, incorporating the financial data imported from other programs. Furthermore, reports can be supplemented with graphic presentations of the data, which provide for easier interpretation. Good graphics can identify trends more readily, provide more meaningful comparisons, save time and money in reporting, and make a more professional presentation to management and to clients.

Value of back-office automation.   Regardless of which accounting and management option is chosen, back-office systems can save valuable time and money, and they may also be used to increase revenue. The same accounting and customer profile reports that are helpful to travel agent management are helpful for business travel management. With increasing frequency, corporations are demanding more from agents in terms of finding the best travel bargains, enforcing company travel policy, and reporting on corporate travel. IBM recently let a $100 million contract to an agent who could best manage its travel needs. Good back-office systems are essential to attracting and retaining such lucrative accounts.

Commission tracking can likewise be improved through accounting/ management systems. Automation can maximize overrides from vendors and otherwise negotiate for vendor favors. Computers make it easier to identify when and where hotel and car bookings are more profitable than air service bookings. Automation likewise enhances identifying and marketing to incentive travelers. Alternatively, back-office systems may identify unprofitable bookings whose costs exceed revenue. In addition, profiling travel vendors as well as clients is profit maximizing.

SUMMARY

Automated travel agency management, which began with teleticketing, has grown to encompass all aspects of the business: operations and procedures, organizational management, marketing, and financial management. Success stories in the application of technology abound. Dun & Bradstreet has proposed to buy Thomas Cook, a sixty-three-agent chain, which, in cooperation with its OAG subsidiary, will give the company a competitive advantage in information technology. Automation was also cited as a motivating factor in the purchase of Execunet Travel, with $17 million of business, by another Chicago firm. Execunet spent $1 million to develop its Smart software, linking Apollo electronic tariffs and a company-designed data base. The data taken from these sources is stored in four separate computer files, one each for lowest airfares, preferred hotels, preferred car rentals, and customer travel policies.

Automation is no panacea, however. As suggested by the examples above, many computer innovations are targeted toward large agencies or those with large corporate accounts. These agents, more so than smaller agencies, are in a better position at present to take full advantage of the emerging technology. The cost of installing and operating a reservations system, a back-office system, or both may be greater than the productivity gains and improved revenue possible with automation. Beyond the cost factors, agents may find that personnel resistance and the complexity of automation make it inhibitive, although these barriers are rapidly being overcome. The cost of computer hardware drops almost as fast as its capability improves. Software, too, is becoming less expensive, more powerful, and, most important, more user friendly. Within a few years, many agencies may be paperless and more profitable due to computerization.

DISCUSSION QUESTIONS

1. What are the functional parts of a computer?
2. How do ROM and RAM differ?
3. What are the goals of automation?
4. What are the primary information formats found in all CRS?
5. How do current CRS differ from videotex?

ENDNOTES

[1] F. M. Collison and K. B. Boberg, "Marketing of Airline Services in a Deregulated Environment," *Tourism Management*, September, 1987, p.197.

[2] "Automation Report," *Travel Weekly*, August 22, 1988, p. 55.

[3] Nadine Godwin, "U.S. Agents Are Taking Another Look at Videotex," *Travel Weekly*, June 24, 1985, pp. 23–24.

[4] H. Apter, "N.Y. Agent Doubles Volume in 10 Months with Telemarketing," *Travel Trade*, March 18, 1985, p. 5.

[5] Nadine Godwin, "Survey Reveals 42 Percent of Agencies Automate Back-Office Functions," *Travel Weekly*, September 8, 1988, pp. 1–4.

SUPPLEMENTAL READINGS

BOOTH, R., "Automation in the Travel Industry," *Tourism Management*, December, 1983, pp. 296–298.

BRADY, P., "Automation: Getting the Most Out of Your System," *The Travel Agent*, July 20, 1984, pp. 40–44.

BRUCE, M., "Information Technology: Changes in the Travel Trade," *Tourism Management*, December, 1983, pp. 290–295.

CHIPKIN, H., "Non-air Suppliers and the CRT," *Travel Weekley's Profit Guide*, July 31, 1985, pp. 75–78.

FELDMAN, J., "Is Electronic Ticket Delivery Inevitable?" *Travel Weekly's Guide to Business and Group Travel*, October 31, 1984, pp. 26–27.

FERGUSON, W., "Should You Buy That Computer?" *Travel Weekly's Profit Guide*, August 31, 1984, pp. 46–47.

GODWIN, N., "Firms Design Software for Corporate Agencies," *Travel Weekly*, June 7, 1984, pp. 1ff.

GODWIN, N., "Documents Show Lines' Priorities in Reservations Systems Displays," *Travel Weekly*, March 25, 1985, pp. 1ff.

GODWIN, N., "ASTA Chapter Urges Videotex Network for U.S. Agents," *Travel Weekly*, May 27, 1985, p. 88.

GODWIN, N., *Complete Guide to Travel Agency Automation*, 2nd ed. Albany, NY: Delmar Publishers, Inc., 1987.

MARKO, J., and R. MOORE, "How to Select a Computing System, Part I," *Cornell H.R.A. Quarterly*, May, 1980, pp. 8–18.

OTT, J., "Airlines, Corporations, Building Ticketing Role of Travel Agents," *Aviation Week and Space Technology*, July 15, 1985, p. 36.

PIEKMAN, R., "A Machine That Demands You Know Your Business," *Travel Weekly's Profit Guide*, August 31, 1984, pp. 42–45.

"Rosenbluth to Offer Direct Data Base Link to Corporate Clients," *Travel Weekly*, August 27, 1984, pp. 1ff.

RUBIN, K., "Consumer PCs to Hook into American's Res System," *The Travel Agent*, September 12, 1985, pp. 1ff.

WEISER, M., "Carriers and Car Rental Firms Strive for Res Improvements," *Travel Weekly*, March 21, 1985, pp. 43ff.

chapter 11

Legal Aspects and the Management of Risk

LEARNING OBJECTIVES

- To understand the contractual relations that travel agencies enter into with suppliers, clients, and sometimes employees
- To recognize where potential lawsuits exist and to understand how to take preventive steps to avoid them
- To understand the importance of disclaimers and other legal provisions to travel agencies
- To understand the concept of risk management as it applies to the travel agency

KEY TERMS

- Agency by Authorization
- Agency by Conduct
- Agency by Necessity
- Agency by Ratification
- Agent
- Assignment Rights
- Breach of Contract
- Business Interruption Insurance
- Consumer Disclosure Notice
- Default
- Disability Insurance
- Disclaimer
- Disclosure
- Employment Contract
- Errors and Omissions Insurance
- Fiduciary
- General Liability Insurance
- Insurance Deductible

- Key Person Insurance
- Life Insurance
- Phantom Flight
- Principal
- Property Insurance

- Restrictive Covenant Clause
- Risk Management
- Strict Liability
- Travel Insurance

INTRODUCTION

Between 1978 and 1983, a record 12 million lawsuits were reportedly filed in the United States for every conceivable complaint—some justified, some frivolous. By 1984, according to a *Forbes* estimate, one civil suit was filed for every fifteen Americans. In that same year, out-of-court settlements reached an average of $1.7 million per case. Since then, the situation has not improved, causing businesses in many communities to demand civil tort reform through state legislation. Every industry, business, and profession, including travel agencies, has been affected by this crisis in product and service liability.

Suits against travel agencies have been increasing due to a combination of factors: the growing depersonalization of travel agency service, which makes clients less hesitant to sue; the general rise of the consumerism movement; the system of tort law in the United States, which is based on court precedence rather than on legislative statute; and the increased accessibility to and low cost of small claims courts. Clients generally look to their travel agent to provide for everything—planning itineraries, guaranteeing reservations, and making detailed arrangements, almost down to the point of assuring that their leisure time will be well spent. When something goes wrong—the sun doesn't shine, the tour bus breaks down, the hotel room is not air conditioned—clients want to sue the travel agent. Given the litigious nature of contemporary society, travel agency owners and managers now need to be as much aware of all major and minor legal implications as they are of how to conduct business operations.

To avoid potentially costly and time-consuming litigation, the manager must know the agency's responsibilities ensuing from relationships with clients, suppliers, employees, and others, as well as the rights accrued to the agency. Legal entanglements of any sort should be avoided, not only because of the time and cost involved but because of the potential damage to the agency's reputation and the strain it puts on relationships with clients and suppliers.

RELATIONSHIP WITH PRINCIPALS

In the normal course of business, the travel agency will enter into contractual relationships with suppliers, clients, and sometimes employees. With regard to suppliers, the relationship is usually one of an "agency." The legal concept of "agency" defines a relationship that is fiduciary in nature (based on trust, confidence, and loyalty) and is between two companies or persons where one, the seller, known as the agent, is authorized by the other, the supplier, known as the principal, to deal with third persons. In the travel industry, this means that the travel agency represents the various principals (airlines, tour operators, hotels, cruises, car rental companies) and is able to act for and in the place of these principals in the sale of their products. Any authorized act of the agency will bind the principal as if the principal had participated directly in the act itself. When the agent acts within his or her authority, the contract developed between the agent and the client is binding only on the principal and the client—not the agent. This is so under two conditions: (1) the client is aware of the fact that the travel agent is acting only as agent and not the ultimate supplier, and (2) the client is aware of the identity of the principal. Under normal circumstances—but there are exceptions that will be discussed later—the agent has no further liability regarding the contract.

The agency relationship may be written, oral, or simply implied by the conduct of the parties. While it requires consent on the part of both the principal and the agent, it does not necessarily imply that the agent will be monetarily compensated for services rendered. The agency relationship can be established in a number of ways, including agency by conduct, agency by ratification, agency by necessity, and agency by authorization. A short description of each follows.

- *Agency by Conduct.* This form of agency relationship is based on the conduct, or behavior, of suppliers. For example, when a tour operator sends travel brochures to an agency and requests that these brochures be distributed to the agency's customers with the agency's stamp, the tour operator (principal) is in effect giving authorization for the agency to act on its behalf to sell tours.

- *Agency by Ratification.* If a supplier such as a hotel or cruise operator accepts reservations made by a travel agency through its reservation system, even though the travel agency may not be an official agency of the supplier, an agency-by-ratification relationship is established.

- *Agency by Necessity.* In an emergency, it is possible to establish an agency-by-necessity relationship between principal and agent. If, for instance, during the course of a tour a situation were to arise that required medical attention to treat an injured passenger, the tour group leader could approve emergency treatment. Even though the tour group leader normally has no authority to take such action, his or her actions are binding on the tour supplier once action is taken.

- *Agency by Authorization.* An agency relationship established by express authorization is the most common form between travel agencies and air carriers. Since 1985 members of the Airlines Reporting Corporation formally authorize travel agencies to act as their agents in selling air travel, pursuant to the provisions set forth in the Agent Reporting Agreement. Outside of national boundaries, the International Air Transport Association has a Passenger Network Services Corporation that represents international air carriers entering into contractual relationships with travel agents.

In the Agent Reporting Agreement, the travel agency agrees to represent the air carriers in selling air transportation in return for a commission paid by the carrier on sales. The carrier also agrees to provide the agent with the carrier's tickets and furnish other documents to be used in connection with sales. Becoming "appointed" by ARC allows agents certain rights to ticket stocks and plates. In exchange, agents are subject to many of ARC's rules and stipulations (discussed in Chapter 2).

When carrier and agent enter into the Agent Reporting Agreement, certain rights and obligations are incurred for both the agency and the airlines. The agent is obligated to use care, diligence, and skill in selling air transportation and to render an accounting of sales to the air carrier on demand. The air carrier, on the other hand, agrees to hold the agent harmless from suits arising out of any injury to a customer caused by the carrier and to compensate the agent for the selling of air transportation. The carrier is also liable for any acts performed by the agent on the carrier's behalf within the scope of his or her authority.

When the agent acts beyond his or her scope of authority or is negligent in the selling of the carrier's air service, he or she may be held liable for these acts. However, if the principal ratifies, either by words or conduct, a contract made by the agent exceeding his or her authority, the agent is absolved of responsibility. If, as a result of negligence or breach of contract on the agent's part, the carrier becomes party to a lawsuit, the carrier may be able to indemnify itself by taking legal action against the agent.

Although the travel agent acts on behalf of a principal and is only an intermediary, the agency may be held liable to third parties (clients) for damages if he or she knowingly misrepresents the travel product by giving false, misleading, or materially incomplete information. In some instances, the agent may also be held liable for inaccurate statements made regarding the quality of travel products sold. The principals are not liable unless they provided the false information, had knowledge that false information was being disseminated and did nothing to stop it, or later ratified through conduct or words the agent's incorrect information. Figure 11.1 illustrates the possible contractual relationships that ensue from the sale of travel products.

Disclosure

In acting as an agent for a specified principal (tour operator, hotel, air carrier) it is legally important for the agent to disclose the principal, that is, to

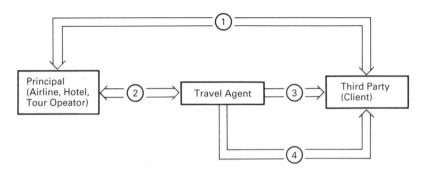

FIGURE 11.1 Contractual relationships. The diagram illustrates four possible implicit relationships: (1) A contractual relationship exists only between principal and third party (client) when agent has acted within specified authority and properly disclosed the principal. (2) In selling the travel product of a principal for a consideration (commission), a contractual relationship is established between the travel agent and the principal. (3) Travel agent is a representative of the principal to a third party in sale of travel products. (4) Travel agent is held liable to third party if he or she acted beyond authority, did not properly disclose principal, or was negligent.

inform clients that he or she is merely acting in the role of agent for the principal. With disclosure, the agent has taken a major step in avoiding liability by obtaining implicit consent from the client to use the travel supplier. For example, take the case of tour products. The general assumption on the part of most clients is that tours are arranged by travel agents. When they purchase a packaged tour, clients are not always aware that the travel agent represents a principal (tour operator) nor do they have a clearcut understanding of the legal relationship between the travel agent and the tour operator. When the client is unaware that the travel agent is acting as an agent for one or more specified principals, he or she may assume that the agent is acting on the agent's own behalf. Consequently, the client may hold the agent liable for any breach of contract (failure to perform) or for any harm caused by the travel supplier. Although a contract made between the client and the disclosed principal is generally still binding on the principal, courts have often interpreted the contract to be binding on the agent as well because of the failure to disclose. In recent years, many cases have come before the courts addressing the concept of undisclosed principal and travel agents have occasionally been held liable for damages suffered by clients.

Many travel agencies now specify their agency-principal relationship by identifying the principal in writing. When executing a contract, the agent may disclose the agency-principal relationship by signing as agent for a principal (for example, "Hawaiian Holiday Tours, per PAX Travel Agency, Inc., Agent for Tour Operator"; "Hawaiian Holiday Tours by PAX Travel Agency, Inc., Agent"). Some agencies go one step further by printing a Consumer Disclosure Notice on the ticket jacket or on the back of an itinerary. Exhibit 11.1 is a sample consumer disclosure notice.

TRAVEL AGENTS'
CONSUMER DISCLOSURE NOTICE
(TO BE PRINTED ON INVOICE, TICKET JACKET,
OR COMPUTERIZED ITINERARY)

(*NAME OF TRAVEL AGENCY*) is acting as intermediary and agent for suppliers ("principals" identified on the attached or accompanying documents) in selling services, or in accepting reservations or bookings for services which are not directly supplied by this travel agency (such as air carriage, hotel accommodations, ground transportation, meals, tours, cruises, etc.). This agency, therefore, shall not be responsible for breach of contract or any intentional or careless actions or damage, delay, or injury to you or your travel companions or group members. Unless the term "guaranteed" is specifically stated in writing on your ticket, invoice, or reservation itinerary, we do not guarantee any of such suppliers' rates, bookings, or reservations. The travel agent shall not be responsible for any injuries, damages, or losses caused to any traveler in connection with terrorist activities, social or labor unrest, mechanical or construction difficulties, diseases, local laws, climatic conditions, abnormal conditions or developments, or any other actions, omissions, or conditions outside the travel agent's control. By embarking upon his/her travel, the traveler/s voluntarily assumes all risks involved with such travel, whether expected or unexpected. The traveler is hereby warned of such risks, and is advised to obtain appropriate insurance coverage against them. Your retention of tickets, reservations, or bookings after issuance shall constitute a consent to the above, and an agreement on your part to convey the contents here to your travel companions or group members.

Source: Alexander Anolik, *The Law and the Travel Industry,* vol. II (San Francisco: Alchemy Books, 1987), p. 1–29.

The timing of the disclosure notification can also be a critical factor. In a technical sense, the agent can avoid liability only if the client understands the agency-principal relationship *before* entering into the contract. Notice of the agent's role as agent, therefore, must be given to the client prior to the moment he or she agrees to authorize the purchase of travel arrangements. For this reason, some agents verbally advise clients of their role as agent early in the relationship, then request that the client sign or initial some form of consumer disclosure notice when the sale is finalized. Full disclosure automatically establishes a legal defense, serving to identify the agent's professional role as that of counselor and agent, while assigning to suppliers the role and responsibility that is theirs for the travel services they provide to clients.

Termination of Contract

An agency-principal agreement may be terminated in various ways. Agreements between agents and travel suppliers made for a specified period of time terminate at the end of the expiration date. When no expiration date is stated, the courts have generally permitted the agreement to lapse after a reasonable length of time has passed and there has been no activity between the two parties that could keep the contract in force.

   An agent's authority can be revoked by the principal at any time. In this situation, however, the principal is liable for any losses the agent suffers under the existing agreement. The principal must also notify all third parties involved that the agency's authority has been revoked to avoid the responsibility of continuing liability. The agent has the option to renounce an agreement at any time as well; in this case, the agent is subject to the same liability as the principal when the principal revokes the agreement. The principal-agency agreement may also be terminated upon the death of either agent or principal and for reasons of bankruptcy, insanity, or other incapacity to perform by either party.

Travel Agent as Principal

In situations where the agent assumes the role of tour operator or promoter of travel shows or in other business situations in which the agency represents itself, the travel agent may be legally interpreted as acting as a principal. One major difference between agent and principal is that the principal acts for itself for profit whereas the agent is generally a sales representative working on commission for suppliers and does not own or produce the travel product.

   If the agency decides to purchase products outright for resale at a profit or to create its own agency package tours, the travel agent, in effect, becomes owner, or principal, of the travel product and therefore assumes responsibility for product liability. Although some travel agents in this situation will have clients sign a statement acknowledging that the agency is still acting as an agent and will not be held liable for actions caused by suppliers, the courts may not always recognize such a disclaimer. It is helpful, therefore, for the travel agency to have a contract with each supplier clarifying the specific responsibilities and liabilities of each party.

RELATIONSHIP WITH CLIENT

When the travel agent has acted fully within the scope of his or her authority and has properly disclosed the fact of his or her agency capacity and the identity of principal(s), the agent has no actual contractual liability. In a legal sense, client and principal are bound to each other. However, because clients make travel arrangements and ticket purchases through travel agents, many feel that the travel agency should bear some responsibility for the harmful actions of principals and, consequently, numerous lawsuits are filed against travel agencies.

It should also be noted that some responsibilities of the agent are not transferred to the principal simply by disclosure. The agent is still liable to third parties for damages resulting from any false or misleading statements made on the agent's part, for fraud or misrepresentation, and for breach of contract, if any, between the agent and client. As previously noted, an agent may also be liable for any false statements made with regard to the quality of travel products, especially if these statements appear to be based on the agent's personal expertise rather than information printed in a brochure. When people use travel agencies for professional services, they feel they have the right to expect that the services rendered or advice given will be informed, knowledgeable, and accurate.

Strict Liability

Many disgruntled travelers have tried to convince the courts that the principle of "strict liability" should be applied to travel agencies, whereby travel agents would be held liable for any damages suffered by clients *regardless of any negligence on the agent's part*. This would mean that, legally, the agency would be viewed as an "insurer" of the quality or safety of travel regardless of fault. Courts around the country, however, have uniformly rejected the application of the strict liability principle with regard to travel agencies. They have reasoned that strict liability applies to defective products, not services, and also that making the promoters of travel at once insurers of the health, safety, and happiness of all travelers would be carrying business liability risk too far.[1]

Case Examples

The following nine examples and composites of actual court cases illustrate the cloudy, often nebulous, relationship existing between the agent and the client and why there is a need to take preventive steps to avoid potential problems.

Case 1. If an agent responds to legal questions, for instance, giving information or advice regarding marriage laws in certain states or on ships, divorce procedures, visa regulations, import or export restrictions, and so on, and the client has been hurt by his or her reliance on such answers, the agent in most cases will be held responsible. Some lawyers might also accuse the agent of practicing law without a license. In general practice, therefore, it is safer for the travel agent to provide clients with referral phone numbers to obtain the correct information.[2]

Case 2.   A fire breaks out in a city hotel, killing ten guests who were located on the highest floors. It had been widely reported in the media that the fire department's ladders could not reach past the fourteenth floor. Later, a couple enters a travel agency requesting to book into the top floor of another hotel in the same city. Without comment or caution to the couple, the travel agent makes the reservation. Unfortunately, a fire breaks out in the hotel where the couple is staying, and they narrowly escape. Upon their return, they file a suit against the travel agency for gross negligence in not warning them. Since the first hotel fire and problem with the ladder length was widely covered in the media, the travel agent, although not expected to know every danger, would probably be expected by the courts to think about the recent disaster when making the reservation and to warn clients of the possible danger of their request, perhaps even in writing. The point here is that in order to avoid being the target of lawsuits, agents must be aware of significant current events that affect the industry and their customers and warn clients when the chances of danger are likely.[3]

Case 3.   A travel agent is approached by a client requesting the cheapest possible airfare for a five-country visit to South America. One leg of the journey uses a small air carrier that has the worst FAA safety record in Latin America. The plane crashes, and the client, who is hospitalized, sues the travel agency. The courts might find the agency liable because (1) the agency has access to safety information, and (2) the agency knew or should have known about the airline's poor safety record and should have advised the client.[4]

Case 4.   An elderly client wishing to book a cruise inquires if the travel agency can help to arrange for someone to share her cabin. The agency complies. During the cruise, the client has $15,000 worth of jewelry stolen from her cabin, and she sues the travel agency for having arranged for her to share her cabin with a thief. It is presumed in law that the agency arranging the accommodations must act with at least reasonable care, which might likely mean the obtaining of references and other available information on each woman. If the agency is unable to prove it used reasonable care in selecting the roommate, it can be held liable for the client's losses. To avoid this situation, the agency should have either (1) booked the client for a single occupancy, (2) suggested an operator who would accept the responsibility for arranging the shared room, (3) recommended that the two clients exchange phone numbers so they could determine their own compatibility, or (4) had the client sign a statement agreeing to hold the agent harmless.[5]

Case 5. An antique dealer who is a seasoned traveler purchases a four-country tour from a travel agency. The tour stops in country *X* where antigovernment rioting occasionally makes headlines. While the client is scouting for antiques, the town falls under siege, during which time visitors are not in any real danger unless they try to leave the hotel. Upon his return, the client sues the travel agency, claiming that agency personnel failed to warn him of possible disruptions in country *X* and that his trip was ruined because he was unable to bring back antiques. In this case, the courts would probably not be sympathetic to the litigant because of his status as an experienced traveler and his business background in selling foreign antiques. Indeed, he might reasonably be expected to know as much as the travel agency about conditions abroad where he does his buying. His trip could, moreover, be interpreted as one necessitating an assumed risk. Generally, when a travel agency has no way of knowing uncertain conditions or dangers to provide information to clients, liability may be averted with a disclaimer.[6]

Case 6. A client buys a one-week trip to Exotica Island. One week before the purchase, an outbreak of cholera on Exotica Island was reported in a national travel industry magazine. The agency does not subscribe to the magazine and therefore did not know about the cholera. While on Exotica, the client contracts the disease and is hospitalized for several months. Upon recovery, he sues the travel agency for negligence in failing to warn him. Where health and safety are concerned, the courts may determine that it is the duty of the travel agency to read all readily available information on areas of travel where the company does business. While the agency could not control the cholera, it could control its ability to be well informed and to warn prospective travelers. The court ruling might also depend on when the travel agency learned of the cholera outbreak, whether the announcement was well publicized before or after the client's departure, and whether every effort was made to warn the client before departure.[7]

Case 7. A family purchases five airline tickets for a European holiday from a travel agency. A few weeks before the trip is scheduled, the air carrier declares bankruptcy, and the family sues the travel agency because no other airline will honor the tickets. The travel agency shows the family the invoice, which clearly states that its role is simply that of an agent for the air carrier. In this type of situation, the courts generally feel that any business doing more than a substantial amount of sales should be run by people who are sophisticated enough to at least read the financial section of major newspapers. Where the agent knew or should have known that the European carrier might default, he or she had a responsibility to disclose such information before receiving money from a client; otherwise, the agent could become liable for the value of the worthless ticket. On the other hand, if the potential bankruptcy of the carrier was not known to the trade until after the fact, the travel agent would probably not be held liable.[8]

Case 8.   An elderly couple consults a travel agent about an extensive trip but expresses fears of recent hijacking. The travel agent recommends taking a cruise, assuring the couple that a cruise is the best option for a good but safe trip because "terrorists would never grab a cruise ship." The couple takes the cruise, the ship is seajacked, and the elderly couple returns home in a nervous state and ready to sue the travel agency. Because most cruise brochures do not contain information regarding safety, except with regard to fires and life jackets, the agent is taking independent action in assuring the couple's safety. The cruise line is generally not responsible for the independent acts of the travel agent. If the couple can prove that the agent's safety assurance was a major factor in their decision to buy the vacation cruise, they might have a case against the agency for breach of contract or breach of warranty, especially if the agency knew or should have known of previously publicized seajacking incidents. The travel agency would have a stronger defense if it could prove that it had inquired about cruise ship security precautions before advising its clients.[9]

Case 9.   In a California case—*McCollum* v. *Friendly Hills Travel Center,* 72 Cal. App. 3d 83 (1985)—the courts ruled on the agent's liability to a third party in what may be a precedent-setting case. McCollum approached the travel agency to arrange for a water skiing vacation at the Cancun Club Mediterranee. The agent informed him that Club Med was fully booked for several months and provided him with brochures on alternative facilities. The client consequently selected another package but specifically inquired whether he would have to take his own skis. The agent checked his reference binder and informed him that he would not.

Upon arrival at the resort, however, McCollum found that the hotel had only one pair of skis available, and these were in poor condition. Nonetheless, he decided to use them. On the first two runs, there was no problem. On his third run, the boat driver increased his speed. McCollum signaled for the driver to slow down, but there was no response; McCollum subsequently fell, twisting his neck, and twenty-two days later he suffered a stroke.

In the ensuing suit, the court ruled that for this specific transaction, the agent was acting as a special agent for the traveler and therefore had a duty to apply reasonable effort in providing the client with necessary information available to the agency. However, the agent's duty to disclose was limited by the fact that the agency is not an insurer and cannot be expected to forewarn of every possible tragedy or danger that may occur. While travel agents have the duty to warn of dangers that they are or should be aware of, the law requires only that agents be loyal, not prescient. The foreseeability of harm was of key importance in this specific case. The client was an experienced skier and had himself inspected and accepted the condition of the skis. It could not be reasonably expected that the travel agent could have superior knowledge of equipment condition in responding to his client's inquiry regarding the availability of equipment.[10]

This last example illustrates that in certain situations the travel agent may be legally interpreted as acting as an agent of the traveler. The traveler may be viewed as acting as principal in choosing a retail travel agency and relying on the agent's judgment. If the courts find that the travel agent is legally the agent of the traveler, then the agent is bound to perform in a "fiduciary" manner and to make the "fullest disclosure of all material facts concerning the transaction in question that may affect the principal's decision." To be relieved of liability in acting as an agent for the traveler, the travel agent generally must prove that he or she had disclosed the fact that he or she was acting solely as an agent on behalf of the disclosed principal suppliers and was not acting as an agent of the traveler.

Other areas where the agent faces potential charges for negligence, lack of knowledge, misrepresentation, and so on, include not advising of the availability of different types of insurance, not specifying in the itinerary the airport or railroad station for a multi-terminal city or stating the wrong one, failure to notify customers of a schedule change, failure to call in ticket numbers to the airline or issue tickets by the deadline for incentive fares, failure to provide the passenger with a written confirmation by the supplier when time permits, and making guarantees about the quality and/or location of accommodations. Especially in the instance of accommodations, it is wiser for the travel agency to use only reputable accommodation suppliers and to know the features and quality of lodging products, striving for accuracy in the description of such products.

Agent Liability Outside of the United States

The agent-principal relationship is a definitive one in the United States. In Europe, consumer groups have banded together to place more liability on the travel agent. The European Economic Community has been engaged in drafting tough tourist protection regulations, including the incorporation of a proposal to hold travel retailers liable, even for events that may not be within their realm of control. This move toward "strict liability" is aimed at improving convenience for travelers who must seek recourse when something goes wrong. For travel retailers it might require placing all money collected from clients in a trust until the customer returns from the trip and is fully satisfied.[11]

One of the strongest examples of a travel consumer protection law is the Ontario Travel Industry Act, passed in 1987, which requires travel agents to inform clients of the laws and customs of each country to which they will travel. The Association of Canadian Travel Agents has been cautioned that the trend in Canada is now away from price and into consumer service with guarantees.

Disclaimers

To avoid legal predicaments in the event that problems arise in the client's planned or expected itinerary, travel agents should use disclaimers and other protective measures. All disclaimers should be drawn up by a qualified travel attorney. The disclaimer is an agreement whereby one party to a transaction (the client) declares that he or she will release the other party (the agent) from liability and responsibility for the transaction under certain stated conditions. In the travel industry, many of these disclaimers are in the form of announcements printed on brochures or invoices, and they are generally closely scrutinized by the courts before they can be upheld in a lawsuit. Disclaimers aside, it should be reiterated that travel agencies do not have responsibility for the negligent acts, bankruptcy, and other defaults of travel product suppliers.

A disclaimer is actually a form of a contract and must therefore meet three criteria in order to be legally enforceable.

1. Mutual or reasonable bargaining equality of the negotiating parties
2. Consideration or something of value
3. Knowledge and full understanding of the terms of the agreement[12]

The client must have full knowledge of, and give free consent to, the agreement before purchase to relieve the travel agent from liability, and the travel agency must prove that it was not taking advantage of the unknowledgeable or uninformed client. The circumstances and language of the release forms are, therefore, important factors in their validity.

Disclaimers that leave the consumer without recourse of any kind when there is a problem with the purchase are viewed by the courts with skepticism. They must also be considered reasonable and mindful of consumers' rights. Furthermore, they should disclaim only that conduct that is clearly beyond the control of the agent and specify clearly who is responsible for providing what services.

The courts will evaluate the disclaimer in terms of the prominence of the disclaimer in the printed material given to the client (ease of notice), size of lettering, readability of the clause and ease of understanding, and legal wording. The language in the disclaimer should be clear and unambiguous. It should also be as restrictive as possible in achieving the desired results; a disclaimer that is too broad in scope has a lesser chance of being upheld in court.

The disclaimer, even if not always enforceable, can often discourage nuisance or frivolous lawsuits, which may damage the successful operation of the agency through adverse publicity, time spent on the case, and legal costs of defense. The disclaimer can also act as a release if the client signs it with a statement to the effect that there is understanding and acceptance of its provisions. This offers the strongest possible protection, and the original copy should be placed in the client's folder for reference as prima facie evidence if needed. Even if the client will not sign the disclaimer or there is no contact with the client in person to obtain a signature, a copy should nonetheless be provided to the client. The alternative to having the client sign the disclaimer is to print it on the ticket envelope or the reverse side of the invoice or itinerary. The point is that as long as the client is aware of the disclaimer and understands its provisions, it will be valid and legal.

Many agencies do not use disclaimers for the simple reason that they may frighten away potential customers. Formal legal documents have a way of arousing suspicion. Some clients will refuse to sign such a document or before signing may want it reviewed by their attorney, creating extra work and undesired problems.

Exhibit 11.2 is a consumer disclosure notice specifying that the agent will not be liable for any actions on the part of suppliers. Exhibit 11.2 illustrates standard provisions covering other specific areas for which the travel agency may disclaim responsibility. Descriptions of certain of these provisions follow.

Airfare fluctuations.   As a result of deregulation, air carriers are permitted to change fares at will. In such a flexible environment for the carriers, it is difficult for the agent to be consistently up to date on perpetually changing fares and schedules. Yet by misquoting prices, selling at unauthorized levels, or giving out old information, however unintentionally, the agent is exposing him or herself to potential liability for failure to secure the best possible fare for a client. Adding to the problem in the case of international ticketing is the fact that currency fluctuations can also result in significant fare changes. While disclaimers may permit agents to rightfully avoid responsibility for obtaining the lowest fares, the agent should also be careful not to promise clients that the fare given is the cheapest possible.

Supplier default.   Carrier bankruptcies have become much more common under deregulation. A provision specifying that the agent will not be responsible if a supplier ceases operation should be printed on the invoice, on the itinerary, or on the ticket jacket. In the event of a carrier failure, clients must then look to their defaulting suppliers for refunds.

Prior to deregulation, the Airline Default Protection Plan covered the shortages of defaulted airlines by requiring some 130 airlines participating in the Area Settlement Plan to provide alternate transportation for passengers holding travel-agent-issued tickets on a defaulted carrier, but at present

EXHIBIT 11.2

SAMPLE PREVENTIVE LEGAL CARE PROVISIONS

[*NAME OF TRAVEL AGENCY*] is not responsible for any fluctuations in fares and rate or price differentials offered to and accepted by customer, nor carriers' subsequent changes in fares/services.

―――――――――――――

[*NAME OF TRAVEL AGENCY*] is not responsible for cancellation of any service/s and/or refunds from any supplier or carrier that may cease operations.

―――――――――――――

[*TRAVEL AGENCY/TOUR OPERATOR NAME*] herein gives notice that it cannot be held responsible for any disruption of travel and/or related services in "troubled areas," due to Monetary Crisis, Political or Social Unrest, Terrorist Activities, Labor Problems, Mechanical or Construction Difficulties, Climatic Aberrations, Local Laws, Diseases, or Novel Conditions.

―――――――――――――

[*NAME OF TRAVEL AGENCY*] has advised me of potential travel disruption due to labor or financial difficulty but I prefer reservations on [*NAME OF CARRIER*].

Source: Alexander Anolik, *The Law and the Travel Industry,* vol. II (San Francisco: Alchemy Books, 1987), pp. 1–16.

no such plan exists. The American Society of Travel Agents (ASTA) has been trying to get a new Airline Default Protection Plan passed by legislation that would establish a federally controlled trust fund financed by a passenger airfare surcharge. The plan, however, has not been adopted for legislation.

Other provisions.   Computer errors that result in mistaken fares, routings, and flights and misconfirmations are now increasingly common with the use of automated systems. Occasionally, flights listed on the CRT may even turn out to be phantom flights or flights that do not exist or operate as scheduled. These situations make a disclaimer necessary to advise that an agency cannot be held responsible for errors originating from automated reservation systems that are under the control of the supplying carriers.

Another provision specifies the need for detailed travel documentation from the client in the event of a mishap. For clients to be properly reimbursed, they must have accurate information from such sources as newspapers or other official accounts of what happened, copies of replacement tickets, police reports for baggage, all receipts reflecting expenses, or any other legal papers served as a result of an incident.

Many agencies also include a statement that all purchases made through the agency are done at the request of the customer, reemphasizing the third party relationship between the travel agency and the client. Exhibit

EXHIBIT 11.3

SAMPLE DISCLAIMER PROVISION

Customer has initiated the specially requested purchase for above-stated travel services to all above destinations, and has been more than reasonably warned by Agency of all dangers associated with above destination occurrences arising after today; and will pay Agency as directed only after having received such advise.

Source: Allan H. Bell, "The Riot Sale," *The Travel Agent,* August 16, 1984, p. 15.

11.3 provides a sample disclaimer that can be used by agencies in the event that a client wants to travel to a destination where there are known dangers.

Airline deregulation has brought with it increased risk for travel agents in terms of liability. Deep-discount air fares, frequent flyer programs, the use of consolidators and preferred supplier arrangements, and a host of other new practices require the use of still more disclaimer notices. Table 11.1 provides a summary of steps travel agencies can take to shield themselves from these additional liabilities. A more detailed discussion on the subject of travel insurance follows.

TRAVEL INSURANCE

In recent years there has been a significant growth in the availability of various forms of travel insurance coverage. It is good preventive legal care for the agent to inform clients of the existence of such insurance. The potential liability for failure to advise of the insurance availability has encouraged some agents to offer the various coverages in writing and to require clients to initial or check off a form similar to that used by car rental companies. (See Exhibit 11.4.) Once transacted, a copy of the form should be put immediately in the client's file. In the event that the agent is sued, he or she can at least claim that the client has been advised that insurance protection was available. If properly done, these forms should stand up in court or at least deter dissatisfied clients from filing a nuisance suit.

Travel insurance sales can contribute to the agency's profit by providing an additional income source—commissions range as high as 50 percent. Moreover, travel insurance provides a certain peace of mind to the traveler. If a medical emergency were to arise during the course of travel, for instance, the appropriate travel medical insurance would cover doctor's bills, hospital fees, and prescription costs. Trip cancellation insurance, while most commonly applied against a default by an air carrier or wholesaler,

TABLE 11.1 HOW AGENTS CAN PROTECT THEMSELVES FROM LEGAL LIABILITIES.

Potential liability	Summary of agent remedy
Deep-discount airfares	Make brief verbal disclaimer at time of sale; follow up with written disclaimer stating that fare must be used exactly as issued (as such, it is nonrefundable or subject to a cancellation fee).
Carrier bankruptcy	State in written disclaimer that suppliers, not agents, are responsible for defaults and they must be addressed for refunds or other recourse. Remind clients that travel insurance may be purchased as safeguard.
Forgotten travel documentation (passports, visas, medical records)	Include in general written explanatory disclaimer, distribute to all clients.
Use of consolidator	Explain in written disclaimer consolidators may not confirm flight or deliver tickets until long after payment; if consolidator goes out of business, agent is not responsible for refunds or other recourse; tight restrictions on ticketing may make client change of plans impossible.
Purchased frequent flyer coupons	State in written disclaimer that purchased coupons may be confiscated by airline and passenger denied boarding—he may be forced to purchase full-fare ticket on the spot.
Lack of travel insurance (medical, baggage, trip cancellation)	Offer various coverages in writing to client; he has option to accept or reject each one individually.

Source: Arthur Schiff, "New Threats Prompt Use of Disclaimers," *ASTA Agency Management,* January, 1988, p. 92.

can also provide coverage for a client against cancellation penalties due to unexpected illness or death of a family member or some other unforeseen problem. Trip cancellation currently constitutes the majority of claims being filed: Approximately 55 percent of all travel insurance claims processed are for trip cancellation, 30 percent for baggage loss or damage, and less than 20 percent for medical-related emergencies.[13]

Travel agents should be aware that although selling travel insurance is usually a routine task, insurance policies cannot be written in the following specific situations.

1. *Ban on Coverage.* Generally when suppliers have gone into default or filed under Chapter 11, insurance companies will issue a warning against selling such policies for the supplier and place a ban on these

EXHIBIT 11.4

INSURANCE PROVISIONS

We recommend that all of our clients check their insurance policies before departing to ensure that accidents or health problems will be covered under their policy. We also offer travel, baggage, suppliers default, and travel medical insurance at reasonable rates. Please check the appropriate box if you wish to purchase this type of insurance.

☐ I accept baggage insurance
☐ I reject baggage insurance

☐ I accept personal accident insurance
☐ I reject personal accident insurance

☐ I accept trip cancellation insurance
☐ I reject trip cancellation insurance

☐ I accept supplier default insurance
☐ I reject supplier default insurance

☐ I accept travel medical insurance
☐ I reject travel medical insurance

Source: Jeffrey R. Miller, "Disclaimers Minimize Agency Liability," *Travel Marketing and Agency Management Guidelines,* May/June 1985, p. 20.

---

policies by sending a notice. The travel agent who continues to sell these policies does so at his or her own risk.

2. *Preexisting Medical Conditions.* Most insurance policies contain clauses about preexisting medical conditions that will preclude coverage of or invalidate a policy in the case of clients with a known medical problem, unless there is medical certification stating that the condition is under control.

3. *Free Trips.* Insurance is generally not available for free trips.

4. *After the Fact.* Insurance cannot be purchased after a contingency has occurred, for instance, after a supplier has gone into default or the client had to cancel a trip.[14]

In summary, disclaimer notices and forms covering such items as the types of available insurance have proven to be meaningful in numerous court cases. The fact that the courts have upheld carefully drafted disclaimers that have been clearly and conspicuously brought to the clients' attention at the appropriate time demonstrates the necessity for all travel agencies to seek legal counsel for the purpose of drafting disclaimers and business forms. The routine use of these forms should then be incorporated into standard office operating procedures.

LEGAL ISSUES COVERING EMPLOYEE RELATIONSHIPS

Employment Contracts

Employment contracts should be utilized by every travel agency. These contracts may cover such elements as compensation, including salary and/or commission or bonus, work days and times, annual leave, sick leave, severance pay, paid holidays, and employee duties and responsibilities. The most important elements for inclusion, however, are assignment rights and restrictive covenants.

An *assignment clause* allows the employer to assign the employment contract to any successor, including a new owner. For the new owner, the assignment right can be particularly valuable with respect to a *restrictive covenant clause*—perhaps the most important part of the employment contract for the travel agency. A restrictive covenant helps the agency to protect its business by prohibiting an employee who resigns from using confidential client lists that are the property of his or her former employer to benefit a new employer. An example of a restrictive covenant in an employment contract might read as follows:

> For a period of two years after the termination of this Agreement, the Employee will not, within a radius of twenty miles from the present place of business of the Employer, directly or indirectly, own, manage, control, or be employed by a travel agency. In the event of a breach of this Agreement and paragraph, the Employer shall be entitled to an injunction restraining the Employee from owning, managing, controlling, or being employed by such travel agency. The Employer shall also have reserved any other remedy available for the breach, including the recovery of damages from the Employee.

It is generaly accepted that an employee cannot solicit his or her employer's clients for another agency while he or she is still working for the former. However, this issue becomes clouded when employment with the first employer has been terminated. An employee has the right, of course, to inform clients that he or she will be changing agencies, but controversy occurs when an employee upon resignation decides to use client information obtained during his or her prior employment to further a new job. Although laws vary among states, the general rule is that an employee after resignation may not solicit clients of his or her former employer, under the following provisions:

1. The identities or special requirements of clients were confidential and not readily accessible to competitors. Courts evaluate this in terms of the employer's efforts in compiling and maintaining the client list and in keeping it secure, as well as how the information was obtained and developed.
2. The relationship between the client and the former employer would have continued without undue interference.
3. There is an enforceable agreement (restrictive covenant) between the former employer and employee that specifically prohibits the solicitation of the employer's customers when the employee resigns to take a job with another agency.

Other factors the court will review in evaluating breach of covenant cases include whether the employee had developed his or her own clients while working for the first employer, whether the ex-employee had copied any client lists, and whether there were "dirty tricks" employed by either party. A restrictive covenant will be upheld only if it is reasonable as to length of time and geographic area coverage. Legal assistance is, therefore, necessary in drafting the covenant.[15]

Employee Termination

Until recently many states had laws that recognized the precept that if no agreement existed specifying the term of employment, the employment relationship involved a mutuality of obligations between employer and employee. Either party, upon proper notification to the other, could terminate the relationship at will with very few restrictions.

Recently the trend in court has been more protective of employees who have been arbitrarily or unreasonably terminated. As the rules of employee termination, which invoke an implied covenant of good faith and fair dealing incumbent on both parties, have wide application to all situations, not only to travel agencies, we will only mention that prior to terminating an employee, the agency manager must be able to give a sound justification, and records should be kept of each and every factual situation that might logically bring the manager to a termination decision.

Good documentation is generally the best defense against a wrongful discharge suit. Agencies utilizing employee handbooks or policy and procedures manuals should use caution in specific wording because many courts have interpreted these manuals to represent contracts. Employers should specify reserved rights by including termination-at-will provisos and identifying actions that will result in immediate termination.[16]

CHECKLIST OF LEGAL PROBLEMS

There are many more legal issues that a travel agency becomes involved with than would seem immediately apparent. Some, but not all, have been discussed in this chapter. The following checklist provides a thorough item-ization of the potential sources of legal problems for travel agents.[17]

- ☐ Acquisitions
- ☐ Advertising—copy packaging
- ☐ Agents and brokers
- ☐ Antitrust matters
- ☐ Arbitration—role in disputes
- ☐ Bankruptcy
- ☐ Board of directors
- ☐ Buying and selling—terms and conditions
- ☐ Checks—forgeries, frauds
- ☐ Contracts and agreements
- ☐ Competitors stealing employees
- ☐ Corporate form
- ☐ Disclosure of information
- ☐ Employer and employee respon-sibilities
- ☐ Employment agreements
- ☐ Franchises
- ☐ Insurance contracts
- ☐ Interstate transportation
- ☐ Laws—federal, state, local
- ☐ Mergers
- ☐ Misrepresentation
- ☐ Multiple corporations
- ☐ Negligence
- ☐ Negotiable instruments
- ☐ Order acknowledgment and con-firmation
- ☐ Override
- ☐ Permits
- ☐ Price fixing
- ☐ Product liability
- ☐ Profit sharing
- ☐ Rebating
- ☐ Records, legal
- ☐ Retirement pensions
- ☐ Risk management
- ☐ Service charge
- ☐ Slander and libel
- ☐ Stockholders
- ☐ Stock options
- ☐ Stock voting rights
- ☐ Taxes
- ☐ Tie-in sales
- ☐ Trademarks
- ☐ Unfair competition
- ☐ Verbal agreements
- ☐ Wills
- ☐ Workmen's compensation
- ☐ Zoning

RISK MANAGEMENT

The selling of travel has many inherent risks, for there are many aspects over which the agency has no control. Various liability factors were dis-cussed in preceding sections, including the quality of pictures and language used in travel brochures and what the client infers from them, the reliability of travel suppliers, potential bankruptcies, employee termination, and the agency's own mistakes, among other elements.

Risk management incorporates the business activities of planning, or-ganizing, directing, and controlling the agency's resources to safeguard against potentially crippling losses. Risk can be defined as a chance of finan-cial loss resulting from many possible causes—fire, theft, death of an owner or key employee, computer breakdown, employment problems, or, as discussed in the previous section, legal damages paid for a mistake or negligence on the part of the agency.

The process of risk management incorporates four steps:

1. Identification of potential risks
2. Assessment of degree and impact of potential risks
3. Decision to asssume, avoid, or transfer risk
4. Action implementation

As a first step, every travel agency should make an effort to identify all potential risk to its business, which should then be evaluated in terms of their probability, frequency, severity, and impact.

In dealing with identified and evaluated risks, the agency has two choices. It may decide to accept the risk through internal control and self-insurance (that is, avoidance, elimination, reduction) or to transfer the risk through insurance. Usually a combination of both options will be exercised, as it is a rare business that can afford to fully self-insure in modern practice. In taking action on risk decisions, consistent policies and programs should be incorporated and followed to protect the agency from disaster. Managers need to impress on their employees that dealing with risk management is every employee's responsibility. Employees should become so familiar with risk-management procedures that their application becomes almost second nature.

Because insurance is expensive, some larger travel agencies with high business volume decide to finance their own risk and emphasize the practice of measures that will reduce their exposure to potentially damaging losses. Important preventive measures cover not only the use of disclosure notices and disclaimers but also specific procedures on what should be done with cash sales (for example, depositing large sums in the bank immediately, requesting that clients who pay cash come in early in the day, keeping the safe door closed at all times to protect cash and ticket stock). (Note: Travel agents are liable for lost or stolen ticket stock if they have not followed ARC guidelines for protecting it.)

Preventive legal care also requires adhering to a strict policy of not accepting personal checks when banks are closed and no verification is possible, not accepting postdated checks or second-party checks, requiring management approval for credit because of its negative impact on cash flow, limiting or placing a ceiling on credit, "aging" accounts receivables, consistently using fraud alert bulletins, ensuring that all vital records are copied and kept off the premises in case of fire, and double checking all tickets for accuracy. To make these procedures operative, constant personnel training is paramount.[18]

Insurance

While the risk-avoidance procedures such as those mentioned can help to prevent disastrous situations, insurance protection provides a backup when something goes wrong despite precautions. Insurance reduces the risk of travel agency operation by trading off a large, uncertain loss for a small but certain loss in the form of a premium to the insurer. Purchased wisely, insurance contributes to the agency's financial soundness and profitability.

The types of insurance protection to purchase, the amount of protection needed, and how much the agency can afford are questions that the agency must review carefully, and they are best considered with the help of professional advice. The overall insurance plan should provide a comprehensive protection package with maximum coverage in crucial liability or loss areas. Most insurance policies specify a stated deductible amount, which means that the agency pays this specified sum of money on a covered loss before the insurance policy coverage begins. In principle, the higher the deductible, the lower the premium; also, the greater risk, the higher the premium.

In selecting an insurance company, the agency must consider such factors as the firm's experience in working with the travel industry, the firm's reputation in settling claims, and the payment plan and terms of the policy. It is often advisable to use the same insurance company for both general liability and professional liability to prevent gaps or duplicaton in coverage. In every instance, the agent must be cognizant of the exact coverage of each policy and the restrictions and exclusions that apply.

ASTA, through its ASTA Group Insurance Trust, is attempting to provide affordable, effective, and comprehensive group insurance coverage for travel agency owners and their employees and families with a series of programs underwritten by a major insurance company. Currently, the trust is providing more than 8000 travel industry professionals with competitive group rates on health, disability, medical, and life insurance plans.[19]

There are various types of insurance that are available and applicable to travel agency businesses.

Errors and omissions insurance.   *Errors and omissions insurance,* otherwise known as professional liability insurance, is similar to what the medical profession terms *malpractice insurance.* It protects the agency by covering claims for damages suffered by the client for financial loss, inconvenience, embarrassment, or other injuries because of an error or omission on the part of the agent. A simple and easily made mistake such as writing the incorrect flight time, failing to make a hotel reservation, or making an error in professional judgment could trigger a lawsuit that seeks not only actual but punitive damages. Even though few claims are actually made in this area, settlements can be high, more or less putting the agency on the line with every sale.

Errors and omissions coverage is extremely important to the travel agent because of the nature of the product sold. Travel products are intangibles, in reality promises for the delivery of services, which do not lend themselves to giving immediate satisfaction as tangible commodities do. Considering the high cost of travel, a client's expectation is likely to be equally high, so the risk of dissatisfaction is always present.

The travel agent, being wholly dependent on travel suppliers for the quality and delivery of the product, has no control over the performance of the supplier. Indeed, the very status of the agent as a professional counselor adds to his or her exposure to the liability risk arising from the sale of an unsatisfying product. Errors and omissions insurance should, therefore, cover not only actual and possible compensatory and punitive damages awarded by the courts but also costs incurred in defense of the travel agency. In certain states, the insurer may not insure against intentional torts giving ground for punitive damage.

Policies for professional liability limit claims coverage to those claims pertaining to acts made while the insurance policy is in force. Claims filed for negligent acts performed before or after the policy's effective dates are not covered. In most policies, there will be a deductible for each claim and usually a specified limit as well. Excluded from E and O coverage is any liability that may result from the mixing of agency funds or the failure of the agent to pay principals or to collect from clients. Actions of the agent involving willful dishonesty or violation of any laws are also excluded.

General liability insurance.   This insurance protects the agency in the event of injuries to clients or clients' property while they are on the agency's grounds or at an agency-sponsored function. It may also cover acts of employees or those of independent contractors that result in damages. Many liability insurance policies also cover certain personal injuries, such as libel, slander, or damages resulting from false, fraudulent, or misleading advertising. The high costs associated with medical care and defending a lawsuit make this type of coverage essential to the travel agency.

Property insurance.   Disasters commonly associated with property insurance include fire, smoke damage, hail, lightning, wind storms, vandalism, flood, and water damage. The extent of the coverage will depend on whether the travel agency operator is the owner of the building or a tenant. If he or she's the owner, the policy will pay the insured the actual cash value of the building (and/or contents if included in the policy) at the time of loss. This is defined as replacement cost minus depreciation. When buying property insurance, the agency manager should be aware that coverage for contingencies and policy provisions may vary widely among different insurers.

Business interruption insurance.   While this form of insurance is not essential, it does add to the security of the business. When the agency's building is either damaged or destroyed and the agency is forced to temporarily close down operations or move its location, the insurance covers certain incurred expenses. The purpose of business interruption insurance is to minimize the impact on the agency's financial status by covering such fixed costs as salaries, subscriptions, computer time, and so on.

To collect on a business interruption policy, the agency must show that the interruption resulted from a damage specified by the policy, that the loss of business occurred as a result of the damage, and that the business would have continued to operate had there not been such damage (for example, a travel agency that was already in the process of declaring bankruptcy would not qualify).

Disability insurance.   Most states now require all employers to cover employees under workers' compensation, which compensates and protects employees who are injured or disabled while performing their jobs. However, employees are compensated only for time lost because of work-related sickness or injuries. Disability insurance, on the other hand, provides workers with an income for life or for the duration of the disability for accidents or sicknesses that are not work related.

Life insurance.   Group life insurance plans can be purchased that will cover all employees at a nominal cost. Another type of life insurance exists called "key person" life insurance that protects the agency against the effects of the death of an owner or principal employee with essential skills and knowledge whose absence would likely jeopardize the health of the agency—in this instance, by assigning the face value of the policy to the travel agency.

Other insurance.   Other types of insurance policies commonly purchased by travel agents are fidelity bonds that reimburse the agency for theft or embezzlement by an employee, employee health insurance, automobile insurance, crime insurance, and rent insurance where applicable.

Travel agents daily face many risks of various types that can be covered by insurance. However, insurance costs today greatly add to the cost of doing business and for the small travel agency may even be prohibitive. The potential risk must, therefore, be weighed and evaluated against the cost of the insurance policy.

During the mid-1980s, an unprecedented number of factors came into play severely impacting the American insurance industry. These factors included, among others, falling interest rates that resulted in a lower return on insurance company investments and dwindling cash reserves, tighter government regulations, rising consumerism awareness, an increase in class-action suits and contingency fee cases with large damage awards, and in the minds of many the general mismanagement of the industry itself.

The woes of the insurance industry in turn had a harmful effect on virtually every type of business, especially those engaged in professional services (medicine, health care, child day care, and so on), as rising numbers of insurance companies that cover professional liability decided not to take on new policies, not to renew existing ones, or to insure for professional liability only at exorbitant rates. While the professional liability insurance situation has settled somewhat since the early 1980s, travel agents need to be aware of the importance of this insurance and the numerous factors that influence the industry's insurance situation.

SUMMARY

A travel agent's relationship as an agent acting on behalf of principals or suppliers to serve a third party, the client, may not be too difficult to understand, but it is cloaked in complicated legal concepts, terminology, and language. Therefore, it is necessary for a travel agency to seek professional legal advice and services in the review of most documents, especially those dealing with disclosure, disclaimers, internal policies, and employee practices. There are a number of practices and policies the agency can adopt to minimize its liability, including the use of disclosures and disclaimers, and it is critical to have a full understanding of these instruments, especially in view of the recent increases in lawsuits filed against travel agents. The process of risk management means taking action to avoid, eliminate, or reduce an agency's exposure to losses and purchasing an adequate insurance package as a means of transferring risk and assuring the agency's survival in today's environment of consumer rights.

DISCUSSION QUESTIONS

1. How do travel agencies differ from other retail operations with respect to the legal relationship with suppliers and clients?
2. What factors(s) determine whether or not the travel agency will be held liable to its clients for travel products purchased?
3. In what situation or circumstances might the travel agent act as principal?
4. What types of travel insurance are available to the traveling public?
5. Why are assignment rights and restrictive covenants important elements in the employment contract?
6. In addition to the purchase of insurance, what other types of risk-management activities can an agency practice?

ENDNOTES

[1]Alexander Anolik, *The Law and the Travel Industry*, Vol. II, (San Francisco: Alchemy Books, 1987), pp. 1–22.

[2]Allan H. Bell, "Don't Answer That," *The Travel Agent*, December 11, 1980, p. 64.

[3]Allan H. Bell, "A Matter of Responsibility," *The Travel Agent*, April 9, 1981, p. 42.

[4]Allan H. Bell, "He Books a Hospital Room," *The Travel Agent*, April 9, 1981, p. 42.

[5]Allan H. Bell, "The Case of the Cruise Thief," *The Travel Agent*, June 7, 1982, p. 18.

[6]Allan H. Bell, "The Riot Sale," *The Travel Agent*, August 16, 1984, p. 14.

[7]Allan H. Bell, "No News Is Bad News," *The Travel Agent*, August 5, 1982, p. 70.

[8]Allan H. Bell, "Ticket to Nowhere," *The Travel Agent*, February 5, 1981, p. 24.

[9]Allan H. Bell, "Seajack," *The Travel Agent*, October 28, 1985, p. 30.

[10]Alexander Anolik, "A California Court Swings Your Way," *The Travel Agent*, December 5, 1985, p. 28.

[11]Bill Bartman, "EEC May Hold Agents Liable for Event They Don't Control," *The Travel Agent*, October 24, 1985, p. 1.

[12]Allan H. Bell, "Disclaimers," *The Travel Agent*, May 24, 1982, p. 32.

[13]John M. Noel, "The Insurance Advisor," *The Travel Agent*, June 10, 1985, p. 24.

[14]John M. Noel, "Selling a Policy's Usually Easy But. . .," *The Travel Agent*, January 3, 1985, p. 34.

[15]Jeffrey R. Miller, "Employment Contracts," *Travel Marketing and Agency Management Guidelines*, March/April, 1984, pp. 14–15.

[16]Alexander Anolik, "Courts Make It Difficult to Terminate Employees at Will," *Travel Marketing and Agency Employees Guidelines*, July/August, 1982, p. 27.

[17]Edward M. Kelly, ed. *Business Management for Travel Agents* (Wellesley, MA: Institute of Certified Travel Agents, 1976), p. 188.

[18]Dwight E. Levick, *Risk Management for the Travel Industry* (Wellesley, MA: Institute of Certified Travel Agents, 1983).

[19]David Swindell, "Group Insurance Designed for the Travel Industry," *ASTA Agency Management*, January, 1988, p. 88.

SUPPLEMENTAL READINGS

ANOLIK, ALEXANDER, *The Law and the Travel Industry,* vol. 2, San Francisco: Alchemy Books, 1987.

LEVICK, DWIGHT E., *Risk Management for the Travel Industry,* eds. Edward M. Kelly and Joan E. Crooke. EPCU. Advanced Study Series. Wellesley, MA: ICTA, 1983.

MILLER, JEFFREY R., *Legal Aspects of Travel Agency Operation* (2nd ed.). Albany, NY: Delmar Publishers, Inc., 1987.

STEVENS, LAURENCE, *Guide to Starting and Operating a Successful Travel Agency,* Wheaton, IL: Merton House Travel and Tourism Publishers, 1983.

chapter 12

Future Aspects in the Industry

LEARNING OBJECTIVES

- To understand the impact that business travel departments (BTDs) and satellite ticket printers (STPs), among others, have and will have on the travel agency industry
- To be able to discuss how current and future trends will affect the structure of the industry

KEY TERMS

- Association of British Travel Agents (ABTA)
- Coupon Brokers
- Default Protection Plan
- Merger
- "Other Persons"

INTRODUCTION

The operating environment of travel agencies is quickly changing. Just as methods of operation successful ten years ago are no longer necessarily successful today, today's successful operations and organization may not resemble tomorrow's. Continuing environmental changes guarantee the further evolution of the travel agency system. Some changes will be primarily industry driven, such as those precipitated by the Airline Deregulation Act domestically and the International Airline Transportation Competition Act internationally. Other changes are being driven by travel trends, that is, traveler choices, some almost entirely new and some merely continuations of long-term trends.

Deregulation

Due to deregulation, the accredited travel agency distribution system no longer enjoys antitrust immunity. As discussed in previous chapters, the Airlines Reporting Corporation (ARC) and the International Airline Travel Agency Network (IATAN) replaced the ATC-administered program, which, until January 1, 1985, had governed airline-agent relations for forty years. Although ARC/IATAN portend many upheavals, their most immediate impact will probably be felt in the area of business travel management. Among other things, agencies are expected to more vigorously pursue the business traveler and improve their ticket delivery systems with equipment such as satellite ticket printers (STPs).

Deregulation will continue to impact the industry's organization as well. Domestic and international tourism can be expected to increase for the foreseeable future, creating a larger client base. On the other hand, technological improvements and competition will make it increasingly difficult for the individual agent to survive. The travel agent must adapt to these changes, altering the services offered to meet changing market conditions.

Rebating

Providing new services is not always sufficient; sometimes agents must resort to rebating, undermining the basic integrity of published tariffs. The problem is particularly acute and longstanding with respect to international travel. Any hope for immediate relief of the rebating problem was dashed when the United States Department of Transportation recently said that it will do nothing to stop such practices in this country, even though it is illegal. Between declining average fare levels and rebating, the travel agent is seeing a diminishing revenue yield per transaction. The problem is compounded by the number of times tickets are reissued—primarily downward in terms of profit. Costs increase; revenues decline. Agencies must closely control costs, and raise revenue, perhaps through service fees, in order to survive.

The institutional, organizational, and financial problems mentioned above are only a few of the many challenges facing the travel agent in the near future. Each is discussed in more detail in the remainder of this chapter. Other problems, however, although excluded from this review, should not be considered immaterial but rather the object of further study.

ARC-RELATED CHANGES

With the disbanding of the ATC in 1985, replaced by the ARC, travel agencies lost their exclusive legal right to sell airline tickets for a commission. In general, the ARC provides a more liberal system of agency appointment, operation, and compensation. The corporate travel sector is taking greatest advantage of the new provisions. Business travel accounts for 50 percent of airline and travel agent sales. Since it also represents one of the largest and most inflationary expenditure items for many large corporations, businesses are trying to better manage their travel budgets. In the process, the traditional boundaries separating corporate travelers, travel agents, and airlines are blurring.

Business Travel Departments

ATC standards forced business travel departments (BTDs) to purchase airline services through, and pay commissions to, retail travel agents even though they would often provide most or all of the services associated with agents themselves. ARC allows corporations to bypass travel agents altogether if they so desire, and vendors are willing, or use this possibility as leverage to obtain better service from their travel agents.

Most promising to BTDs, and most worrisome to travel agents, are restricted access agencies and "other persons" categories created by the ARC. Neither must be open and accessible or be clearly identified to the public. Self-sales are unrestricted and commissionable at the discretion of the airline. "Other persons" do not technically even report through the Area Settlement Plan as do travel agents. In essence, a corporate travel department can become a commercial travel agent. One corporation, McDonnell Douglas, has already converted its BTD into an agency.

Many firms may find it uneconomical or impractical to create an in-house travel agency. While at first it would seem beneficial to the commercial agent, closer examination suggests that it may not always be so. Some firms are leveraging their agents instead—International Business Machines (IBM) is a case in point. In 1985, IBM consolidated the four divisions of its

Information Systems Group, with an annual travel budget exceeding $100 million, for the purpose of purchasing travel services.[1] Selected retail agents were chosen to bid on a central contract to manage the entire year's budget. Pricing provisions of the contract have not yet been disclosed, but some current contracts provide for rebating one-third of airline commissions and 100 percent of hotel and car commissions to the firm. In addition, IBM service demands include a minimum of two ticket deliveries per day, assured lowest airfare, updated corporate traveler profiles, the provision of assistance in credit card matters, and even lost-baggage support.

These examples are not meant to suggest that the retail travel agent is doomed in the corporate sector but rather that the travel agency must adjust its product or service if it is to survive. Foremost, agents will no longer be able to remain primarily order takers. BTDs can and will buy their own travel requirements if this is the only service offered. Some have suggested that the future will see retail travel agents bulk wholesaling airline seats, providing their own frequent flyer traveler incentives, issuing agency credit cards, and improving billing systems. Whether with these services or others, agencies must provide convenience and savings to the traveler while enhancing brand loyalty to the agency.

Impact of Frequent Flyer Programs

One system of generating brand loyalty, the airline frequent flyer programs, has created numerous problems for the industry.[2] The administrative cost of managing the records of frequent flyer programs is seen as being quite high by many firms. As corporations begin purchasing travel services the same way they have purchased all other products in the past, travel agents should expect this to be an area of negotiation. Firms such as IBM will require the travel agency to incur the cost of managing the corporate program. The profit potential from providing such a service is obviously quite large; the cost of providing the service is equally very large.

While frequent flyer programs create a demand for travel agent services on the one hand, they diminish it on the other. Legal or not, frequent flyer coupons often end up being used by someone other than the person who earned the award. The least significant part of the problem is the individual selling his or her coupon to another traveler, thereby depriving the agent of a potential sale. More significant are coupon brokers, such as the "Coupon Bank," who operate nationally. These companies simultaneously divert customers away from traditional agents and drive down the prices in markets where they operate. The end result is more commission revenue.

Retail travel agents have a powerful ally in their competition with coupon brokers—the airlines. The frequent flyer awards programs were initiated to encourage brand loyalty. Instead, airlines have seen the programs cut already thin margins and have been forced to increase average fares, thereby discouraging some travel markets. As a result, several of the major carriers operating in the United States have gone to court to close ticket brokerage houses. Retail travel agents can only hope that they will be successful; if not, then brokering may be an option to explore for themselves.

Satellite Ticket Printers

A final issue in the ARC-BTD arena is the use of satellite ticket printers (STPs). The STP is analogous to the telefax in principle and in process. Although many airlines deny any link between BTD and STP, it is quite obvious that the greatest potential for the STP lies in replacing traditional means of delivery to corporate clients. They give even the smallest agent the capability of fast delivery to any client anywhere in the country. They are no panacea, however.

Traditional delivery systems to service dispersed clients have relied on overnight and second-day delivery couriers and regular mail service. While the latter is sometimes slow and the former has been considered somewhat expensive, each has proven workable and economical in most instances. The STP, however, is nearly instantaneous, but it is also expensive, perhaps prohibitively so for all but the largest agencies and their clients.

Exact cost data about STPs is difficult to obtain due to their relative newness. Current costs for an installation are estimated to range up to $1200 per month. In addition, costs will be incurred for phone lines, dial-up phone charges, office space, and employee salaries. Often the employee salary may prove a double burden, as an STP is operative only when the home office is open. Therefore, an agency on, say, the East Coast would have to stay longer to provide STP service to a client on the West Coast during the latter's normal business hours. Giving consideration to all of these factors, it has been estimated that the cost of issuing fifteen tickets per day per STP is $1.40 per ticket, a cost that would fall to $1.00 per ticket if twenty-five tickets per day were printed.

Cost may be the least problem with STPs. ARC rules stipulate that each STP is provided with a separate agency code. Thus, an agency would have individual codes for the central office and for each STP located on the premises of a corporate client. Sales for each agency (code) are, of course, reported to ARC. As ARC is made up of airlines, the airlines would know exactly how much business, and the nature of business, for each corporation served by an STP. In a sense, a travel agent would be helping the scheduled airlines collect market data on a customer-by-customer basis. With travel agent commissions being the third largest cost item for airlines, and one of the most rapidly escalating, it would not be surprising if the airlines, protestations notwithstanding, used the information to deal directly with corporations, bypassing the travel agent altogether. It must be emphasized that all major airlines have disavowed direct dealings with corporations, but the future market may prove to be different.

The greatest obstacle to extensive use of STPs is the liability issue. ARC imposes absolute liability on the agency for any loss, theft, or forgery of any traffic documents where the STP is located. Insuring against liability for ticket stock is probably not possible. Until the ticket is issued, the stock has no determinable value; therefore it generally is not insurable. The STP attendant could be bonded, but this is of limited value, protecting the agency only if the attendant is at fault. More promising is for the agency to negotiate the commercial contract with liability in mind, getting the corporate client to indemnify the agent.

The promise of STPs is great. In the short time that they have existed, growth in their number has been explosive. According to ARC, in 1986 there were 289 STP locations. In 1987 the number increased to 867 and by July 1988 there were 1670 ARC-approved STP locations. With STPs, small agents can distribute nationally, able to compete, at least in this regard, with much larger agencies. Some foresee the cost falling by one-half in the near future; experience with other high-technology developments gives this argument some credence. Liability issues may be negotiable, particularly with small- and medium-size clients. STP and all ARC-related factors, in conjunction with other more general aspects of airline deregulation, will reshape the structure of the travel agent industry.

INDUSTRY STRUCTURE

In 1978, at the start of deregulation, there were 14,804 travel agency locations in the United states, accounting for approximately 40 percent of ticket sales. By mid-year 1988, there were an estimated 31,699 locations including STPs. If current trends continue, retail travel agents will generate 85 percent of airline sales by the close of the decade. When combined with the increasing percentage of hotel, tour, car rental, cruise, and train services purchased through travel agents, these figures present a very optimistic future for the industry. Nevertheless, some deregulation-spawned factors are not so bright.

Airfare Impacts

Ironically, but not too surprisingly, agencies' profit potential rests with the same group that first endangered agent profits—the airlines. The fare wars that broke out following deregulation are the most immediate cause of red ink in the travel agency business.

Fare levels have dropped dramatically since 1978. In 1977, 60 percent of all revenue passenger miles were purchased by travelers paying the standard coach fare. By 1986, over 90 percent of passengers were traveling on fares discounted an average of 62 percent.[3] To the traveler, this is good news indeed; to the travel agent earning a 10 percent commission on gross fares, this is bad news.

At nearly one-half of all agencies, a survey conducted by ASTA in 1988 showed the profit spread ranged from $2 to $5, and this was only at the most profitable agencies! Ultimately, agent profitability depends on rising airfares, but even increasing fares would not solve all problems.

The cost to write a ticket, as disclosed by the ASTA survey, is around $25 to $35 at most travel agencies. The break-even point is then a $250 to $350 itinerary, assuming that there are no rewrites. With transcontinental service commonly available at under $500, it is easy to see why the number of agency failures is increasing. In fact, a record number of travel agencies— more than 1400—closed their doors in 1986.

Travel agents can look to several sources of action to improve their revenue picture. One area of promise is the current trend toward stability, as well as the slight increases in airline fares recently evident.

Override Agreements

If agents are to be proactive, rather than reactive, they must take positive steps to bolster revenue rather than rely upon a fare structure beyond their control. One step that is finding increasing favor is the use of a preferred supplier list to maximize override commissions.[4] (This topic was discussed briefly in Chapter 5, Marketing.) Although they have been around for many years, the use of override agreements has risen dramatically and in concert with lowering airfares. Today, approximately 54 percent of travel agencies receive overrides from domestic air carriers while 48 percent earn overrides from international airline sales. For carriers, overrides build agent loyalty and strengthen the sales distribution system. Travel agents may realize even greater benefits.[5]

Most obviously, override agreements with preferred suppliers give agents the opportunity to earn higher commissions. Overrides can run from as low as 1 percent extra commission to well over 5 percent (representing a 50 percent increase on the average commission of 10 percent). Beyond this, agents also often gain access to seats and tour programs at lower prices than are offered to other agencies. Cost economies also typically accompany a move toward preferred suppliers. Agency owners and managers are better able to direct the agencies' business, and the agents' time toward particular vendors, thereby decreasing search time and increasing revenue.

Even with focused selling efforts, many agencies may not realize sufficient volume to earn overrides. The key rests with agency size: Large agencies, doing large amounts of business, are well positioned, but what of the small agency? Some must close their doors, expand their sales base, or specialize in a particular niche. One possibility is to buy other agencies, another to run a franchise operation. A primary motivating factor in establishing

Uniglobe, a chain of more than 500 franchise agencies, for example, was the desire to increase profits through override agreements.

Service Fees

A second avenue to increased profits, not yet as widely used as overrides, is the use of service charges (as discussed in Chapter 5). Some agents argue that lawyers do not offer free advice to clients and therefore neither should they. Travel agents are professionals whose time represents money. However, some problems must be anticipated before instituting a fee schedule.

Unless all agents in a particular market adopt service fees under a uniform schedule, an agency charging fees probably will lose clients to agents not charging fees. Even if a fee schedule can be maintained both legally and operationally, agents could face the prospect of clients dealing directly with airline ticket offices. In constructing fee schedules, therefore, a travel agency must be careful that revenue gains are not offset by revenue diversion.

Service fees also may take agencies into a new legal arena. Agents are used to being agents for travel suppliers, such as the airlines. An agent's liability and attendant insurance costs are well known. By assessing a service charge, however, the agency becomes an agent of both the travel supplier and the traveler. Although this legal point has yet to be firmly established in court, it is one of which the agent must be aware.

Facing new and increasing liability, a travel agency can take several steps to protect itself. The first, easiest, and least costly step is to advise clients, preferably in writing, of the dual agency status being maintained by the travel agency. Beyond this, the travel agency charging service fees should reexamine insurance coverage to ensure it has adequate errors and omissions insurance and liability insurance. The cost of obtaining this coverage may outweigh the gains of service fees, particularly when these costs are added to the potential diversionary impact mentioned above. Service fees, at this time, are best implemented carefully and selectively by the typical travel agent. The following is a list of guidelines for agencies choosing to utilize charges.

1. Service charges should not be discussed with staff of other agencies. Local agencies should not devise a joint service-charge policy as it may be construed as illegal price fixing.
2. Charges should be simple and discussed with staff and/or major clients before implementation.
3. A sign should be posted near the entrance advising clients about the service charges. A short statement on itineraries and invoices also helps remind clients about the charges.

4. Be prepared to lose business, although quite likely, most of this will be unprofitable business.

5. When explaining the new charge policies, present them in a positive matter-of-fact way.

6. Be flexible with the charges policy, especially with the agency's best clients.[6]

Mergers and Defaults

Competition in the airline industry is decreasing through merger and bankruptcy, frequently with mergers between a profitable and a bankrupt carrier. Less known, but equally as damaging to travel agents, are defaults of tour wholesalers. In 1986, approximately twenty operators went bankrupt. In all cases, little protection was accorded the agent and its client.

The collapse of Braniff in 1982 was the last time agents were protected from carrier default. When Continental closed its doors, agents were not protected, either from their angry clients or from the worthless ticket stock they held. Bankruptcies since that time, such as People Express, Frontier, and others, have found the travel agent equally vulnerable.

At this time, there appears to be little that can be done to protect against the default of carriers. The Air Transport Association has often talked of reinstating the Default Protection plan that worked so well in Braniff's case. Since it would make little competitive sense for the healthy members of the industry to adopt a plan to help the financially weak airlines, travel agents should not look to the airlines for protection.

Congress may provide the answer; the government has funded a study to determine the feasibility of a default protection plan administered by the Department of Transportation. Sample plans call for a surcharge of $0.25 per ticket to establish the fund. Despite the ardent support of ASTA, however, unless the current deregulatory mood changes, the travel agent can expect little help any time soon from the government.

TRAVEL TRENDS

Although challenges wrought by deregulation and other industry-related changes pose difficult problems, travel agents face an even larger set of challenges. The demand for travel agent services is, of course, derived from the demand for travel and tourism services. An agency, through effective management, may be able to cut itself a larger piece of the travel pie, but it has little effect on the size or nature of travel itself. Ultimately travel agents profit from or become victims of travel trends, some of which are favorable while others are not.

Travel Statistics

In 1987, records were set across many measures of domestic travel. Nearly 1.2 billion person-trips were taken, an increase of approximately 6 percent over 1986 levels. Travel industry receipts rose even faster, climbing some 7 percent, outpacing the growth of GNP. Within this total, business travel was the fastest-growing sector, climbing 10 percent, outpacing growth in vacation travel, which rose by only 2 percent.[7]

The growth in travel is not without negative implications. The total number of nights spent away from home rose only 4 percent, less than the growth rate found in trips taken. The number of vacation nights spent away from home actually declined by 3 percent. The disparity between total nights and vacation nights away from home is explained by the growth in nights away from home in the business travel sector.

Shorter Vacations

Americans are turning toward weekend and shorter vacation travel. Thus, while total travel is increasing, trip duration is declining—the average trip length during heavy summer travel months is only 870 miles round trip. This trend is expected to continue in the foreseeable future as the number of two-income and career households increases, forcing people away from long trips in favor of taking a "getaway" weekend when work schedules permit.

The challenges posed to travel agents are obvious. How do you insert yourself into the revenue and distribution stream created by short trips? Furthermore, will the price of a single itinerary, even if booked through a travel agent, generate sufficient commission revenue to be profitable? It is not difficult to envision that travel agents are looking to a future of selling more travel products with each at a relatively lower price than today's longer itineraries, to make a given level of profit.

Vehicle Travel

Shorter, more frequent trips likewise reinforce the private automobile as the predominant travel mode in the United States. Of all travelers in 1987, 82 percent went by automobile, truck, or recreation vehicle and 14 percent by air, with the remainder divided between long-haul rail and bus service. In spite of predictions to the contrary, which have been rendered by experts for at least two decades, Americans have not foregone their automobiles in favor of air travel.

If Americans are traveling shorter distances, taking shorter-duration trips, traveling primarily by automobile, and, even when traveling by air, having increased direct access to reservations systems, a real question arises as to whether travel agents will have any useful role to play in the future. The answer would seem to be an unqualified no for agents unable and/or unwilling to exploit favorable trends and new profit protential.

Marketing for the Elderly

Agents can and must look toward providing travel products and services for the elderly. There are nearly fifteen million people who are comfortably retired in the United States.[8] Another three million are among the pension elite, that is, retired people who receive money from three sources: Social Security, pensions, and assets. These segments generally have the largest amount of leisure time available for travel, are able to take longer trips, travel internationally, and are in a position to travel during off-peak or short periods. The U.S. Bureau of Census 1988 Statistical Abstract, in fact, showed that the number of new passports issued to Americans aged 60 and older escalated from 360,000 in 1970 to 1,039,000 in 1985. The market for the elderly has become attractive to suppliers and should likewise be of interest to agents.

The graying of society is not strictly an American phenomenon. It is estimated that one-quarter of the European population will be age 55 or older by the year 2000. Twenty years thereafter, the Japanese market is expected to have similar characteristics. At present, only one in nine Japanese is 55 years or older, yet between 1975 and 1983 this segment rose from eight million to eleven million people.[9]

Agents must therefore look to the special travel needs of the elderly. In keeping with the fitness trend, health-related tourism is expected to grow as the baby boomers reach maturity; in addition, inclusive tours may enjoy a resurgence as people look for convenience in booking and traveling. For example, only one-sixth of the population in Europe has taken an inclusive tour. The propensity to purchase these services should increase as the general population ages.

Grand Circle Travel in Boston, Massachusetts claims to be the first American marketer of direct travel packages for the mature and has developed an "extended vacation abroad" concept, popular with retirees. In thirty years of business, Grand Circle Travel has sent more than 500,000 people on vacations around the world, doing an annual business of $40 million.[10]

Business Travel

The tried-and-true business sector also offers new opportunities. Although competition, ARC provisions, and BTDs present some difficulties, the business travel sector holds significant promise for retail travel agents. Improved information technology and a generally freer pattern of trade suggest that global business will increase and become increasingly mobile. As businesses search out new sources of supply and markets, managers will be asked to travel to ever more locations. Yet, recent studies indicate that most business managers are relatively ill prepared for and uneducated about business travel. This segment is growing, however, and with this the need for assistance in managing travel effectiveness and efficiency. Business travelers are evidently in need of expertise, something travel agents do or should possess.

Beyond helping businesses manage travel budgets, agents should look to the changing nature of business travel for profits. Women represent an increasing share of business travelers, and hotels have already begun to alter their marketing mix in light of this fact. Can travel agencies say the same?

Business travelers are traveling more frequently with spouses or partners than at any previous time. Travel agents, then, must design offerings to meet the the needs of both parties. At its simplest, perhaps marketing appeals directed at the business person's secretary must be augmented with appeals to the spouse.

Meetings and Incentives

Perhaps nowhere is the increasing tendency to travel with spouses more evident than in the meetings and incentive travel segments, growth markets in their own right. Those agents who have yet to develop expertise in this area may wish to do so. Although highly competitive, the incentive market is now and should be even more profitable.

THE INTERNATIONAL TRAVEL BUSINESS

The greatest challenge, whether in the leisure or business travel sector, is for the travel agent to adapt to the international travel picture—probably the greatest devleoping sector in the industry. The number of trips is growing. Trips are longer. Itineraries are higher priced. But the risk of selling international travel is also greater, and growing larger relative to the selling of domestic travel.

Globalization of travel will have several implications for travel agents. Not surprisingly, legal issues present the most immediate concerns. Throughout much of the world, but especially in Europe, countries are applying strict liability laws to travel products and their sales. In essence, these laws hold tour operators and, in some cases, retail travel agents liable if anything goes wrong on an overseas tour. Whether entering the international arena individually or as part of a consortium (which is increasingly common), advocates in the travel industry believe agents must establish a total risk-prevention plan to cover themselves.

A major part of any protection plan will be to understand the laws of all countries in which an agency conducts business.[11] Currently most disputes in which a U.S. agent becomes embroiled will be heard in U.S. courts.

There is no guarantee, however—in fact very little hope—that international disputes will be held in these same courts, so international tribunals and laws will come to bear in the profitable operation of U.S. travel agencies.

Japan Travel Law

Japan law offers an interesting contrast to the United States with regard to travel agency law. Whereas the United States favors a laissez-faire position, Japan enacted the Travel Agency Law (TAL) in 1952 to ensure fairness in business dealings. As amended in 1982, the TAL regulates the industry in order to secure fair transactions between travel agents and tourists, safety in travel, and benefits for tourists.

The TAL primarily is a consumer protection law. It obligates agents, through their association, to settle complaints made by travelers or suppliers. The government has formulated standard general terms and conditions for contracts between travelers and agents, and most agents have adopted these standards. Those agents choosing to develop their own general terms and conditions for contracts must have them approved by the government.

Travel agents in Japan are classified into one of three categories. *General travel agents* may deal in domestic and international travel products. *Domestic agents* are restricted to selling domestic services. *Travel subagents* operate as representatives on behalf of other travel agents. The primary distinguishing characteristic differentiating the groups is financial status—general agents are required to have assets in excess of Y30 million, whereas domestic agents must have at least Y3 million.

U.K. Travel Agency Network

Not all foreign distribution systems are as radically different as those in Japan and the United States. For example, the travel agent networks in the United Kingdom and the United States are similar in many respects. Definite trends are visible in both countries toward mergers and acquisitions. In 1985, 2936 Association of British Travel Agents (ABTA) members operated 4082 outlets. Six of the largest companies—Thomas Cook, Hogg Robinson, Lunn Poly, Pickfords, American Express, and A. T. Mays—control 20 percent of the retail market.

Agencies in both countries are following a path toward increasing specialization. Lunn Poly has pursued a decidely maverick policy by focusing almost exclusively on holiday travel. Business accounts were sold to Pickfords; coach and rail ticketing was dropped; agency outlets are referred to as "holiday shops." This unique strategy helped make the company one of the fastest growth in the United Kingdom, expanding fivefold from 1981 to 1986.

Hogg Robinson chose to target business markets although it still services leisure accounts. Automation in reservations and transactions accounting systems, effectively employed for business accounts, has increased profits. Further profits in business travel markets have been gained through membership in the U.S.-based Woodside consortium.

U.K. and U.S. agents differ mainly in the nature of services they provide and sell. U.K. agents derive on average over one-half of their total revenue from selling inclusive tours. Airline sales, although important, generate less than one-third of total revenue and their contribution is declining. The profit picture of a typical U.S. agent is dominated by airline sales with relatively little income from inclusive tours. The U.S. agent, however, tends to package travel components on site to meet the needs of individual travelers. Advanced computer reservations systems (CRS) give U.S. agents this ability, which is as yet unmatched in the world.

The globalization of travel is facilitated by airline-developed CRS. Major American vendors, such as American and United, are pushing to get their systems into Europe and Asia. Carriers in those areas are responding to the challenge by forming their own CRS consortium; Galileo and Fantasia are just two of several systems recently introduced. These systems and those yet to be developed are the keys to the future and to profits.

SUMMARY

Travel agents have access to more information, which is more accurately compiled and more readily accessed, than at any time in history. The information age promises the ability to cope with changing travel trends, industry practices, laws, and markets. The range of technology now available, and that will be available in the foreseeable future, equips agents to identify growth markets as well as expand in existing markets. Travel agents also will be better prepared to offer individualized service to counsel rather than merely take ticket orders. The future for travel agencies promises continuous and rapid change. Managers will need all of the tools discussed throughout the text, and others, to remain profitable.

DISCUSSION QUESTIONS

1. What categories of agencies are recognized under ARC?
2. What are the major issues surrounding the continued growth of STPs?
3. How can a preferred supplier list be used to improve profitability?
4. How does agency liability change if the agency charges a service fee?
5. What travel trends appear favorable for retail travel agents? What trends are unfavorable?
6. Contrast the travel distribution systems in the United States, the United Kingdom, and Japan.

ENDNOTES

[1]E. Lassiter, "IBM Pulls Switch on Retailers," *Travel Weekly*, January 31, 1985, p. 1.

[2]F. Collison and K. Boberg, "Marketing of Airline Services in a Deregulated Environment," *Tourism Management*, September, 1987, pp. 198–199.

[3]Ibid.

[4]D. Barclay, "Agency Group Enters New Age of Exclusivity, Focused Selling," *Travel Agent Magazine*, June 27, 1988, pp. 28–29.

[5]"ASTA Survey Gives Figures on Overrides, Ticketing Costs," *Travel Weekly*, September 1, 1988, p. 27.

[6]Adapted from Sylvia Blishak, "How to Levy Service Charges Without Losing Customers," *Travel Marketing and Agency Management Guidelines*, May/June, 1986, p. 17.

[7]C. Goeldner, "Travel 1987: The Year in Review," *Journal of Travel Research*, Spring, 1987, pp. 44–47.

[8]Charles F. Longino, Jr., "The Comfortably Retired and the Pension Elite," *American Demographics*, June, 1988, p. 25.

[9]"Tourism in Japan 1986," *Japan Travel Blue Book 1987* (Tokyo: Travel Journal Inc., 1987), pp. 132–136.

[10]William A. Davis, "Cashing In on the Mature Traveler," *Honolulu Star Bulletin and Advertiser*, September 18, 1988, pp. 1–8.

[11]"Industry Lawyer: U.S. Firms Must Learn Other Countries' Rules," *Travel Weekly*, June 20, 1988, p. 15.

SUPPLEMENTAL READINGS

BOBERG, K., AND J. CAVINATO, "Business Travel Management: Evolution under Airline Deregulation," *Transportation Journal*, Winter, 1986, pp. 12–20.

"Falling Commissions Will Spur Service Fees, Predicts Attorney," *Travel Weekly*, June 4, 1987, p. 24.

"Overrides Changing the Way Airline Agencies Do Business," *Travel Age West*, May 18, 1987, p. 3.

SALTMARSH, G., "Travel Retailing in the U.K.," *Travel & Tourism Analyst*, September, 1986, pp. 49–62.

Glossary

Accreditation   Approval by conferences or associations allowing the sale of tickets and other travel services.

Affinity Group   An organization, formed for virtually any purpose other than travel, which subsequently elects to sponsor group travel programs on scheduled or charter aircraft and qualifies for certain group travel privileges.

Agent   A person authorized to sell the products or services of a supplier.

Agent Reporting Agreement   An agreement between travel agents and airlines, via the Airlines Reporting Corporation, which specifies the rights and obligations of both parties.

Airlines Reporting Corporation (ARC)   Formed by the Air Transport Association to preserve essential domestic services performed by the Air Traffic Conference prior to deregulation; as a regulatory association for travel agents, ARC establishes agency requirements with respect to professional personnel standards, agency accessibility to the public, and financial and security standards.

Airline Tariff Publishing Company (ATPCO)   A company jointly owned and operated by airlines to consolidate, publish, and distribute fares and cargo rates, along with associated rules, to the travel industry.

Air Taxi   Aircraft carrying up to 19 passengers, operating usually within a limited radius of 250 miles.

Air Traffic Control   A service operated by appropriate authority to promote the safe, orderly, and expeditious flow of air traffic.

Air Transport Association (ATA)   The trade association representing all scheduled airlines in the United States under whose jurisdiction the Airlines Reporting Corporation was established after the dissolution of the Civil Aeronautics Board.

Airbus (Aerial Bus)   A jumbo jet carrying twice as many people as a 707 or DC-8 and specializing in short- and medium-length trips.

Airline Codes   The system of abbreviations for airlines, airports, fares, and so on used by airlines and travel agents throughout the world.

Airline Deregulation   By the federal law enacted in 1978, the elimination of the CAB and governmental regulation of the airlines and other suppliers with regard to routes, fares, and other specifics.

All-Expense Tour   An inclusive tour that includes many services for a stated price; probably most, if not all, meals, sightseeing, taxes, tips, and extras.

American Automobile Association (AAA)   An organization that provides its members with a variety of services—travel information, maps, highway and legal services, insurance, trip planning, and so on—related to owning and operating automobiles. AAA also operates a multi-branch retail travel agency organization.

American Plan (AP)   A meal plan that includes three meals daily with the price of accommodations.

American Society of Travel Agents (ASTA)   A trade association of U.S. and Canadian travel agents and tour operators.

Amtrak   The name used by the National Railway Passenger Corporation, a quasi-public corporation established by Congress in 1971 to assist the declining railroad industry.

APOLLO   The computer reservation system developed by United Airlines and introduced in 1976.

ARC *Industry Agents' Handbook*   Published by the Airlines Reporting Corporation for travel agents, the handbook specifies the requirements to become an ARC Industry Agent and provides guidelines and procedures for appointment.

Area Settlement Plan   A system of banks authorized by the ARC through which travel agents and approved suppliers report and remit airline tickets.

Association of Retail Travel Agents (ARTA)   A trade association of American travel retailers.

Automated Ticket Machines (ATM)   Automated vending machines selling computer airline tickets, generally located in airport terminals.

Average Room Rate   Total revenues from room sales in a hotel, or collective room revenues of a destination, divided by the total number of available rooms. Average room rates may be computed on a daily basis for an individual property or an annual or seasonal basis for a destination.

Back-to-Back   Describing a program of multiple air charters between two or more points with arrivals and departures coordinated to eliminate aircraft deadheading and waiting; that is, when one group is delivered at a destination, another is ready to depart from that point.

Bed and Breakfast (B & B)   A meal plan that includes breakfast with guest house or other lodging accommodations.

Bermuda Plan (BP)   Hotel accommodations with a full, American-style breakfast included in the price of the room.

Bonding   The purchase, for a premium, of a guarantee of protection for a supplier or a customer. In the travel industry, certain bonding programs are mandatory: For example, ARC insists that travel agents be bonded to protect the airlines against defaults.

Bucket Shops   Firms selling heavily discounted air tickets or tour packages, usually below market value.

Bulk Fare   A fare available only to tour organizers or operators who purchase a specified block of seats from a carrier at a low, noncommissionable price and then have the responsibility of selling the seats, including a commission in their marked-up price for the seats.

Business Class   A class of service on airlines that is usually situated between first class and economy (coach) and offers such amenities as larger seats, free cocktails and headsets, and early check-in privileges.

Business Travel Department (BTD)   An in-house travel agency for a business or organization.

Cargo Liner (or Freighter)   A vessel principally engaged in transporting goods, licensed to carry a maximum number of passengers (usually twelve).

Certified Travel Counselor (CTC)   Professional certification awarded to travel agents who have successfully completed a study program developed and administered by the Institute of Certified Travel Agents.

Charter Service   Nonscheduled air transport services whereby the party or parties receiving transportation obtain exclusive use of an aircraft at published tariff rates and the remuneration paid by the party receiving transportation accrues directly to, and the responsibility for providing transportation is that of, the accounting air carrier. This term also has general application to any other mode of transport, such as motorcoach, ship, and train, where the entire capacity or a minimum number of seats are hired by contract for exclusive use.

Child   Variably defined. Airlines normally classify a child as two through eleven, but some suppliers classify the range to fourteen, sixteen, or even up to eighteen years of age.

Circle Trip   A trip involving more than one destination and returning to the origin city. Example: Tampa to Atlanta to New Orleans to Las Vegas to Tampa.

City-Pair   The terminal communities in an air trip, that is, the origin and destination on a one-way basis.

Coach Service   Transport service established for the carriage of passengers at fares and quality of service below that of first-class and business-class service. It is also known as economy service.

Commercial Rate   A special discounted rate offered by a hotel or other supplier to a company, group, or individual traveler on a qualified basis.

Commission   A payment received by travel agents for the sale of air transportation, hotel accommodation, tours, rental cars, and other products and services, usually computed as a percentage of sale made by the agent.

Commuter Airline   An airline that offers frequent round-trip service to or from smaller communities and some larger airport hubs with a published flight schedule of such services, principally to serve business commuters.

Computer Bias   Giving preference, as in listing a certain airline's schedules first in a Computerized Reservation System.

Computerized Reservation System (CRS)   An electronic information system connecting individual travel agencies to a central computer, making immediate inquiries and reservations on an airline, hotel, car rental, or other possible travel services.

Conference   An association of air carriers designed in principle to provide a set of operational rules that are fair to operators and to prevent injurious competition among operators. A conference may establish and enforce agreed-upon rules, ethical practices, safety standards, and documents, as well as serve as a clearinghouse for information. It may also establish travel agency rules and regulations.

Conference Appointment   A process whereby travel agencies are approved by conferences (for example, IATAN, ARC) to represent a group of carriers or other travel suppliers to sell its services.

Configuration   A particular type of specific aircraft, ship, and so on, differing from others of the same model by virtue of the arrangement of its components or by the addition or omission of auxiliary equipment such as "long-range configuration," "cargo configuration."

Consolidator   A person or company that forms groups to travel on air charters or at group fares on scheduled flights to increase sales, earn override commissions, or reduce the possibility of tour cancellations.

Consortium   A group of persons or travel agency companies that pool together their resources to obtain some travel benefit such as higher commissions, advertising, twenty-four-hour call-in service, or other services.

Consumer Disclosure Notice   A written statement frequently used by travel agencies to inform clients that they are acting merely as "agents" for a principal (that is, airline, hotel). With such a disclosure notice, agents take a major step in avoiding liability by obtaining implicit consent from the client to use the supplier.

Continental Breakfast   Usually a beverage with rolls, butter, and jam or marmalade. In Holland and Norway, cheese, cold cuts, or fish are sometimes included.

Continental Plan (CP)   Bed and breakfast, meaning hotel accommodations as specified and breakfast according to the custom of the country.

Convention   A business or professional meeting, usually attended by large numbers of people. In Europe the more prevalent term for convention is "congress."

Cooperative Business Corporation   Formed as a joint-stock organization to establish and maintain a working relationship among its members.

Corporate-Owned Chain   A fully owned group of retail chain member outlets featuring common signage and advertising, usually (but not always) operating under a unified marketing concept and standardized management policies and practices.

Coupon Brokers   Travel companies that buy and sell frequent flyer program coupons.

Courier (Tour Escort, Tour Leader, Tour Manager)   A professional travel escort.

Cruise Ships   Ships used specifically for pleasure cruising, as opposed to point-to-point transportation.

Currency Restrictions   Limitations established by a country to control the amount of money taken in, out, or exchanged within a country.

Customs   The formal procedure whereby all persons entering a country must declare their possession of specific kinds or amounts of items purchased in another country under the jurisdiction of a government agency that has the right to inspect, restrict, seize, and/or impose taxes on goods brought into a country. Also refers to the normal manners or behavioral procedures of a society.

Customs Duty   A tax on certain goods being imported.

Day Rate   A special rate for a room used by a guest only during the day up to a specific hour, such as 4:00, 5:00, or 6:00 P.M.

Deadhead   A rail, bus, or airline term for a carrier returning with an empty cabin or cargo payload.

Default Protection Plan   A system established to protect travelers and travel intermediaries in the event of a supplier default. There is currently no system operating; however, several plans are being reviewed.

Demi Pension   The same as Modified American Plan.

Deposit   A partial payment to hold space, usually refundable if cancellation is made by a prescribed time.

Direct Selling   The sale of travel products by suppliers (airlines, hotels) directly to the customers, without the use of travel intermediaries such as travel agents.

Disclaimer   A legal concept whereby one party (that is, the client) to a transaction declares that he or she will release the other party (that is, the agent) from liability and responsibility for the transaction under certain stated conditions.

Domestic Airline   A carrier providing service within its own country.

Domestic Independent Tour (DIT)   The same as FIT, but more commonly used in the North American context of an independent, prepaid trip within the country.

Domestic Trunks (Domestic Trunk Operations)   Domestic operations of the domestic trunk carriers. This group of carriers operates primarily within the geographical limits of the forty-eight contiguous states of the United States (and the District of Columbia) over routes primarily serving the larger communities.

Duty-Free Imports   A government-specified list of item categories and their quantities that may be brought into the country free of tax or duty charges.

Duty-Free Stores   Retail stores in which merchandise is sold only to travelers who are leaving the country. Merchandise is sold completely or partially free of the taxes and duties that would otewise be imposed by the country in which the store is located.

Economy Hotel   A hotel with limited facilities and services targeted at budget travelers, also referred to as second-class or tourist hotel.

Economy Service   Transport service established for the carriage of passengers at fares and quality of service below first class and business class, also known as coach service.

Efficiency Unit   A room that has kitchen facilities, similar to a one-room apartment. Also called a studio.

English Breakfast   Usually includes juice, hot or cold cereal, bacon or ham, eggs, kippers, or sausages, toast, butter, and jam or marmalade.

Entry Requirements   The official documents required to enter a country, which may include a passport, visa, or document showing inoculations.

Errors and Omissions Insurance   Also known as professional liability insurance, this insurance protects the agency by covering claims for damages suffered by the client for financial loss, inconvenience, embarrassment, or other injuries because of an error or omission on the part of the agent.

Escorted Tour   A tour that includes the services of an escort, also called a conducted tour.

Escrow Accounts   Funds placed in the custody of licensed financial institutions for safekeeping. Many contracts in travel require that agents and tour operators maintain customers' deposits and prepayments in escrow accounts.

European Plan (EP)   A meal plan that does not include meals with the price of accommodations.

Exclusivity   Restriction imposed by the Air Traffic Conference that prohibited airlines from paying commissions to entities lacking ATC accreditation and standardized ticket stock. Prior to deregulation, travel agents and airlines had exclusivity on the sale of air transportation.

Excursion   Usually a side trip out of a destination city; may be used interchangeably with tour or sightseeing.

Excursion Fare   Usually a round-trip fare with restrictions such as minimum and maximum stay and advance purchase requirements.

Excursionist   A temporary visitor remaining less than twenty-four hours in the destination visited and not making an overnight stay.

Exit Restrictions   Restrictions (such as an exit Visa or large exit tax) imposed by a country to curb outbound travel.

Familiarization Trip or Tour   A trip or tour offered to travel agents, tour operators, incentive planners, travel writers, and so on to promote a new product or destination and the services of the suppliers, usually at a discount price or FOC (free of charge). Also called a "fam trip."

Family Plan   Special money-saving arrangement for family travel, applied differently in various phases of the industry. Generally, members of a family are entitled to discounted fares, accommodation rates, and so on.

Fare   The amount per passenger or group of persons stated in the applicable tariff for transportation, including accompanying baggage unless otherwise specified.

Federal Aviation Administration (FAA)   The Department of Transportation agency that regulates U.S. civil aviation. Among other things, FAA licenses private and commercial pilots, certifies aircraft and monitors their maintenance, certifies and monitors airport traffic control systems and their personnel, and enforces airline security regulations.

First-Class Hotel   A hotel offering a high standard and variety of services. In Europe a first-class hotel ranks below a deluxe or grand luxe hotel. In Asia, first class may mean a four-star property where five stars denotes the top classification.

First-Class Service   Transport service established for the carriage of passengers at premium fares, for whom premium quality services and seating accommodations are provided. Term also applies to the lodging industry in a similar context.

Flag Carrier   A term usually referring to the national airline of a country.

Flat Rate   A special room rate for a group negotiated in advance where all rooms in the property, which may or may not be subject to certain restrictions, are priced at the same rate.

Fly–Drive   A package that includes airfare and car rental (and sometimes accommodations).

Foreign Independent Tour (FIT)   An international trip with the itinerary prepared to the individual traveler's specifications. Some suppliers refer to FIT as "free and independent travelers" to denote travelers who have made independent arrangements.

Franchise   The right to market a service and/or product, often exclusive for a specified area, as granted by the manufacturer, developer, or distributor in return for a fee; prevalent in the fast-food service industry.

Franchisor   An entity that grants vested right to use a recognized brand name for an extensive, contractual time frame. The franchisor typically provides a franchisee with a complete business package, including operational plans and support services. A franchisor is regulated by the Federal Trade Commission.

Frequent Flyer Program (FFP)   A program whereby bonuses, usually free travel with certain restrictions, are offered by the airlines to passengers who accumulate travel mileage. Hotels often participate in FFPs by offering similar incentives for hotel patronage based on room nights. FFPs are also termed as FTPs, or Frequent Traveler Programs.

Full-Service Travel Agency   An agency that offers a full range of services and products related to international and domestic travel.

Gateway City   A city that functions as the primary entry destination for visitors to an area because of its location, population, and air traffic patterns.

General Sales Agent (GSA)   An exclusive sales representative of a principal for a given area.

Ground Arrangements   Land services such as transfers, sightseeing tours, and so on.

Ground Handling Agent   A company that provides local transportation, sightseeing, and other services to a client at a destination.

Ground Operator   A supplier that provides local transportation, accommodations, sightseeing arrangements, and other services to a client at a destination.

Group Inclusive Tour (GIT)   A prepaid tour covering transportation, accommodations, sightseeing arrangements, and other services. Special airfares are provided to the group, requiring that all members must travel on the same flight round trip and must travel together during their entire time abroad.

Guaranteed Reservation   A guarantee to the traveler given by the hotel, usually based on advance deposit, that the room will be held all night in case of late arrival of the traveler. With a guaranteed reservation, the traveler must pay for the room whether or not it is actually used.

Hostels   Accommodations where the facilities may be somewhat similar to dormitories, usually associated with youth travel.

Hotel Garni   A term used to designate European hotels that do not have a restaurant.

Hub and Spoke Concept   A concept involving the establishment of a particular city as a central point to which longer-haul flights are scheduled and which serves as a connecting point where other flights are deployed or made to smaller cities. The routing of schedules through a central connecting city ensures heavier passenger loads.

Incentive Companies   Professional firms assisting clients with designing, promoting, and executing of incentive travel programs.

Incentive Travel   Travel providing an incentive reward for sales or work performed by sales staff, distributors, or members of other organizations when the sales or work performed exceeds particular quota levels.

Inclusive Tour (IT)   An advertised package or tour that includes accommodations and other components such as transfers and sightseeing.

Independent Arbitration Panel   A panel of three independent persons with the authority to hear appeals brought by agency organizations when the ARC has adapted rules or fee changes such organizations deem to be unreasonable.

Individually Owned Chain   Each member outlet, for example, hotel, restaurant, travel agency, within the retail chain is individually owned but features common signage and advertising, following a unified marketing concept, and operates in a uniform manner.

In-plant Branch   An operation established by a travel agency to serve the client at its own location but using the client's own employees to do the agency work. In this situation, a split commission system is arranged.

Institute of Certified Travel Agents (ICTA)   An organization established in 1964 that is concerned with developing and administering educational programs for travel agents, in order to confer professional certification.

Interline Agreements Agreements involving two or more air carriers who cooperate on specific actions such as interline travel rights and privileges or share airport facilities or other resources.

Intermodal Using different types of transportation, as in a tour using a combination of rail, air, and motorcoach services.

International Air Transport Association (IATA) A trade association of international airlines that promotes a unified system of air transportation on international routes; sets fares and rates, safety standards, and condition of services; and appoints and regulates travel agents to sell international tickets.

International Airlines Travel Agent Network (IATAN) The trade name of the Passenger Network Services Corporation (PNSC) created by IATA as the international counterpart of the ARC in appointing and regulating travel agencies.

Itinerary The travel schedule provided by a travel agent for his or her client. A proposed or preliminary itinerary may be rather vague or very specific. A final itinerary, however, spells out all details—flight numbers, departure times, and so on—as well as describing planned activities.

Jitney A car, van, or small bus to carry a small number of passengers.

Joint Fare A fare agreed upon by two or more carriers to provide service from origin to destination, or a fare for an off-line connection (within a country).

Joint Marketing Organization A company that markets the products of selected suppliers through its ranks of member agencies.

Junket (1) a promotional low-cost tour package offered by a particular sponsor such as a gambling casino, hotel, or other travel supplier; (2) a nonessential trip usually taken at the expense of the public taxpayer.

Late-Show A passenger or customer holding a reservation who arrives at the check-in desk after the designated time.

Limited-Service Travel Agency An agency that specializes in selling only one type of travel product, for example, domestic airline tickets, and generally offers discounted tickets as the primary basis for attracting clients.

Load Factor The ratio, expressed as a percentage, of carrier capacity sold to total capacity offered for sale. The two most common measures are the number of paying passengers to number of available seats and the number of seat miles to revenue passenger miles. Example of the latter: If an airline operates 100,000 seat miles and its sales total is 50,000 revenue passenger miles, it is operating at a 50 percent load factor.

Meeting and Convention Planner   A professional consultant who specializes in the planning and execution of conventions and business meetings.

Minimum Connecting Time   The amount of time required to change planes, established by regulation.

Modified American Plan (MAP)   A meal plan that includes two meals daily (usually breakfast and dinner) with the price of accommodations.

Motorcoach   A bus designed to carry passengers for touring, frequently equipped with toilet facilities.

National Tourism Office or Organization (NTO)   Also known as National Tourism Administration (NTA). The primary government agency charged with the implementation of national goals and public policy with respect to tourism.

Net Rate   A wholesale rate before markup for resale.

Net Wholesale Rate   A rate usually slightly lower than the wholesale rate, applicable to groups of individuals when a hotel is specifically mentioned in a tour folder. Rate is marked up by wholesale sellers of tour to cover distribution, promotion, and so on.

Nonscheduled Services   Revenue flights that are not operated in regular scheduled service, such as charter flights and all nonrevenue flights incident to such flights.

Official Airline Guide (OAG)   A publication that provides current data on available airline services between city-pairs. There is also an electronic edition of the OAG.

On-Time Performance   The number and percentage of aircraft, flights arriving on time, or flights arriving within fifteen minutes of the carrier's published scheduled arrival time for any specified flight or group of flights during any specified period.

Open Jaw   An arrangement, route, or fare, authorized in a tariff, granting the traveling public the privilege of purchasing round-trip transportation from the point of origin to one destination at which another form of transportation is used to a second destination, at which point the passenger resumes the original form of transportation and returns to the point of origin; or from such destination to another destination that is in the general direction of the original starting point.

Option   A tour extension or side trip offered at extra cost.

Out-plant Operation   An operation where the agency client performs most of its own itinerary work, then transmits the information to the agency, with the agency doing the actual ticketing. The commission is generally split according to a negotiated arrangement between the client and the agency.

Overbooking   The practice of preselling more hotel rooms (or airline seats) than the hotel (or airline) has to offer.

Override Commission   An additional commission paid above the normal commission to travel agents by suppliers based on incremental quantity or volume of sales.

Package   Prearranged elements of a trip such as hotel accommodations, meals, sightseeing, and transfers, less inclusive than a tour.

Parador   A Spanish word referring to castles, abbeys, or other historic buildings that have been restored for use as lodging accommodations.

Passenger Name Record (PNR)   The record of an airline reservation stored in a computerized airline reservation system. The record contains all pertinent information such as passengers' names, travel times, flight numbers, and cost of ticket.

Passenger Network Services Corporation (PNSC)   See IATAN.

Passenger Ships   Ships whose primary purpose is to transport people from one destination to another as opposed to simply pleasure cruising.

Passport   Issued by national governments to their citizens for out-of-country travel as verification of their citizenship.

Pension   A French word widely used in Europe meaning guest house or boarding house.

Person-Night   A statistical term denoting one paying guest staying one night at a destination.

Preferred Supplier Program   An arrangement whereby an agent, working in concert with a supplier, agrees to give preference to that supplier's travel products. In turn, the agent gets incremental commissions or overrides above the standard.

Principal   The dominant participant in any given situation. More specifically in travel: (1) a primary producer of any unit of travel merchandise—an airline, a hotel, a shipline; (2) any person (or company) who assumes responsibility for a travel program; (3) anyone who pays a commission to another for selling a travel program.

Queue System   An eletronic ticketer file common to airline reservation systems; can be thought of as an electronic mailbox or card file in which carriers place messages for the agent and agents place messages for themselves.

Rack Rate   The regular published rate of a hotel. When special rates are quoted, they represent a discount from the rack rate.

Rebate   The practice of charging, demanding, collecting, or receiving less compensation for air transportation, or for any service in connection therewith, than the rates, fares, or charges specified in the air carrier's currently effective tariffs.

Recreational Vehicle (RV) A motorized self-contained camping trailer or a truck or van used for traveling. Also an off-the-road vehicle such as a dirt bike or dune buggy.

Regional Carrier A carrier serving a particular area only.

Retail Travel Agency A travel agency that sells travel products on a retail basis on behalf of his or her principals—airlines, cruise lines, hotels, car rentals, and so on—for a commission to the general public.

Reentry Permit A document allowing alien residents to return from trips outside the country.

SABRE The Computer Reservation System developed by American Airlines and introduced in 1976. (Acronym stands for Semi-Automatic Business Research Environment.)

Sailing Permit A document required of U.S. residents having "resident alien" status who are traveling abroad, attesting that they are not delinquent in the payment of any income tax liability.

Satellite Ticket Printer (STP) A printer at another location other than the main premises that can dispense tickets for travel products for travel agencies.

Seasonality High and low seasonal fluctuations in market demand due to the time-of-year specifics of the area's attractions and their ability to attract visitors.

Self-Drive A car hired to clients without the driver. Conditions of hire vary from agency to agency and may be based either on mileage or on an hourly or daily basis.

Side Trip An optional trip offered to participants of a tour.

Sightseeing Company A local tour bus company providing guided sightseeing in a city, town, area, and so on.

Sightseeing Tour A tour within the city limits showing clients the main places of interest, scenic and historic places, churches, museums, monuments, and so on.

Sliding Commission Scale A commission system whereby the percentage of commission to a travel agent increases as the volume of sales of a particular supplier increases.

Special Fare In contrast to normal fares, special fares have various restrictions—for instance, advance purchase, specified length of stay, limited or no schedule change privileges, and limited or no cancellation rights.

Special Interest Tour A prearranged, packaged itinerary designed to appeal to or respond to a request by a group of persons who have a particular interest area of study or activity, for example, culture and the arts, sports, preservation, wilderness, shopping, cuisine, and so on.

Stockholder Licensee Group A corporation whose members are stockholders, providing a vertically integrated format, with an elected board of directors to ultimately judge the business decisions of management and to whom management reports.

Structure Fare   The particular fare charged for trips of varying distances and the relationship between coach fares and fares for the other classes of service. The manner in which the fare level should be distributed to, and recouped from, the passenger transport services operated by the air carriers. Used most often in rate making.

Subscriber-Based Network   An organization that provides subscriptions such as airline and hotel guides and publications such as hotel facility listings to travel agencies for their corporate travelers.

Suite   A living room connected to one or more bedrooms.

Supplier   One who offers the products or services sold through the travel retailers or in some cases directly to the public.

Supporting Document   Any document used as supporting evidence in a transaction—for instance, a birth certificate, health certificate, passport, visa, voter registration card, military discharge papers, and so on.

Through Fare   The total fare from point of origin to destination, which may be a local fare, a joint fare, or a combination of separately established fares.

Ticket Stock   The supply of tickets an agency keeps on hand and for which the agency has legal responsibility.

Timesharing   The concept dividing the ownership and use of a lodging property among several investors; generally each timesharing purchaser is able to use the unit for a specified interval (for example, two weeks) each year for a specified period of time.

Tourism Plant   Facilities, amenities, and services explicitly built and provided for tourist use in a given area.

Tourist   A temporary visitor staying at least twenty-four hours in the country visited and the purpose of whose journey can be classified as leisure—recreation, holiday, health, study, religion, sport, business, family, mission, or meeting.

Tour Basing Fare   A reduced-rate excursion fare available only to those who buy prepaid tours or packages, including inclusive tour, group inclusive tour, incentive group, contract bulk inclusive tour, tour basing, and group round-trip inclusive tour basing fares.

Tour Breakage   Usually operators' fixed cost items such as meals, transfers, admissions, and so on, costed into the package but not used by the purchaser. Tour operators often put an estimated percentage return of breakage in their costing elements. Breakage may represent either increased cost efficiency or extra profit for the operator.

Tour Broker   A person or company that organizes and markets tour products.

Tour Desk   The desk at a hotel or airline that is used for selling tours and packages.

Tour Escort   A person designated as the leader of the tour group, usually for the entire travel experience, although he or she may be assisted by other guides.

Tour Operator   An operator that provides services including responsibility for the delivery and/or operation of all facets of the tour, usually providing an escort. Tour operators may also be wholesalers as well as local operators.

Tour Package   A joint service that gives a traveler a significantly lower price for a combination of services than could be obtained if each had to be purchased separately by the traveler. Thus, the total price of a tour package might include a round-trip plane ticket, hotel accommodations, meals, sightseeing bus tours, and admission fees.

Transfers   The services of transportation from an airport, railway station, or other terminal to the hotel of the clients.

Travel Advisory   A caution issued by some authoritative body, for example, the State Department or a foreign ministry, regarding the safety, changing conditions, or practices of a specific travel destination that may be detrimental or harmful to travelers from the advisory body's country.

Travel Agent Arbiter   Person designated with the responsibility to rule on ARC complaints against individual travel agents and also individual agents' complaints against ARC.

Travel Agent Commission   The payment by airlines and other travel suppliers to a travel agent of specified amounts of money (usually a percentage) as compensation for the agent's sales of travel products.

Travel Agents' Handbook   A manual published by IATAN setting forth procedures and guidelines for IATAN-appointed agencies.

Traveler Profile   Characteristics describing various travel market segments.

Travel Industry   The composite of organizations, both public and private, involved in the development, production, distribution, and marketing of products and services to serve the needs of travelers.

Travel Industry Distribution System   The process of moving travel products and services from suppliers to ultimate consumers.

Travel Insurance   Regular insurance tailored to cover travelers and their personal effects. May be sold by a regular broker; however, most travel agents and tour carrier personnel are specially licensed insurance *agents* with the power to issue such policies and immediately *bind* the insurance company.

Universal Air Travel Plan (UATP)   A credit card program operated by airlines, primarily for frequent travelers.

VFR   Classification of travelers whose purpose for travel is to visit friends and relatives.

Videotex   An electronic transmission process whereby written and image material is displayed on a video screen.

Visa   An endorsement on a passport or document used in lieu of a passport by a consular official indicating that the bearer may gain entry into the country of issue.

Voucher   Document to be exchanged for goods or services, substantiating that payment has already been made. Also called an exchange order.

Wagon-Lit   A European Pullman. A sleeping car on European railroads, consisting of a private bedroom, including pillows, blankets, and a sink, to accommodate one or two people.

Wholesaler   A company that usually creates and markets inclusive tours and packages or buys services in bulk for sale (or resale) through travel agents. Often used interchangeably with tour operator, but several distinctions might be drawn: (1) A wholesaler presumably sells nothing at retail; a tour operator often does both. (2) A wholesaler does not always create his own products; a tour operator virtually always does. (3) A wholesaler is less inclined than a tour operator to perform local services. Industry distinctions for this term are far from clear; many travel companies perform any or all of the functions of travel agent, contractor, tour operator, and wholesaler.

Wide-Bodied Aircraft   A generic and commonly used term applied to any and all of the newest generation of jet aircraft with a fuselage diameter exceeding 200 inches and a per-engine thrust greater than 30,000 pounds (for example, Boeing 747, McDonnell Douglas DC-10, Lockheed L-1011).

Index